1

———

When I was seven years old, I shut my eyes, crossed my heart and sat the future next to me like a present, waiting to be unwrapped.

It was a vision of a life, so vivid that it presented itself to me as if pure, sweet inevitability. Had I known the meaning of the word, I would have written "destiny – do not open until forty" on the box in bold, permanent marker while I waited with it patiently.

Inside the box, I am forty years old, doing what I was put on this earth to do. I am managing a football team at the very highest level. I am folding my arms on the side of a pitch, looking pensive, conferring with my assistant, who occasionally holds random fingers up in the air and signals at players. In the background at our place of work, there are stands – limbs and bobbing heads, shouting and screaming, with the smell of burger vans and smoke and stale lager and grey heavy clouds merging in the air. The senses spell football and football alone, it takes on a homely, background haze, but I cannot see any of that specifically in my current focus. You see, I am too tightly locked into the proceedings on the pitch. In front of me, as the game is halfway through the first half and still revealing itself, I witness everything in a hyper-realised aspect ratio. While my mind ticks, I might manage an appreciative glance, wave and clap at the fans while they sing my name. It's nothing unprofessional or arrogant. It's just a gesture to assure them the respect is mutual. Then it's back to work. How can I explain this to mortals? I see the dimensions of a football pitch cut into highly evolved sci-fi-like squares, appearing to me while I read probabilities. Sometimes, I swear, with the footballing gods as my witnesses, I see phases of play and whole periods of possession unfold before they have even happened.

As the game intensifies, I prowl up and down my technical area, shaking my head before allowing myself a wry smile. The wry smile betrays the complex technical conversation I am having inside my head, one only I have access to. I am trying out theories in fast forward, throwing some away with a little in-joke to self as I do. It is all enacted with subtle cinematic dexterity for everyone watching. I land on a plan that, when I eventually communicate it into short, sharp, concise instructions, I will use to sculpt the course of this football match, and then the season, and maybe the future of football itself and sport as we know it. These are not my words though, these are the words of Des Lynam and Alan Hansen in the studio. (I haven't done the maths yet that Lynam and Hansen will probably not always be doing the football television coverage and analysis in the future). Inside the unwrapped present, in 2025, I am forty and Des Lynam and Alan Hansen and everyone else in football are the same age that they were when I received the box – a timeless, blissful, football-themed Groundhog Day preserving them all. In the post-match interviews, their praise is repeated to me by an evergreen touchline reporter. I refuse to take personal credit, telling them instead to focus on my team and

Praise for *Whatever Will Be, Will Be*

"A book so beautiful that it finally made me understand
what football means. An exceptional writer."
— Bella Mackie

"So much more than a book about football. A book about aging,
community and memory. Rich in detail and great jokes.
I wish I had written it."
— Josh Widdicombe

"Mesmerising and unputdownable, like *Fever Pitch* meets
The Sportswriter. I commend it in the highest terms."
— Amol Rajan

Whatever Will Be, Will Be

A Matter of Life and Football

Felix White

First published in Great Britain in 2026 by Cassell, an imprint of
Octopus Publishing Group Ltd
Carmelite House
50 Victoria Embankment
London EC4Y 0DZ
www.octopusbooks.co.uk

An Hachette UK Company
www.hachette.co.uk

The authorized representative in the EEA is Hachette Ireland,
8 Castlecourt Centre, Dublin 15, D15 XTP3, Ireland (email: info@hbgi.ie)

ISBN: 978-1-78840-559-1
eISBN: 978-1-78840-561-4

A CIP catalogue record for this book is available from the British Library.

Typeset in 10.75/16.5 pt Miller Text by Six Red Marbles UK, Thetford, Norfolk

Printed and bound in Great Britain.

10 9 8 7 6 5 4 3 2 1

This FSC® label means that materials used for
the product have been responsibly sourced.

Contents

backroom staff before, unprompted, asking myself questions that I then answer in a bizarrely diplomatic fashion. That's what us football managers do – we ask ourselves questions and then answer them, before asking ourselves another. Do I believe that we will still be in the mix for all trophies come the end of the season? It really isn't for me to say, I'm just concentrating on next week, which is a huge game for everyone in and around this football club. Do I believe it's right and proper that we approach every game as a cup final? Absolutely, yes. Is there any truth in me being approached by European giants Real Madrid? Look, there's no chance of me leaving. I give you my word now. My demeanour softens, playfully acknowledging the camera before turning back to the interviewer. If they had got in touch, I tell you this for sure, I wouldn't tell you. Winks back to camera.

I am gracious in victory, humble in defeat. Sometimes I wear a tracksuit pitch-side and sometimes a suit. It's very hard to pin me down like that. I will not be pigeonholed into any genre. Such is my innovation on the pitch and off, I might even go half and half, like Bryan Robson has just done on being appointed player-manager at Middlesbrough. Suit and tie on the top half and shorts, socks and football boots on the bottom. By 2025, perhaps that will have been normalised. Maybe it's what everyone is doing. I am happy to imagine that all of us football managers are wearing suits on our top half and football kit on our bottom half as we fly around on airborne scooters in this unwrapped version of the future. But trivial things such as aesthetics and futuristic travel practicalities aside, the burden I wear tells the world that I understand the enormity of the task at hand and that, in meeting the challenge, I can dig deep and rely upon both intuitive empathy and elite levels of competitive resilience. I set my stall out and take each game as it comes. Any player can come to my door with a problem, and I will make sure they leave unburdened, free to express themselves, to enjoy their football, to die for a cause, while I take their issue and roll it around in the holistic map of my mind before I come back with a conclusion for them. And as for all the employees of the club, I treat them with the same love that I would our top goalscorer. We are all a family here. This stuff permeates through the place.

My ambitions skipped the natural seven-year-old football fan's dreams of being a footballer. I had played football and had broken the news to myself. I'd sat myself down and had the chat. You're not going to make it, son. You are absolutely terrible at football. I was, in truth, quite scared of playing football. Some quirk of physical jitters had rendered me unable to kick a football with the "laces", my only option being a very cautious pass with my instep, like a broken computer game controller with only one button accessible. Despite throwing the ball against the back of the house and heading it back at it, I had no natural physical instinct to head a ball. Why, after all, would any sane person do that? In a game situation, ball falling from the sky, everyone's eyes searching for it, I would make sure I was far enough away from the ball to make it physically impossible for me to head it, before running back towards it as if I was desperate to get there at all costs. I always just missed it. Through sheer consistency of attendance and an ability to reel off every Premier League player in every squad, I made it into the school team, neatly shepherded away at left back, where my role required standing in a line and occasionally celebrating goals wildly that I had played no part in whatsoever. I was overwhelmed and out of my depth at under-elevens school level, let alone at some elite level, and I knew it. It was no cause for alarm. Elite management was where I was going to be.

So, my first steps into this leadership role – though inevitable – would not be the route pretty much exclusively travelled for a football manager, after an actual football career. My journey – and it was a journey – would have to be from outside. That was OK. It would be a more inspiring story when it had magicked its route there. And as a nine-year-old in 1993, there was only one accessible route into football management I had come across – play-by-mail Fantasy Football, advertised in *Match* magazine. It bounced off the page like a job vacancy. Pure Fantasy Football. Play by mail. Manage your own real football team alongside a network of thousands of managers across the country. One pound and seventy-five pence a week. Could I have those coins on the shelf, please, to Sellotape into a letter and send to this office in Chesterfield? My finger tapped the vacancy urgently.

Every week it would arrive, with a satisfying, substantial, hearty thud on the door mat. A very serious, thick envelope of stats and numbers and football results. I imagined a huge contraption, a heaving, spluttering, NASA-like beast of machinery that was spitting out these numbers and football results back to me, as if I had some sort of weekly communication with a mechanical footballing deity. There, I put my happiness, my entire sense of self held in its hands. Every week I fill in my team with thought and precision. Instructions and substitutions for very specific different outcomes. Man marking or zonal marking. Tactical inflections. Formation ultra-detail. I ask the postman every day, from this moment until its eventual arrival, if he has next week's mail. I ask him as if I am expecting a letter from a loved one who is away at war. It is unbearable. A week feels like a year. Pacing the room; rocking back and forth in the foetal position; scrawling potential new ideas for next week on the wall. When the envelope eventually arrives – match result with detailed report, this week's league, transfer lists – I tear it open like a wild, hungry animal. I then pore over all of it, turning from animal to analyst, like it is the *Financial Times* or something of similar compulsory adult importance. Every week, next to the league tables across the imaginary globe are the names of real people, other managers, and the phone number of each.

Every phone number is a landline – this being just before the real dawn of early mobile phones. The direct phone-to-phone aspect with other managers is going to be an important tool for me. I have been handed the unenviable challenge of bringing brighter times to Partick Thistle in Scotland. They have few resources and a squad not blessed with options. I know I'll have to be savvy in the transfer market. And so begin months of returning home from primary school and making landline calls across the United Kingdom to complete strangers. Players are desperately sought after; hardball is played; deals are put on the table, then botched, then bartered, then rearranged. I'll give you £1.5 million for him. In the morning, I wake up to notes by the phone in the living room on tiny pieces of yellow sticky paper. The Aberdeen manager called, my mum has scrawled, her multiple sclerosis starting to affect her handwriting, making it barely legible. He says two million and you've got a deal. I take the note with me. Hold it in my palm. I look at it throughout classes, scrunched in my hand, the words like a code to decipher. Is this a deal worth doing? I will have an answer by 3.30, at the end of school, I decide. Deadlines are good.

All the other senior play-by-mail managers seem to be extremely adult men. Inside every phone call is a portal to another universe. Their wife or child picks up the phone. Yes, I'll get him, who is it please? It's Felix White, manager of Partick Thistle. When they come to the phone, some of them speak in hushed tones, or I hear them picking up a receiver in another room, a private room. A click. A change of voice. Let's talk transfers, but first, in future, could you just say you're a work colleague, please, my wife doesn't approve of the Fantasy Football stuff. No problem, I say, assuming a trustworthy voice of impeccable responsibility, affecting the seriousness of a child cold war spy, looking around the room as I do so. Let's get this transfer sorted, and your secret is safe with me. £1.75 mill and we have a deal. Not one of the other managers ever asks my age. I do not know how many of them, if any, are also nine-year-olds pretending to be adults.

I reach the top four of the Scottish Premiership with Thistle – a remarkable achievement considering the budget and modest history of the club. When I walk around Partick – not the nine-year-old real me, but the fantasy forty-something – I can't move for people thanking me for the job I've done. It really does feel like a second home here, I tell them. Other clubs have no doubt tried to lure you away, so thank you for staying, they say. Honestly, I tell them, all of that stuff is flattering, but it's tomorrow's chip paper, and I've committed to a project here that is more important to me than any personal accolades. Of course I'll sign this for you; send my love to the family and here's to three more points on Saturday. Slightly north of Glasgow had become a fantasy spiritual home for me, a place where I imagined an actual community thanking me for something I'd done in an alternate reality.

Buoyed by this experience and my subsequent perhaps societally concerning withdrawal into my computer and *Championship Manager* – mail that took a week to receive bowing to computer games that only took half an hour to load – I tentatively stepped into the real world of football management. I had recently moved schools, from one side of Wandsworth Common (Allfarthing) to another (Honeywell). We had moved house to help with my mum's MS. She couldn't get up and down the stairs any more. Still having ties at Allfarthing, a lightbulb hit me. I could arrange a game of football between my little brother's class at Honeywell and my friend's little brother's class at Allfarthing. Me and Steven Bow arranged it all like an invitational. We were going to manage seven-year-olds and pit them against each other on a Saturday morning. Reality and fantasy clashed wildly in this exhibition match and – after receiving an angry call from a parent telling me that they were perplexed by all these team sheets their child kept bringing home in anticipation – I spent the early Saturday morning on Wandsworth Common frantically assembling a football ground out of cones and any loose items that could help mark the pitch. The parent had also informed me that they had phoned the houses of the players supposedly playing in this game, and the information had not been passed on to any of the other parents. I had overlooked a lot of the admin of football management. The other team were much better organised, with their parents turning up to see their children and a rough footballing system in place, whereas I, panicked and crestfallen, scrambled last minute to arrange my squad making the game. We were out of our depth before the game even began. I lost count at 15-0 and, having to referee as well as manage, I completely lost control of the game, the same parent coming over to me after the loss, looking disappointed and saying to me, "This is going to destroy them, Felix." In hindsight, I'm not sure it did. I think it didn't matter anywhere near enough to any of them to destroy them. But it did, in its own way, destroy me. If it was this hard to manage at this level, if the actual world of real management was so brutal and confusing and full of logistical nightmares, how would I ever actually manage Partick Thistle successfully? I left embarrassed and ashamed, dimming my memory of it, pushing it into the unspoken, unprocessed depths of my stomach.

Sheffield Wednesday played Sheffield United in the FA Cup semi-final that year, both teams appearing in *Roy-of-the-Rovers*-ish Technicolor at Wembley. I had as much connection to Sheffield as I did to Partick – absolutely none whatsoever – and yet, for whatever reason, something about this game spoke to me extremely directly. One side of the city, Wednesday, in blue and white stripes and the other, United, in red and white. It was a very succinct, simple explanation of rivalry and geography and the meaning of football. Tottenham had been beaten the day before by Arsenal, a North London derby that also gave a neat storyboarding to the whole thing. In the opening minutes of the semi-final, Chris Waddle – long-sleeved, tall and thin, collar half upturned – lined up a free-kick seemingly miles away. Everything looked further away at Wembley. The crowd from the game. The space between players. The general distance of the pitch. It all appeared, even from the television, to be elasticated and warped and more daunting. Waddle, marked in difference by his long-sleeved shirt, runs towards the ball and, as if it has all been pre-determined, like it has already happened in the annals of time, catches it perfectly with his left foot. It's like it has its own flight path, a flight path somehow pre-destined – moving towards the goal with an exact purpose I had not seen a ball take on before. It was as if the goal had always existed. It was like life was unimaginable before it. Sheffield Wednesday led 1-0 in the opening minutes. It was one of the most beautiful things I'd ever seen.

Sheffield Wednesday played Arsenal in the FA Cup final that year. Arsenal had already won the League Cup in its first year sponsored by Coca-Cola, beating Wednesday in the final there too. Like those semi-finals, there was a nice continuity to it all, as if it were very rudimentary storytelling to captivate a child, that the teams had reached both finals. It was really tidy and understandable and attractive. That day the coverage on BBC lasted four hours. It was rare to have four hours of football. A real annual occasion not to be missed. Hours before kick-off, every single movement of the teams' activity was covered. They're eating! They're having breakfast! They're having lunch! They're swimming! Lee Dixon is shaving! They're getting on the bus! Lee Dixon is getting on the bus clean-shaven! They're an hour away! They're getting off the bus! Lee Dixon is still unshaven! Referee Keren Barratt is having a light snack! He's planning on changing for the game at ten to two! The teams are in suits! Now they're in tracksuits! The FA Cup final, in effect, was an early warning sign of a world to come, of content for content's sake, of celebrities doing routine things fetishised for us all to watch. It is oddly addictive even then. I am sat centimetres from the screen. In between every other link of Sheffield Wednesday or Arsenal players doing something incredibly ordinary, or giggling in packs, almost every sentence is designed to reinforce how important the FA Cup is. There are montages from over the years, moving from black-and-white to colour, John Motson is shouting "It's there" over all of it, every time a goal goes in. Hartlepool United recorded a single when they reached the fourth round, we learn. Half an hour into the coverage, pre-made little mini-docs on the teams' histories with the competition are aired. Quite genuinely chilling music is played as time is reeled back to meet Sheffield Wednesday's last finalists of 1966. They were 2-0 up, we are told over a continuously ominous backing track, before Everton shocked them to win the game 3-2. Gerry Young is sat in stark light, being asked, "All the reports seem to blame you for that third goal, do you blame yourself for it?" "Oh aye, of course," he says. "I did let the ball go, didn't I." He says it as if he can still see it, slipping to let Derek Temple through. Among a precedent and premise of pure feelgood, it is absolutely poleaxing in its lack of feelgood factor. It really must stay with you then, I thought, gulping, the reflection of Gerry Young's face burning its way into my retinas.

Just by being told the back story, I already knew that Sheffield Wednesday, who I was strangely attached to, were losing this game. I probably could have told you they'd lose the replay in the last minute of extra time, as it exactly transpired. It was the same when, in October of the same year, commentator Brian Moore foresaw Holland's Ronald Koeman taking a free-kick against England, Arsenal's David Seaman in goal. "He's going to flick one now." Moore said it again, as if trying to frighten an armed burglar while helpless in his underwear, then a third time. "He's going to flick one." Koeman did flick one and England were not going to qualify for the World Cup. Just like Waddle's goal, as soon as it was in the net, it was as if it was always in the net, as if it always had been in the net, as if the ghost of Gerry Young danced around it, telling me that I would never forget this either. In his way, Rilke was part wrong: "Let everything happen to you: beauty and terror. Just keep going. No feeling is final." Beauty and terror. When it came to football, both feelings were, in their own way, both very forever and very final.

There was an instantaneous second universe to live in because of football. It was one that I could land in now at all times of day, every minute of every waking hour, waiting for that envelope every week. But it was not just an imaginary land to keep only to yourself. It was a real world with possibilities more brutal and more magical than imagination would ever have you believe. Football, in one year, had already shown me all it could show me, all anything would ever be able to. Fantasy and reality and grace and hurt and mundanity and deep feeling and escape and everyday. There was already nothing more to tell. And yet I wanted it to tell me it all again and again. While I waited for that box to be opened, praying the football gods were kind, there was a conversation to be had with almost any adult – an opinion to be shared, a vortex to be surfed. A world to be joined.

I still have never been to Partick, on the north side of Glasgow. In my head, though, I am still checking out there regularly, meeting the people of Partick, telling them "Thanks so much" and "Really, the pleasure is all mine."

2

Extra Preliminary Round

Saturday, 3 August 2024
Frenchfield Park, Attendance: 210
Penrith vs Pickering Town

Thirty years later, it wasn't that I was looking for anything. Not that I knew of.

It might have had something to do with being on the edge of forty. We are back in the van, my new band, 86TVs, retracing the path The Maccabees, my old band, had hauled ourselves up twenty years ago. Everything is so familiar – the same venues, the same splitter vans, the same hotels. It is as if every passing day, I collide with my younger self, remembering and recalibrating a chaos that happened exactly half my life ago, only to find myself back in the same place with half the energy. This time, it involves less drug taking. Well, less recreational drug taking. There is much more medicinal drug taking. I have a bag I take everywhere with me that is full of medicine.

It rattles when I move, when the van moves, when anything in its wake moves. It sounds like a bag full of thousands of miscellaneous keys for homes I do not know the doors to. It sounds how my joints feel every time I get up from my seat in the van, a sound that seems to come from depths unknown. I used to wonder where that sound came from that old(er) people made when they moved, that particular *urgh* and *oomph* on standing up or sitting down or walking or coming to a stop, and I now know. It is the sound of having lived, of having to continue to live. It is the sound of how doing anything at all, even just standing up, has suddenly, in its own way, become some sort of mountain to climb. The vitamins were purchased from a Holland & Barrett the day before we left, a half-hour unaccounted for, where all I know is I must have grabbed everything at eye level and left £350 worse off. The rattling has been with me ever since. I am determined not to get ill on this tour – the most recent strange self-imposed ultimatum I have given myself – but I am losing my voice all the time. Screaming once escaped me like a tsunami, ready on demand, just begging to be let out as if it was some sort of rushing, unplugged grief. Now it must be almost manually coaxed out through whole days of not talking. So, instead of talking, in the name of making each show, I just stare out of the window, steamer in hand. I like being in motion. It settles me in some inexplicable way. I am going somewhere; I have proof of it. I must be. And as I do, jarred against a past life and daydreaming of a new one, I do it among pots and pots of honey, like a wounded cartoon bear.

It will not occur to me until later on in this tour that taking this number of vitamins, most of which are the same as the other, is fraught with its own minor dangers and health implications. It's the tamest sort of double dropping, but it can leave you nauseous, with stomach cramps and dizziness, retching to scream, finding nothing in my voice from the time I've done it last night. I promised I wouldn't scream because it wasn't a massive show and I should save my voice, only to reckon in the moment that I might actually be dead tomorrow – after all, no one knows, and aren't they all massive shows? On a fix of the natural adrenaline surging through my body that gives me these hour breakthroughs of pure purpose and clarity and joy, I scream anyway, trying to do it louder than I ever have before. Somewhere behind the screams that give way again for the day-long silence are the questions that persist, pecking away, growing every day, closer to the core. Why do I not have children? Am I fat? Am I losing my hair? How do you slow time down? Why do I choose to take on forty-five jobs at once?

It doesn't matter that we've only been on tour for six days. Service stations are all we know. It's your modern-day travelling band equivalent of holding a blade of grass to the sky and determining which way the wind is blowing. There are no other means of external perception, no other ways to know where and when the outside world is at. The packets of Perfectil (skin, hair, nails) are definitely not going to do it. The hotel receptions offer no indication; just an endless "Can I change my room, there's a weird smell in here/there isn't a roof on it/there are handprints on the mirror." The shows themselves tell you that it is evening, and there are people here, thank god, there's people here – sometimes we crane our necks around the dressing room door to the stage and excitedly shut it, shouting to the rest of the band,

"There are some young people here!" – but that's it. Service stations are the only real litmus test of a world outside. It's like coming out of a cryo chamber pod and being told the world is operating as if it is a Thursday afternoon. Or, if everything at the services is shut down, for example, we are travelling through a weekday night. If a spat-out hen party is waiting by the toilets, shivering in T-shirts and antennae, it's a Friday evening. Today's case is a specific feeling and hum for one time and one time alone: the way Lancaster services is bombarded, running children and queues and a million general intentions colliding in one space, it can only be twelve o'clock on a Saturday.

We leave the van, I make the noise as I stand up, the "definitely feels like I'm starting to get old a bit, actually" noise, and disembark from the middle of the van, sliding the door across, looking out onto the mass of cars parked outside, "Welcome Break" written high and large. It's like Noah's Ark in here. There are at least two of everyone. Army cadets, school trips, families, stag dos, hen dos, The Bears rugby team, The Bears football team, miscellaneous teenagers. I love service stations. I love that there is nowhere else to be. That there are no other options. I like that it is OK to behave like a child and slide twenty pence pieces into arcade games that ask you to hook an unhookable teddy bear onto an unhookable claw. I like that everyone is going somewhere from somewhere else. No one has arrived at the thing. There are no unmet expectations here or broken dreams or harsh realities – there is just being between somewhere and somewhere else.

I'm rubbing my eyes, waiting for my fourth white americano of the day when, the shapes and chaos moving across me, I begin to realise something. If this is roughly noon on Saturday, that means football across the country is happening at three. Everyone knows football is happening at three. I bet there's football somewhere near the Kendal Calling festival. We're not on stage until six. The level we are back at, we will likely have some sort of shared Portakabin, which will either be a reflective hellish heat or an over-air-conditioned cold where I will be thrown deeper into the temptation of setting light to my vitamins as some sort of warmth to gather round. If there was football near Kendal, I could get there, maybe? I could watch football and get back in time for our set?

A surge of potential runs through me. A slow swell of possibility – of glorious, mundane, familiar escapism for two hours. Of the taste of fried onions and that smell only football programmes have, a dream of being in a space where people shout things like "Release" and "Who wants it?" into the air among listless daydreaming and petty confrontations and all the other good stuff. I check on my phone. What grounds are near Kendal Calling? One is a half-hour drive from the festival. Penrith Town. Please be at home, I pray. I need this. They are. The extra preliminary, very first round of the FA Cup, at home to Pickering Town.

I google the reviews. There is one. "If you like pies or chips, you are in for a treat." The van is back moving now as I do, Lancaster Services and the Noah's Ark a speck on the disappearing horizon. We are moving through the beautiful hills of England, shades of green and brown set on top of each other, big grey clouds furnishing them. There are enchanted trees hanging off the end of natural ledges, giving way to farmhouses unshrouded by anything at all. Sometimes roadside trees hide the view for a stretch and then reveal massive mountains behind them that weren't even there before. It is a non-transactional relationship, just being you and the view, a film developing in front of your eyes to whatever you are listening to.

The instructions about the game are vague. As the background flashes between the trees and the roadside and the mountains, I am hunched over my phone, researching. It is the actual opening round of the FA Cup, an extra preliminary round designed to ensure more amateur teams can fit in there. I call the Penrith number. It rings and rings. I am about to give up when, in a slightly bumbled collection of sounds, someone picks up the receiver. After a second, the voice answers as if their home phone number has been rung in the middle of the night. In one "Hello?" delivered after hesitation, the man manages to sound part concerned, part disturbed and part put out. There is a game, yes, he says. There will definitely be tickets on the door, yes. And finally, it's £7 adults and £4 concessions.

I ask the rest of the band at the entrance to the festival, where wristbands are being handed out. Does anyone want to come and see Penrith vs Pickering Town in the extra preliminary round of the FA . . .? I don't even need to finish the question. Everyone's attention has trailed off even before I have reached the end of it. Who, after all, wants to come and see Penrith vs Pickering Town in the extra preliminary round of the FA Cup? I half reconsider. Do I really want to? Then it speaks to me. The gut feeling that people tell me I should be able to feel on bigger, actual life decisions. The little voice everyone says you're supposed to listen to. The one that everyone says when you know, you just know, and I nod, but absolutely do not know what the fuck they are talking about. It arrives here, though; it whispers, but whispers insistently – not then, not in any of the actual serious life moments I've had, of course, but now – about non-league football and it says to me, definitely go to Penrith vs Pickering Town in the extra preliminary round of the FA Cup. It's what you must do.

The face of the cab driver, waiting outside the festival site, appears to half spark when I tell him where I'd like to go. For ten minutes, there is silence. We drive back through the trees and farmhouses I've just come from. I am the passenger sitting next to a stranger. Shot through with a feeling of excitement I get sometimes when I'm outside London, I think about how much of my life I have spent in passenger seats next to strangers and never learned a single thing about them. I am unsure if I should start a conversation, or let us sit here in the nothing. Is the silence because there is some sort of unremedied football grief? Does it trigger a silence in him, or does he just not like football, or is he just happy in this silence?

And then, unprompted, he begins. He was a ballboy when the ground was in the town centre, he tells me. They were a really good team then. The non-league Penrith beat Third Division Chester 1-0 in the first round of the FA Cup in 1981. In the next round, he had travelled on the team bus to Doncaster, where a frozen pitch should have had the game called off, but they played on anyway and Penrith were cruelly beaten. He journeyed back through the snow with his heroes, all of them hurt in their own way, slightly changed. He reels off some of the squad names, unrecognisable to me, putting weight on their first names as if they were fallen war heroes. I can picture each one just by his delivery, the dewy-eyed matter-of-factness with which he drops each line: Geoff Fell, he'll forever be a legend. I do not need to see Geoff Fell to know that he has a strong handlebar moustache. Brian "Billy" Williams was the manager, he tells me. God, Billy Williams worked miracles. A rhythm starts in him, hands suddenly tapping on the steering wheel. His hands stop drumming, he glances to his left, for a fleeting second his eyes on mine. The memory breaks his stride. A bridge between a remembered world and the real one drawn. "The team's gone downhill, these days we're just about holding our own against Stalybridge Celtic." He continues, "In those days, the ground was in the middle of Penrith, it was the centre of everything. People would hear the music from the ground and come out. It was sold to the club that if they moved to the outskirts, they'd have a state-of-the-art ground." It was all, as ever, down to money. "The club was promised loads and it was never really given to them. It turned out the new ground was built on a floodplain, so the pitch is now artificial. It's really out on a limb out here." He tells me this as he turns off the motorway, a town nowhere in sight, and into what appears to be a field populated by occasional sheep, dotted in blue. As he drifts through the scattered blue, a small football ground appears in the distance. It's Frenchfield Park. "Oh," he says in half surprise, "there's some cars here." As I settle up – he has to drive around the mostly vacant car park in search of a spot that his card machine works in – he remembers something, as if bestowing some sort of loaded information onto the lost protagonist of a children's adventure film. He winds the window back down and says, "I would try and sort a car back now if you can, it's not London round here."

You can feel that the playing area is at the bottom of a floodplain, gently surrounded. The gates at Penrith open out onto the pitch, players training, with the hills overlooking behind the goal on the far side to the left, trees framing the touchline opposite. There is one stand, optimistically but accurately described as "the main stand", a bank of maybe a couple of hundred blue seats. There is no sign of the closure of it through last October, when a fan fell through the bottom of it. He was uninjured and investigations were inconclusive. On the side of the boards, as you walk towards the stand, it is written, "Ask not what your club can do for you, ask what you can do for your club."

The first thing I see on site, maybe the first part of action of the FA Cup campaign of 2024–25 seen by anyone, is the Penrith goalkeeper, stood there for isolated drills, reaching forward to catch a ball hit straight at him, only to let it slip through his hands and bonk him on the head. He shakes his head, like a character in a *Wallace & Gromit* film who has just crashed through the floor, looks around for the ball for a moment, then goes to retrieve it as if nothing has happened.

I am keen to heed my taxi driver's parting words of cinematic foreboding and immediately ask the woman at the gate how easy it is to get a taxi back to Kendal Calling. She puffs out her cheeks, as if she has been handed a puzzle, and takes me to a small office. There are two men in what appears to be both an official match office and a club merch stall. Scarves and shirts hang on one side among newspaper clippings from the club's history. One cutting, with frayed edges, proudly sits at eye level – Penrith vs Manchester City 1981. I explain my situation, unsure whether I've walked into some sort of official private area or the club shop. The man in my eyeline puffs his cheeks out too. "You can try here," he says. I recognise him as the voice from the phone. He gently passes over two mobile phone numbers, our hands making brief contact, his rugged and worn, mine expectant and grateful. I thank him and call both. Neither are available to take me back to the festival once the game is over, they say. And no, sorry, they don't know anyone else. When I walk back into the room, slightly crestfallen, on the edge of sudden panic of being stranded at Penrith AFC when I'm supposed to be on stage at Kendal Calling, with visions of walking down the M6 to try and get back in time, the man to my left sits up from his chair a fraction. He is holding an envelope of notes, which he is counting. I tell him my predicament. I'm a musician. I need to get back for a show after the final whistle. "Aye, no problem," he says. "I'll drive you, just come and find me when the whistle is blown." I'm slightly shocked at this generosity and feel an inclination to say thank you but no thank you, but sensing my options limited to just this, thank him enthusiastically, tell him that's really kind, to which he half acknowledges before flicking the envelope of cash with his fingers. "I've just got to go and get the players paid," he says, and walks through the opposite door. My friend from the phone, with the rugged and worn hands, looks back up at me. "You've got lucky today," he smiles. "That's the chairman, that's Billy Williams."

When I walk out of the office and back into the fray, past the programmes that cost £1 (they're out of them for now, but they can "reprint a few, if you like?"), Penrith AFC suddenly appears to be a surreal local football mirage. Walls and seats and tiles and benches are painted a bright blue, the same bright blue as the scattered blue-dotted sheep on the hills above, looking down on the flood-prone pitch. A linesman walks off the pitch during warm-ups, clutching a hamstring. A young woman is covering the game, huge headphones on, a team sheet in front of her, a tiny box connecting her to what must be some form of local radio. I tiptoe to a seat, distant enough not to intrude on what essentially feels like a community barbecue or outdoor party, but close enough to suck it in, to feel its warmth.

There is an unbelievable friendliness, the sort that throws a Londoner completely – an amalgamation of nods and winks and grandparents and children all huddled together. The back of the stand gives way to a community hall of sorts, used as a general play area for kids and, just as I am peering into it, "She's Electric" by Oasis is turned off abruptly and a Tannoy squeals. There's a man in his eighties, sunglasses and white hair, sitting by the sliding doors, half in the inside, his legs overlapping onto the stand. He is waving a microphone around away from him as if he's swatting a fly, trying to stop the squealing. It doesn't stop, but relents just enough not to be cutting a horror film frequency through the air, and he begins to read off a sheet he holds with his other hand. He tilts his eyes just over his dark glasses and, like a bingo caller, starts to announce players' names and their numbers. It is extremely hard to make out the names of the players through the PA, but no one seems to mind. Pickering Town play in bright yellow, against the blue of Penrith. Both teams, against the floodplain and the sheep, resemble vivid hallucinations.

When the game kicks off, it is alarming at first for a game of football to be unfolding without the usual white-noise mush of crowd sound that I have grown to associate it with. Every single noise made from the pitch is audible. The absolute intensity of it for a second stuns me. Semi-romantic phrases are thrown into the air incredibly aggressively, players shouting things like "I need you!" or "Here if you need." It is genuinely surreal that on this warm summer afternoon with the kids and isolated men folding their arms over the hoarding on the side of the pitch, half-watching the game, the air is split by this sort of instant blood curdling. It looks really difficult, really hard work. The idea I sometimes daydream when I watch Premier League football and begin to genuinely assume I could actually fit into this team is torn to shreds when faced with the harsh reality of it at this level, tens and tens and tens of tiers below.

Although Pickering Town are a threat down the left-hand side, Penrith take the lead in the first five minutes, a slide rule pass to Luke Hunter splitting the Pickering defence before he looks up, sees DJ Taylor completely unmarked on the penalty spot and squares the ball to him. Taylor scores. "That's Shaun's boy," the woman to my left says, leaning back over a seat to nudge someone. Her friend nods. When Penrith go two up twenty minutes later, Connor Hammell's dink chipping the goalkeeper in a one-on-one, she leans back again to the same friend. "Picked his spot there," she says. Her friend nods again.

A few minutes later, Pickering Town feel like they should have a handball given in their favour. It is not given and their manager is apoplectic. Penrith's manager walks up to him, both hands in a submissive gesture, and says, with all the sincerity in the world, that he "swears to god that was not handball" and then puts his hand on his heart. The incident happened on the other side of the pitch where it would have been almost impossible for anyone in the dugout to know. This does not appease the Pickering manager, who grunts and channels this injustice into shouting, "How many times do I have to tell ya!" at almost every single one of his players for the next ten minutes. It is 3-0 by half-time, the cup tie already as good as done. The reporter appears not to have heard from her local radio team and, huge headphones still cuddling the entirety of her head, she stares into the void and waits for news.

In the bright blue burger van, a woman with heavy eyelashes and bright lipstick hands a packet of crisps to the next person in the queue. She squeezes it quite tight, scrunching it into the palm of her hand, and then looks impressed. "That's a nice full bag, isn't it" – she makes her eyes big – "because some of them have got nowt in them." He receives his nice, full and now totally crushed packet of crisps less enthusiastically.

During the second half, I suddenly become washed out into a state of being incredibly invested. The sunglasses-wearing white-haired man is back with the Tannoy as the players take to the field again, using his finger to count the players. "Wait a second," he says down the microphone, "16 and 12 have come on, but we don't know who's come off?" He repeats it, the second time more urgently, before the Pickering Town substitutes turn around and shout back that they have replaced numbers 4 and 11. Another squeal, wrestling with the feedback, waving the microphone around like a wand, and then an audible clearing of his throat: "Substitutes for Pickering Town, number 12, Sam Calvert, and number 16, Kieran Stares, on for number 4, Matty Garbutt, and number 11, Joe Wood." There is no need for him to have announced this because everyone has already heard the conversation before, down the microphone.

The plight of Penrith is now important to me. The place is doing the magic thing that football can do. There is nowhere else to be, nothing else happening in the world. The only thing that matters is Penrith vs Pickering Town. People shout "Foul throw" together with sudden authority. A man loitering at the back goes around telling whoever will listen that this has been very impressive, "given the last few seasons". He has the air of a man who walks around with his finger to the sky, telling anyone who will listen that it "looks like rain is on its way". As he does, finding people to tell, my attention is forcibly drawn to a sideshow developing where the Penrith and Pickering benches both demand possession of the spare ball. The Pickering manager hides it behind his back, rolls it in the opposite direction of the Penrith bench. The Penrith manager sends his assistant to go and get the ball. There is a little scuffle over it. The assistant comes back without the ball and is sent back to go and get it again. Meanwhile, the game is continuing out in front of them.

Little moments of genuine brilliance, of actual acrobatic endeavour, decorate the play – Kieran Stares bringing the ball out of the sky like Dennis Bergkamp before being fouled, his manager attempting to complain while still hiding the spare ball behind his back. In this very competition, people will be bringing the ball down like that regularly, as it gradually evolves from amateur to the elite. They already are. There is a kid running around as the last minutes play out, the last indignation for Pickering being an absolute sitter going wide of the post. He is excitedly telling everyone the news: "It looks like it's Crook Town in the next round." Then he says with telling eyes, as if imparting quite secret information, "They're winning 4-1." The reporter does not look like she knows this. She still stares unmoved, waiting for news from her station. I feel like walking up to her, to check that she is still breathing. The messenger finally runs up to the man I have been promised a lift from, the man I now have gathered was the legendary manager and now chairman Billy Williams, tapping him on the shoulder, excitedly telling him the news. Williams receives it with interest without engaging the child in any further conversation, as if it's a mistake he's made before. When the final whistle blows, I am tentatively making sure he is in my eyeline, just in case he has forgotten. He hasn't. He punches the air low down at the result, as if winding a boxer with a borderline low blow, then turns to look for me, sitting in the stand, and waves me over. It's a comforting gesture, as if he always gives me a lift to Kendal Calling.

Billy Williams puts the keys in the ignition and reverses out of the ground. The game has only just finished minutes earlier. "So, you're playing Kendal Calling, are you?" he says, driving back past the sheep. "My granddaughter is there. I'll tell her I've met one of the bands." I tell him that our album is currently number three in the album charts, but we will not stay there as the week progresses, and that *NME* have just reviewed it, saying they like it but it's quite "overstuffed". I don't know why I tell him these things, but I feel like I owe him at least some context for my shotgun seat in his car. He is used to this little shuttle run, it turns out, usually having to play emergency taxi to groundhoppers who are trying to go to every ground in the country. "I have so much respect for people like that," he says. "Football means so much to them. It's important to me that anyone that comes to Penrith for the first time feels like they've been looked after."

I am back on the same road, the one that links Penrith and Kendal Calling, for the third time, my company bizarrely having switched from the rest of 86TVs to the cab driver who was once a ball boy, back again now to the chairman of Penrith, Billy Williams. *I wonder where it would lead, if I kept going,* I think. If I just checked out of all other commitments and decided to ferry lifts back and forth between the two of these places forever, slowly dispersing personal information to strangers and seeing what came back. I tell Billy about the cab driver, about how he name-checked him, and his memories of being a ballboy, about the FA Cup first-round win against Chester and travelling to Doncaster. Billy's ringed fingers on the wheel tap a couple of times, flicking across the wheel in the same fashion I have learned flamenco guitarists play. He talks about Chester exactly like the blissed-out cab driver before him, but then immediately changes his tone for that doomed second round. "We shouldn't have played that game. The pitch wasn't playable." He winces, fingers tapping a touch quicker. "It was in the days when all this new footwear was coming out and our lads didn't have the right gear. We didn't stand a chance really." This is what football does, pulls time tight towards you, even a 1981 FA Cup run, and nowhere more so than in a place like Penrith, as I travel this road for the third time, looking across at ancient trees that are almost completely sideways from wind wearing them down.

Billy Williams has played for Penrith, managed them and owned them. He has been involved with the club since 1967. In those days, he says, he "didn't have a pot to piss in" and would play twice in a day, but "the memory can play all kinds of tricks, can't it." Billy, like the rest of Penrith, laments the move away from town. When he retired, he "should have been living the dream" but was instead "bored out of his head". He got involved with the club again, desperate to keep it afloat. The cup tie somehow connects all of it, the future, the past, the present, wrapping it into a vision of hope. "There's hundreds of clubs in the country desperate to win today, it's a really big deal to create interest in the community," Billy says. He pauses, checking the traffic, eyes meeting mine for a second, the festival nearing. "This will be met with laughter, I'm sure" – his eyes back on the road – "but I've been writing to Pep Guardiola, asking if there was any chance of a game." The Manchester City–Penrith game still looms large in folklore between the Lake District and the Pennines. They dream of another one. We pull into the festival ground, where one extremely bored twenty-something in a hi-vis jacket directs us half-heartedly towards a grassy bank where cars are dotted as aimlessly as the sheep at the football ground. "When I got involved with this club, I got told a story about a lad's mother who came to the ground with a letter," Billy says, following the man's wave. "Her son, I think it was, had played for Penrith and then went to serve in the First World War. The letter read, 'Oh to pull on that shirt again.' He died four days after it was written, in France. I think about him often. I wonder about how old he would have been at that Chester game, and whether he would have been there. I always think, if we keep working hard, you never know, we might have a day like that again one day. I've been here since 1967 and the important thing to me about our club is it still gives people pride, and a real sense of belonging. We all want that, don't we?" I nod. We do. I thank him and leave the car, forgetting to offer him something for the journey. As I lean back in through the window, wishing him luck in the next round, he points his ringed index finger back at me. "Just remember Penrith, son," he says. "It'll be there in your memories." And he is gone, back towards the football, and I turn towards the festival. We are onstage in an hour.

3

Preliminary Round

Saturday, 17 August 2024
Hanbury Stadium, Attendance: 279
Haywards Heath Town vs Deal Town

Have you ever been so sad that, in the tiny moments it relents, you can see the state you are in from outside, and just for a split second, it becomes very funny to you? When The Maccabees ended, I was so incredibly bereft that I had moments like that. I was comic-book bereft. It was like The National had written me into one of their songs; I was like a television version of a person with a broken heart. Sometimes I would almost take myself outside of my own body and think, *This is actually really living, isn't it, feeling something as deeply as this.* I felt like my life might be over, reasoning that I had lived a childhood dream for fourteen years, if not one as a football manager, then one maybe even better, having formed a band with my brother and friends in our teens, dreamed a thing between us that turned into our actual lives, and as recompense for it, my life was now finished at thirty-four. I walked around with the odd sensation of someone who thinks they might have just left a bag on the train but can't remember if they ever had one with them in the first place. The end of the band was, obviously, not my decision; after we toured our fourth album, which had gone to number one, and at the peak of our success but at the end of our collective tether, we parted ways with some farewell shows, our biggest ever.

There was a break-up thrown into the mix too, one that happened at almost the exact same time, for good measure. It was a call that also struck me like an astronomical surprise, but shouldn't have done. It was always going to be too much for me, she said, probably completely within reason. I remember leaving her house, winded to the point of absolute hollowness, in the middle of the night, feeling as if I no longer recognised the body I was in, like everything was completely foreign to me, my feet and legs walking without being attached to my body, a hazy filter placed over the entire world. In the immediate aftermath of both these abrupt endings, I felt like I was becoming see-through, like I might just disappear one night, curled up in the corner of my flat.

My life was thrown into the first phase of extremely delayed, serious grieving for my mum, who had died seventeen years earlier, almost exactly when the band had begun. There was no feeling of anything like this when it actually happened, only the occasional kick of mad adrenaline through deadened skin, the odd prolonged stare into space in the classroom. Back then, I felt an alien sensation carry me through the funeral and the days around it, before I chose to carry on, to work hard, to make something new, fuelled by a heartbreak that must have been so painful I couldn't even really feel it. I wielded it like a secret, fiendish desire to run into the world and see how much I could get out of it.

Seventeen years later, though, these endings forced upon me, it had caught up with me, as if I had been forever two strides ahead of a devilish little goblin, hearing its breath and footsteps behind me for almost two decades, ready to swallow me up as soon as I stopped running. And when I stopped, it swallowed me whole, into a cavernous, reflective, tragicomic black hole. With it, I had all kinds of visceral flashbacks about the end of her life – her trying to keep her head still through the worst, deepest part of the multiple sclerosis. Her trying to speak, but not being able to, her head swinging left and right dramatically. Her arm wildly moving too, out of her control. I dreamed, regularly, that she was with me in a room, looking after her dad, wearing very specific clothes I recognised her in. I open a door in the dream, asking if she could come outside the room with me. She couldn't come, she would say, but I could tell her about what is out there. I would wake up covered in tears, my face wet. Every day, the feeling of rejection from the end of The Maccabees and my relationship bring me towards a realisation of the profound pain and desperation that she must have felt, but somehow smiled through every time I entered the room, her body failing her, her life ending as mine began, her somehow still willing mine to get better.

People who have suffered early grief, I have learned, can really struggle with anything ending at all. A job. A relationship. A meal. A walk. A day. Suddenly, it might strike you that everything ends, and how unbearable that is. Life might become a manic gathering together of every safety mechanism you can find to guard against it. You might try emotional distance, an addiction to a level of busyness and over-exertion. Over time, and the therapy that I am still in, I began to recognise that all the surviving had served me in my formative years, had helped me reach things, get inside and towards anything I loved, communicate with it all in an urgent and meaningful way. But the very same impulse had left me unusually terse and tense with much of the closest part of my internal world, or anyone who dared get too near for too long, not committing to anything that might actually come with a genuine risk of loss.

This feeling at the end of The Maccabees, leaving our last show at Alexandra Palace as if I was walking out of one skin and not yet into another, was, it turned out, a productive energy to be handed at that age. I decided, again as I had when I was seventeen, that alongside the immediate wallowing and the retreating and the occasionally registering how dramatic I was being, I was not going to let myself be a person who used to be in a band, complaining about it ten years later at the end of the bar. I was going to become something else. I was going to use the feeling like a gift, not waste the life that was still in front of me. And so I decided I would say yes to absolutely everything.

This approach – of just saying yes – happened to meet me at a very productive age, sat right in the middle of hurt and hope and energy, and took me further than I could have imagined with work and projects and opportunities. Work has been increasingly wild and varied and full of exploration and discovery, and new versions of connection and being part of things I love. And nonetheless, I have been having strange episodes recently, often when all the jobs collide, of feeling almost physically sick – a kind of panic that none of this work has solved anything, that I don't seem to be happier. When the work subsides, I feel worse and worse. I write lists and lists of all the stuff I need to do. All the money I should be making that I am not. All the goals I need to achieve and am not. I tell myself that when this all works, that this is good because I don't have time to dwell on anything like I did with The Maccabees in the time off, to make it too precious, to hold it too tight, because I will have to go straight into the next thing. This is, in part, true, and a good line, but with it, I bounce around harbouring people's "Wow, you're doing so much" as validation, a point to be proud of, when sometimes it is intended as more of a "Are you OK?" There is always somewhere better to be. Somewhere else that would be more loving, more rewarding, more exciting. The same way walking in London encourages you to never look up, never see the sky, never acknowledge the tops of buildings, I have a sudden sickly sense of having not looked up for the seven years since, and that with every yes there was a no that I couldn't see – a no to children or to calm or to reflection, no significant signposting in my life that comes with marriage or children, just endless working and doing. Though much of it is growing, finding myself more and more capable in multiple disciplines, something bigger and more than a guitarist in a band, nearing forty, my life does not feel pinned down to anything. And with it, endless resentments and jealousies continue in the background of my mind, attaching themselves to an unexpressed shame, the way these things like to do when you are tired, letting them in through the cracks. Meanwhile, some friends die, some friends get sick. Nothing in life stops for you, even if you choose not to recognise it.

My latest hurricane of work is finding its own uncontrollable momentum and, as I balance it all, constantly flapping against a tide, I decide that what I really need, what will put my mind to rest, where I remember feeling good, was that game I saw – Penrith in the FA Cup. That was fun, fun like I used to know. I have recollections of looking up then, seeing the sky, and too being invested in something, watching it all unfold, switched off from all those gnawing little habits and darker thoughts. Maybe that's where it is, the space and time that I am looking for, the excuse to be still, in the next round of the FA Cup. I decide that I'll go to the next round too, see what it has for me.

I have always known Haywards Heath existed, I must have gone through it close to a thousand times, I just have never stopped there. Mark Stephenson, a friend of mine from a hardened line of Crystal Palace supporters, in a flash of an early adult vision of being a football reporter, took his first and last steps on the career path as a local reporter there and across much of the south coast. He enjoyed this a lot, despite the main takeaway being that non-league clubs – despite their popular image of cosiness or homeliness – were largely quite unwelcoming places, where no one would tell you the wi-fi code or what time the ground shut or what bus to get home or where anything helpful was. You were completely on your own. There would always be a man, he said, probably in his fifties, reporting for a rival paper who would not look at or talk to him, and he could never read whether it was the perceived threat or his poor social skills. The managers took themselves incredibly seriously, almost (non-ironically) exactly mimicking the mannerisms and expressions of Premier League managers. They would do very sincere post-match interviews with all the irritability and implied pressure of how it was done on television. The level of ego, he said, was ridiculously high. He once got locked into the ground at Crawley Town after everyone had left, scrambling to finish his match report. He had to find a number on their website and plead with them to come back and let him out. They did so very reluctantly. He went on to do some reporting of League One games, which he found a very similar experience and decided he probably wasn't going to be a football reporter. This is the thing with football that you come to learn with age. It doesn't need you. It is so universal, so sure of its own worth, so assured of its place in the national psyche, that it rarely makes an effort to welcome people in. It does not really need to. People come to it, arms outstretched, completely subservient, asking for their hearts to be broken.

I studied for a year at Sussex University before dropping out because The Maccabees signed a record deal (and I did no work whatsoever). Haywards Heath was a place you would try to never be. If the train stopped at Haywards Heath on the way in from London it was, best case, a longer journey or, worst case, the train was going to terminate there unexpectedly and you were to board a rail replacement bus. Everyone hated that bus. The bus felt like it took for ever, my memory of it being always at night, always dark, always nauseous, bumping from unpopulated stop to unpopulated stop. And with it, Haywards Heath developed a reputation in my mind as shorthand for an unwanted in-between or, if I was being more honest, the middle of absolutely nowhere.

On this train journey, one I have been on in the multiple hundreds of times, I notice, as if for the first time, that the route to Haywards Heath from London is surrounded by beautiful, beautiful open fields. It's like that moment you wake up, as a forty-year-old and suddenly realise the value of walking. Walking for no reason. Just because you can. Walking, slowly, because you are alive. The space makes a mockery of all the effort I have made in life – to make something, to harness attention, to stay in people's minds, to crowd my time with activity. *If I owned all that space now*, I think, like it was a metaphor for having that time again, *I'd leave it exactly as it is*. Just have nothing there, and look out into it, stretch my arms out, look up at the sky and say, Thank god I'm alive.

The train station gives way to a car park, like the space between that I had projected on Haywards Heath. People do not stay here, they stop here and then pass through. Planes fly overhead, from Gatwick Airport, on their way somewhere from somewhere else. As I walk out of the station and towards Hanbury Park, filling in the transience like a black-and-white map that is suddenly being coloured in and given dimension, I cross the road and walk towards a park. There is just a pathway in front of me, no clues yet of what is to either side of me. And then, as if beamed in from another decade, a cricketer appears. He walks out, from right to left – a batter, fully dressed up in batting gear, from helmet to gloves to pads. I am questioning for a second whether he is real until, when the path opens up, a pavilion is revealed to the right and to the left a cricket pitch circled by benches, framed by an incline of twenty-foot hills.

I have time, so I walk the incline, past the pavilion, towards the benches, as the batter that I have just believed to be a mirage walks out. There are a handful of people watching. I like how strangers will sit and watch village cricket. It fills me with appreciative, comedic serenity that people will sit and watch anything really, if it's in front of them. It is like sitting in front of the sea. It's just big and there, and it's a relief to become a dumb witness to it. There is a run-out, the bowler effecting it. I have a perfect view of it, better than the umpire's. It is definitely out, but the umpire gives it not out. The bowler is pleading, trying to get the attention of anyone who will validate his anger. Would it be weird if I shouted and told him I agreed with him? Maybe it would. I think to turn to the older man on the bench to my left, drinking a Stella, a plastic bag of cans next to him still to get through, to ask him whether he thought it was out too. Too late. He's gone, and he's taken the beer with him. I let the bowler simmer in his injustice and soon leave in the drinks break after he has bowled said batter, watching the same batter I had seen arrive, leave, out twice for very little.

I'm walking past Maplehurst Nursing Home and down Oathall Avenue. The road opens out to idyllic little pictures of England through driveways. There are families out, mowing the lawn. I walk past a tattooed man with four children. I order myself in opposition to these things, consciously or otherwise. I am not these things. I'm not tattooed. That was a choice. I don't have children. I can never work out whether that was. We don't acknowledge each other. A driver on Barn Cottage Lane stops as I cross the road. He has his window down. He does a very lovely "Cheers, mate" as I let him past first. One of those soft, gentle, kind ones. The ones that you sometimes feel are all you need in life, just a series of sincere, kind, understated acknowledgements with strangers, before you pop back into the little bubble of your own life. Two boys and a dad are racing a remote-controlled car up and down the vacated road that he leaves in his wake.

There are no signs of a football match whatsoever. Beyond the remote-controlled car there is utter, complete silence. Until, as I edge closer, I hear in the distance, in unmistakable football Tannoy tinniness, the chorus to "Empire State of Mind" by Jay-Z featuring Alicia Keys. This was not written for Haywards Heath Town. I follow the sound. There is nothing else anywhere, at first not even any sight of it, just the sound of football.

Entering the ground is like entering a Stuart Roy Clarke football photography book summing up footballing culture in the 1990s. Every scene I walk through is a perfectly framed image. Families are huddled together as if it is a fair, people looking like they are half done up for a night out and half making every effort to be as totally tracksuited as possible. Everything is deep blue and white. Even in the urinals, the cleaning pod is the same deep blue as the club colours, the urinal and corresponding wall harsh white. The Eiffel 65 song from the nineties is playing, a remix, the words changed from what I remember them to be to "I'm blue and I'm feeling alright, gonna be the best freaking night of my life". Being in football grounds early, way before kick-off, is a gentle reminder of being a child, when it felt like all music was just about having the best freaking night of your life, like there was nothing more aspirational to write a song about, when the future world to inherit was just one of packs of boys and girls getting ready for nights out. I turn to my left again, and there is the man from the cricket, the one with the Stellas. If he were not staring into the middle distance so vacantly, bar the odd twitch or scratch of his nose, I would ask him now whether he thought that run-out was out. I better not, all those beers are gone.

Deal Town, the away team today, wear black and white and have brought a smattering of away fans who all have an air of friends and family. They are herded up by an enthusiastic older man who has brought a drum.

In the programme, chairman Steve Isherwood talks of memories of yesteryear in the FA Cup with Bury. The manager, Naim Rouane, alternately chooses to bathe in the memory of a thrilling tie away at Hassocks that ended with a penalty saved. There is a pull-out poster of Josh Spinks – defender – with a space designated for him to sign. Haywards Heath are joint top, second only on goal difference, in the Southern Combination Premier Division, and haven't conceded a goal yet. Impressive. With time to kill, I'm reading it from cover to cover, like I used to, but also to get the lie of the land. I feel a bit like a bad detective reading a newspaper with holes cut out for my eyes.

A football match at this level – a crowd big enough to give the thing real, scatty occasion, but sparse enough to individually grow accustomed to every person there – is a very specific sort of experience. It speaks of both loneliness and community, conformity and eccentricity, of the tractor beam pull the game has on a certain type of person. For something so certain of its mainstream place in everyday culture, when people are not crammed too tight, not yet just a baying mass, a cultish left field-ness reveals itself. The crowd is an odd combination of tribes – of geezers and families and

Marvel-Comics-wearing geeks and loners. It is enough to turn it inwards and wonder which of those I am. Am I any of those? Maybe the loner? Definitely the loner today. One man is sitting completely alone on the bank opposite me, behind the car park. Being separated by the width of a football pitch, the only stand with seats being mine, gives the odd sensation of being on a ship, and him just a dinghy at sea, waving at him just because that's what people do when separated between shore and sea.

Meanwhile, as the players warm up, the Deal Town drummer is explaining to anyone he can find, bragging, that Deal Town are "doing brilliant in the league" at the moment. He hands the drum to a young girl, maybe seven years old, in a Haywards Heath top, and asks her to bang the rhythm, but pointing a jovial finger right up to her face says, "You've got to say Deal Town, OK?" The finger is quite close to her and, like a muzzled dog, she barks at him: "No." He puts his finger down quickly, as if he has nearly had it bitten off, a wide grin on his face that says he has found a competitor. "Yes," he shouts back louder. She stares back at him. "NO." They reach a stalemate, and he takes the drum with him as he goes.

In the middle of all of this, the Haywards Heath team warm up. They seem to be a mix of much older men, maybe part-time footballers, and children with their hair done in the image of Premier League footballers. There's a Jack Grealish. A few Jack Grealishes, actually. A Phil Foden. A Gareth Bale. They circulate around each other in drills while the manager looks on. You can always tell who the manager is. It's the way their hands are behind their back. It's a small tell. It says, I'm watching, I'm appraising, I'm a man of power choosing not to use it at this moment in time. But I will wield it. Mark my words, I will wield it.

The players run back into the dressing rooms, past a gate that is closed across the walkway between stand and pitch, like a level crossing or a moat. It separates the stand from the tuck shop. It goes up when they are coming through. The welcomes to Deal Town are read out over the Tannoy in the tone of someone channelling the energy of a nervous child on their first day at school. Some stuttering ums and erms and sos between the teams. Then the Brazil World Cup football advert is played. The one where their players did keepy-ups and tricks and passed to each other across the world. The two of these things, unintentionally, kick a lovely sentimentality into the air, as if the difference between reality and imagination is all adjustable, bridges that are walked over easily, just by the choice of the right song.

Then, obviously, it's "Freed from Desire". In 2024, it's always "Freed from Desire". It's a strange reach for football at this level, to give it the ambitions and intentions of a banging nightclub. As the song plays out, the players run through the tiny drawbridge, which is drawn back up. A little girl in a Barbie T-shirt leans on it, her hand aloft to high-five players. Some ignore her, assimilating the body language of elite footballers in a zone that has no time for anything so trivial, others stop and speak to her as if they are the local butcher asking after her family. "Hay, hay, Haywards Heath Town" comes from somewhere. A chant. I look around, puzzled. It doesn't feel like there are really enough people there to make a noise, but the noise still happens, as if it is piped in somewhere from the gods.

The Roy Hatt Family Stand keeps the sound in better than the main stand at Penrith. Where in Penrith, on kick-off, the kind of brutality of football suddenly opened its jaws, all thumping and shouting and general sounds you might associate with war, here there is enough singing and general ambience that shields the naked reality of a football match. Prams are pushed up and down the touchline by young fathers, half watching the game, half watching their children. The Deal Town drummer walks past, banging his drum up and down.

I begin to realise there actually are enough people here – just – for the usual chanting to take place. That's not piped-in sound. It's real. Haywards Heath sing "Shall we sing a song for you" at the twenty friends and family here to watch Deal Town. By the tuck shop, two kids with their dad are restlessly running up and down the corridor between the pitch and the stand. One of them, he can't be much more than two years old, is wearing Crocs. I watch this from my seat between the man from the cricket with the Stellas – a healthy distance between us, him still not having moved – and a father and son on my right. They support Deal Town. The father is wearing a T-shirt emblazoned with a superhero and has a backwards cap on, sheltering long, metal rocker-style hair. The Haywards Heath right back, Max Blencowe, is brought down clearly for a free-kick and, when trying to pick himself off the floor, the dad stands up and shouts at him, "Someone get princess his tiara." The son nods approvingly, half-smiles. Deal Town are cautious in their approach and the Superhero Dad starts to become agitated with them. When one too many passes has gone sideways, he stands up again. "This isn't the fucking Euros," he says. "Pass fucking forwards." He is referencing the England team who are currently, somehow, advancing to the knockout stages of the European Championship despite criticism of their negative style. If you needed an encapsulation of the public's attitude to football in England, it is there, in the exasperation of a Deal Town fan who expects his side to be more ambitious, more technically capable and more entertaining than the European Championship finalists, England.

As Haywards Heath fans behind the goal begin to taunt the drummer, singing "One song, you've only got one song" at him, Superhero Dad jumps to the rescue: "We only need one song." He rubs his belly inexplicably. "We're simple." He stops and then projects his voice again: "Winning is simple, isn't it." No one seems to have any idea what he means, I make sure not to stare too long.

A back and forth develops between him and a six-year-old child, a Haywards Heath fan, who cups his ear at Superhero Dad. Superhero Dad isn't pleased about this, and he and his son begin to shout "Down with the Heath", as if they're in some sort of re-enactment of a medieval battle. Then, like an emperor with cavalry, he sends his son off for chips. His son walks past the Deal Town drummer, each of them catching the other's eye. Superhero Dad is not watching the game now and has followed this little acknowledgement. He has set it up. "What you looking at my son for, you fucking faggot," he shouts. It's the first time the drummer has stopped drumming. He just looks back confused, and chooses not to answer.

When the boy returns with the chips, his dad has advice for him. "You never make it personal or abusive," he tells his son. "It's just normal non-league chirp, this is just how it goes." The son nods earnestly, listening, maybe wondering how shouting "you fucking faggot" at someone, for no reason other than that they are a stranger who happens to be in your line of sight, isn't personal or abusive.

There is a strange clause here in football, where language and abuse are often somehow given a free pass – "this is just how it goes" would be considered verbal assault if not framed by a pitch and a terrace. It is not easy for clubs – big or small – to pick up isolated incidents, and these days they all have a zero-tolerance approach to any form of abuse, which is of course not always the easiest thing in the world to police. I was not at football in the seventies or the eighties, where racism and homophobia were famously commonplace. But in moments like this, it is not difficult to imagine how terrifying it once was, the embers of it still flickering across football pitches everywhere.

There is an odd danger to the atmosphere that starts to show itself. There was no tangible away support at Penrith vs Pickering, no more opposition than the strange battle for the spare balls that took part between the management staff. Here, the off-field face-off is more pronounced. The suggestion of a crowd, multiplied by the distance between people, is making it feel like everyone is an island to take pot-shots at, at a second's notice. Anyone could be a "fucking faggot", just for walking past a child. It's treacherous. There are shape-shifting rules at play, where the finger might land on you, knocking me out of the slightly saccharine, touristy isn't-everything-lovely-at-football that wrapped me in Cumbria, reminding me that football is also an excuse for some people to turn up, tell a few strangers they could knock them out, then leave again.

Outside the Roy Hatt Family Stand, it is almost like a seaside resort. The burger stand, painted blue of course, does relatively steady business, framing the general lazy milling that covers the perimeter of the game. An old man climbs the stairs of the stand as the first half, still 0-0, draws to a close. He slips on a step, falling upwards and just about catching his fall on a seat before he meets concrete. It's the only action in the first half that doesn't meet pointed, particular abuse. As he is helped to his feet, there is just the silence of him slowly processing his own embarrassment and perhaps mortality as he finds a seat unsurrounded by anything at all. That's what I'm worried about, I think. Dying with no one around. Maybe I should have children.

The players switch for the second half, and the fans that are making the noise from behind each goal swap. As long as the game remains 0-0, both a boredom and a tension concurrently start to spike in the air. It's interesting how close the two are to each other, how it is hard for me to distinguish one from the other. The Haywards Heath manager leaves his technical area, with his hands on his heart, pleading to the referee with the absolute sincerity that managers do, the same way the Penrith manager did, that it is a Haywards Heath throw. I have never once, in over thirty years of watching football, seen a manager say with a similar sincerity that the throw-in is for the opposite team. I wonder if they ever do know really, or whether a mist of want clouds them all, always giving the illusion that life is throwing a series of awful injustices at them.

A very aggressive, unbelievably irate man in his mid-twenties is shouting at Deal Town's number nine, Aaron Millbank, who has been pushed to the ground: "Are you going to cry?" The fan in the stands turns to the ref, who is doing the running backwards thing that referees and referees alone do, away from the stand. "Ref," he shouts at the man fading into the distance, whistle in his mouth, "he's going to cry." When the referee, obviously, takes no further action, the man just cranes his neck up at the sky and shouts "Oh, fuck off, you cunt" at nothing at all.

I walk around the ground, trying to get the vantage point of the solitary man by the car park, the Superhero Dad and his son becoming figments across the great divide of the football pitch. The man on the hill comes up to me. "See him, number 18?" There is a player warming up – Teddy Wood. "He's my mate." The man puts an arm around me. "How are you, my boy? Who do you support?" I take a guess at the right answer: Haywards Heath. "Good," he says, "not that shit", and sniffs towards the Deal Town supporters.

This is what the game has turned into: a collection of whodunnits and random accusations of who is going to cry. The deadlock is broken twenty minutes into the second half. Haywards Heath complete a slick move, pulled back for and finished by Darius Goldsmith; side-footing the ball elegantly into the top corner. Ten minutes later, Alex Plummer, who has a central midfielder give-me-the-ball-and-I'll-run-this-show type of energy, executes a perfect finish to kill the tie.

They are two really good goals. Two goals good enough to pop the boredom and airbrush the tension, resetting an atmosphere, the consensus now bowing to a couple of beautiful, semi-miraculous things that have happened. It is funny how the ripple of a net will do this. It can change everything, make us all reassess who we are, who we were seconds before bookmarked now as a definitive thing of the past.

I turn to leave, Hanbury Park and Haywards Heath and all its transitional in-betweenness with me. When I leave, the two children in Crocs and Newcastle kits are wrestling under the table, hands in each other's faces. There are people going through the scores as they leave the gates. "Rob!" Rob turns. "4-2 to Sittingbourne!" Rob clenches his fist meaningfully, not dissimilar to how Billy Williams did weeks ago. I find my phone and scan the scores. Fuck, Penrith lost.

When I am back at the train station, I cross paths with a woman who is trying to get four children out of a lift. She forces one child back into the pram, and the child hits her as she does. *Maybe I don't want children actually*, I think.

4

First Qualifying Round

Saturday, 31 August 2024
Champion Hill, Attendance: 1,270
Dulwich Hamlet vs Leatherhead

Sometimes this summer on a Saturday, I will lie on the grass in the garden at my girlfriend's in Camberwell, trying to suppress the ever-growing list of things that I need to do, a checklist swirling around my head, trying to push it to the bottom of my conscience. I will hear a roar occasionally. A football-ish roar. I've always been confused about what that sound is. Millwall? Millwall is miles away. Palace? I know that can be loud. That's miles away too. If everything bounced around London like that, though, all you would hear would be loud crowds and sounds bumping into each other. South London would sound like a jet plane taking off inside a zoo on fire. I lie there, face up, watching the wild green parrots that somehow populate what is overhead and I genuinely think, lying there, looking at the sky, that I might be imagining it.

It's only on entering Champion Hill for the next round – a practical getaway to a game to continue this FA Cup pilgrimage – that I realise, oh, it's Dulwich Hamlet. *That's* where the sound is coming from. It's from behind that big Sainsbury's, a football ground hiding behind it as if it's playing a game, a place caught between wanting and not wanting to be found.

The atmosphere at Hamlet leans towards beer festival stylings or a footballing arts fair. There are couples covered head to toe in tattoos, people with dogs, souvlaki stands, "Punk football" written on banners, a brick brewery enclosure on the south side of the ground saying "Support local, drink local". "Welcome home" and a heart greet me in chalk on the right-hand side of the turnstile as I enter, banners and St Pauli-style graffiti everywhere. Above the Tommy Jovers stand, which is mostly full before kick-off, "In our house we are all equal" is written large.

Where once non-league football would have seemed a bizarre, trainspottery activity – or even appeared to be on the south coast only a month ago – here it is a joined-up, mini cultural happening. There are no parents with children shouting "You fucking faggot" at anyone who looks at their son. Instead, a father walks with his son across to the Portakabin, gently whispering, "Gosh, there's a lot of shouting here, isn't there?" The son nods.

In the first minute of the game, the assembled, environment-conscious ultras behind the Hamlet goal begin the chants: "Wemberlee . . . Wemberlee . . . we're the famous Dulwich Hamlet and we're going to Wembley." It is the first time Wembley has been mentioned on my run – that two-syllable word that can be rolled into three – an end point that all dreams lead towards. They will have to get past Leatherhead and nine realistically unwinnable games to do so, but of course, that is in the delivery too. There is a knowing irony stitched into it here, a kind of revelling in the smallness and localness of it all. A man explains to his friend, both pitch-side, as the concourse next to the pitch is used almost like a sort of family ice rink waiting area, that "this is quite unusual, actually", tapping into the unique selling point Hamlet and the general growing popularity of localised football provides – its opposition to the usual perception of football.

Dulwich Hamlet play with plenty of width, their central midfielders finding wide players who hover, waiting, on either flank. I lean over the barrier inches away, holding a cup of tea. If I reached out, I could interfere with play. It's like that feeling you get standing at the edge of a station platform, the compulsion to jump, to wonder what would happen if you did. I bend fantasy in my mind, play out the cause and effects of the compulsion. From this extremely close and tight vantage point, there's a sense of the split-second decision-making required even at this level. There is so little time to make decisions, so few airs and graces, so much random shouting of the word "winners" thrown out into the sky. I hold my tea tighter. I do not reach out. I watch as Hamlet number 10 Anthony Jeffrey skips past three Leatherhead defenders, a boyish fantasy being unwrapped, before threading the ball through to Jerome Binnom-Williams, who misses to the right.

There is a polite gap on the fence between me and another solitary man in a Dulwich Hamlet shirt. We have left it there intentionally, the sort of grace that you learn in London, living always crammed against so many people, to gift each other any distance at all, even if it be an extra metre, to do each other the favour of no eye contact, of no communication, to block off your peripheries like a horse that need not be startled. A man, though, maybe ten or fifteen years older than me, squeezes between the two of us, leaning over the barrier towards the football. He is sighing at it and making gestures and saying odd words as if he is fishing, waiting for a catch that might lead to conversation. I sense it and I can feel the Hamlet fan senses the same, both of us tensing, not giving in to the trap. I have the fear, and I can feel that he has the fear too, that whatever conversation develops with this man might never end and will involve a lot of listening. Eventually, no natural ins given, he just begins an unsolicited conversation. My luck is in: he has decided to turn his head to the Hamlet fan and not me. "I go and see Croydon a fair bit," he opens. "It's obviously lower level, but I really have to say it's a great turnout, isn't it." This man is like a solitary walker you bump into looking over an awe-inspiring view, desperate to explain everything in front of you, each description and detail and historical reference making it less inspiring, ideas darting around your mind of how you might escape. "I haven't seen Leatherhead before," he says, "which is weird because I actually have loose connections to the area." The man then starts reeling off the names of divisions. It's unclear whether these are leagues Leatherhead have been in or Croydon have been in or whether, like a six-year-old child, he's just telling you all the stuff that he knows exists. South East Counties Prem. South East Counties One. South East Counties Kent Division Two. My Dulwich Hamlet fan friend sees where this is going. "Actually," he says, "I'm moving back to New Zealand and this will be my last game." He's walked into a bigger trap than he could have imagined. The man has been to New Zealand. He's been to New Zealand to watch sport. He lists off rugby grounds, areas of interest, to which the Hamlet fan nods and feigns interest, now squinting out at the game as if it is very far away at sea and a rescue boat is disappearing into the horizon. This man is not just from Croydon and does not just have loose connections with the Leatherhead area. He is one of those incredibly well-meaning people who wants to go around the world talking about travel arrangements and weather and agreeing with people about very obvious things to agree on and leave saying, "Well, that was very pleasant, wasn't it, and I've made some new friends." I am starting to berate myself for my own scepticism for this clearly lovely man, so I evacuate, with a sense of disloyalty to my fellow island football supporter, leaving him to listen. As I leave, the man is saying, "I've enjoyed this chat so much, I think I want Dulwich to win, despite my loose connections to the Leatherhead area." The other man has contributed roughly a sentence to this chat, which is to tell the man he's going to the other side of the world after this game. "Anyway," his new, worldly, talkative friend says, "some people take this all far too seriously, don't they. They really do."

Tom Cullen, a friend of a friend, is stood by the corner flag on the opposite side to the entrance of the ground. I have been told I have to track him down, because his story with the club has been unlike any other anyone will have with any football club. "If you come to London young, like I did, it can be very lonely," Tom tells me when I ask him how he came across Champion Hill for the first time. He looks out onto the pitch, over a banner tied to the barrier that reads "Up for the cup". "I think the reason people get into football in general, but especially non-league football, is because they feel a bit alone." Tom found himself at Hamlet initially as something to do. "They were so welcoming here that immediately, it was something to set my watch to." Not being someone who half-commits to anything, within months Tom was at Hamlet for every home game. "And I just knew people were going to be there that I had begun to know. It gave me a sense of community and purpose that I really needed at that point in my life." He became a member of "The Rabble", so called because a committee member once condescendingly threw that name at a group of ten Hamlet fans, who picked it up and took it on proudly. He nods to where they stand now, behind the goal, a group in the hundreds, the end packed, himself slightly separated from it.

The passion grew in Tom and, before he knew it, he was going to home and away games, to every single Dulwich Hamlet game every Tuesday and Saturday, until, he says, "It just turned into a religion, if I'm honest." He was introduced to Liam Hickey, Dulwich Hamlet's director. Tom's passion for the club seemed to personify something about a new group of fans and a sense of optimism about what had previously been a tiny football club. After a vote in the match day committee room – "It was unanimous, apparently, even though they asked me to leave the room and took ten minutes to ask me back in" – Tom was swept head first into taking on more formal roles at the club, which he took to with a sort of idiosyncratic fervour. As play unfolds in front of us, the series of events he describes spiral dramatically, from the early days of being welcomed into The Rabble to taking on the club's social media channels, using the club to voice anti-racist and anti-homophobic support more directly and then using the club account to tweet at someone who did not agree that they were a "fucking idiot" and a "fucking bellend". They messaged saying that wasn't very professional, to which he replied, "Semi-professional, actually." This instinctive, emotional use of the club's social media, designed as a reaction to the diplomacy other clubs had used until then, helped align Hamlet in people's minds as an antidote to the ills of modern football. A few years later, Tom, completely unpaid, is almost solely responsible for getting Hamlet out of some serious ground ownership issues and financial hole after financial hole, as the club ironically grew and grew on the pitch and in the stands. Hamlet ended up hosting Carlisle United in the first round of the FA Cup, for the first time in the club's history, having to help the BBC work out how to get their production and cameras and infrastructure into Champion Hill to cover the match.

As we try to keep concentrating on the match, his story is such a race-through of barely believable court cases and regulatory loopholes and emergency meetings, that I cannot keep up. It's like Tom can't either, his history with the club so vast and so all-encompassing that a whole book would not cover it. He is part of long, collective, loving work to keep the club afloat. All parties involved, including the owners, have worked positively with the club to secure its future, and work on a new stadium is imminent. The club is now in the best financial shape it has been in for fifty years. Tom had to step down recently, giving heed to the fact that the obsession with saving the club had colluded with a drinking addiction, and neither was healthy. "A lot of the good and the bad over my life is intrinsically weaved with the football club," Tom says, the game continuing. "My proudest and darkest moments are all wrapped up in pink and blue."

With an entertaining game balanced at 0-0, Anthony Jeffrey has been causing constant issues for Leatherhead. The terrace behind Tom buzzes like a big social, parents and prams and pints and the odd "I do like Peckham Helles, to be fair"-type conversation forming the background for a game. Even looking at a beer now makes me tired. Just looking at the pints in plastic cups makes me half cross my eyes at the thought of it. I can't remember when suddenly a pint turned from being fuel to appearing as a kind of ageing potion, lulling you towards it but then making you feel nothing but heavy, your eyes suddenly given the effect of being Vaselined over, knowing that in a few hours you are going to feel fat and sad and probably won't sleep. Meanwhile, Jerome Binnom-Williams misses a penalty, only to pass home a much more difficult chance on thirty-five minutes and give Hamlet the lead. He celebrates in front of three girls, one of whom bangs a Wellbonds Scaffolding advert in delight.

Dulwich have had all the possession in the second half, but Leatherhead somehow equalise through Sebastian Karczewski. One of the three girls who has just celebrated the Dulwich Hamlet goal also celebrates this goal and then, with just over twenty minutes to play, the ball drops to Karczewski in a rare Leatherhead attack, the way football matches can feel like there is a godly entity conspiring against you and just handing the ball to the opposition no matter what you do, and a clinical bit of finishing makes it 2-1 to Leatherhead. As the game becomes tense, the general drift dissipates and focuses a bit, the way it tends to in football matches. Suddenly the time that has been spent, the general small-talkiness, the fancy-seeing-you-heres, has accumulated into something meaningful. The sky goes gnarly, the game becomes enclosed. The floodlights, just turned on, and the closeness of the players' faces gives them the complexion of boxers hanging in there, clinging to their opponents, buying time, searching for something that cannot come from plans or tactics or drills but something deeper inside, the internal finding something else that is required in close football matches.

Leatherhead's fans, who, as I am again realising is a given at lower league football, congregate behind the goal their team is attacking and switch for the second half, are shouting at Hamlet number 8 Sean Bonnett-Johnson. He just stares back, clearly absorbing each sentence, the crowd not big enough to blur it into one block of abuse, and he rolls his eyes, spitting water from a bottle out of his mouth – a water fountain that only footballers seem able to do. Jeffrey switches to the right and keeps causing problems, haranguing the Leatherhead goal, looking for a way to keep Hamlet in the FA Cup. It's the first sign of desperation in the tournament – that cup knockout feeling of every touch feeling important, somehow heavier, everyone snatching at everything, something irreversible about to finish. In the eighty-fourth minute, during a period of prolonged pressure, he is given slightly more space from outside the penalty area and drills the ball into the right-hand side of the net. It is my goal of the tournament so far. And there it is – the noise – the noise I've been hearing from the garden, one of a bona fide, actual football stadium, a non-league club turning itself into a community concern, where results matter and the very essence of caring about your club, unified noise, turning and hugging strangers, meets the darkened sky. The PA announcer is hoarse when he calls the goal. If it stays this way, he says, there'll be a replay at Leatherhead on Tuesday night. It's a 7.45 kick-off.

It does stay that way. It's a good thing no one knows as they are leaving the ground, with the joyful unrolling of Wembley from two syllables into three, "Wemberlee" spilling out into the big Sainsbury's that hides Champion Hill from the road, that Leatherhead will win the replay 1-0.

5

I remember how it crept up on me. How it infiltrated my system. How it locked its soft fingers around me and told me this is where everything is safe. How time slowed down as it did, until an entire room had been paused and I could almost walk around it, inspect everything, get close to people in the crowd, check their heart rates, observe their faces, sit inside the world as it remained unmoving and unrushed. I remember how, as the shows got bigger, every sensation inside every person in the room appeared to become immediately perceptible. How certain energies of singular people in a crowd could hold a disproportionate amount of power, depending on what you were looking for. How one person yawning or rolling their eyes could be picked out of thousands. Or, alternatively, you might see a person crying, staring straight at you, and look back at them for a few songs, beginning a communication that would be inarticulable anywhere else, just between the two of you, like being in a lucid dream where you are consoling a stranger and telling them you know how it feels. I remember mostly how I just wanted to stay there, where everything was simple. Where I knew what the world was asking of me and what I was asking of it. Where it was completely unimportant to me what was happening anywhere else and, like an unimaginable gift, I felt I knew where I should be. On stage, with The Maccabees.

It did not matter whether we were playing to no one at all or in rooms whose capacity was very gently growing over years and years, from South London pubs to arenas and festival main stages across the world – playing on stage with The Maccabees always gave me this feeling. On the day of every show, the anticipation of it all, the knowing that I was going to walk into this, would leave me uncomfortable and sick, questioning what I was doing, telling myself I hated it, actually, that I didn't know what I was doing, until the moment we walked on stage and some sort of switch that had been hidden until then would flip inside my head, cushioning the edges of daily existence, a tunnel guiding me into something very simple and definable. It sometimes occurred to me that what I was experiencing was a sort of falling in love – the absolute helplessness of it, being exposed to a feeling that is so overwhelming that it's actually not very nice at all. I might try to stop it on occasion in the build-up to a show, this absurd sickening reckoning with want and need, and tell myself I didn't actually crave it, before being tractor-beamed into it every time. As I shimmied from sickness to a wide-eyed, pre-hit state of readiness, I would grow addicted to hearing the many overlapping conversations in a venue before a show, making sure I found a moment just to sit behind the stage and listen to all the lives waiting for a gig, forming one sort of force field of togetherness, everyone there for the same reason. It was like a challenge – to know that, by the end of a show, you might take all those separate lives and, for a brief moment, connect everyone together, get everyone to participate in the same thing, to feel like they are all with you, all a part of you, until you all disperse back into the world again and have to deal with bills and finding receipts and how do I get rid of the mice in my flat and fuck, all the toilet roll has gone.

A gig is a very simple thing. It has a schedule. There is routine and rota and ritual. It's a communication, an exchange – all nicely arranged and ordered, pure in its relief and pure in its escape. It was not only an extremely addictive experience for me, but the central, most consistent one of my entire adult life. I locked into the absolute focus of it with grief-stricken gratitude. Everything danced around this one event every evening, and I was in the middle of it. The rhythms of every day on tour. From the submarine seasickness of waking up on a bus, dusty and nervous, the wandering around foreign cities or fields praying to the gods that I was going to find somewhere to brush my teeth, to the general unfolding of myself hour by hour, every day convincing myself to move from subhuman to an unimaginable attempt at something superhuman, until I was walking onto the stage, putting on the guitar, opening my arms and letting love in. As we had formed The Maccabees as teenagers in bedrooms, it could sometimes feel to me like a very rough and ready manifestation of childhood friends putting their hands together on a Ouija board and trying to reach another spirit. We had committed, of course in an extremely haphazard way, to making something bigger than ourselves, between us. Sometimes I could actually feel that pact, getting odd bolts of revelations on stage that we were all putting our hands at exactly the place we had committed to putting them on our instruments, at exactly the same time, and that playing music together was this sort of surreal commitment, where you had absolute dependence on each other doing the same thing at the same time, and how many variations of it could go wrong at any one time. On a stage, in the protection of being in a gang, all putting our hands together at hopefully the right time, me initially using it as a loose re-creation of the Oasis and The Clash and The Futureheads and *Old Grey Whistle Test* videos I had grown up watching, was where I found oceans and oceans of repressed feeling. I learned that I could not only scream, but scream long and loud and hard, and that I wanted to do this continually, on and off the microphone, as if the world was ending, but with a sense of celebration too. I found myself desperate to lock eyes with anyone, to unflinchingly stare and look into people, to dig into something in life that was not accessible anywhere else. This was sometimes quite alarming – and probably annoying – for people who had just come to watch a show, standing there unwittingly with a pint. But this is what it brought out of me – everything at once – desperation and need and pure joy and panic and revelation and sadness and anything else that was unnameable but until then had sat like a block in the middle of my throat, while I tried to cough it out. And it chose to turn itself into one huge, screaming smile. I think I might even have known when we were first playing shows at seventeen that this was going to never let go of me. That I had found something that saved me, but also had now forever disorientated me, like a kind of cursed pill. The rest of life would feel incomparable and no matter how hard it pushed me, I would always choose it, and would always walk towards that light, even when the light moved further away.

*

They say that footballers die twice, the first time being when their careers are over. I know this feeling. When The Maccabees ended, it didn't just feel as if a family and a friendship and a job and a passion and a singular focus had been taken from me, there was also this fiendish little need that had been long since rooted in me. The absolute need to be seen. The absolute existential dread of disintegrating from view. The fix of serving my body adrenaline and endorphins every night at nine o'clock for fifteen years and then, without warning, taking it away.

I was, by chance, the age at which footballers and cricketers tend to retire. I don't know whether I would always have found a way to dovetail sport and music, whatever the situation, going off on daydreams about all the ways that goalkeepers are drummers, or wingers are guitarists and strikers are singers, but this colluded deeper affinity in me. I felt a strengthening of my already extremely embedded affinity for sportspeople. I found myself at any sort of football match and the county cricket, staring into the abyss, searching for the thing I was missing. If going to a gig is slightly too painful, too present, too jealousy-inducing, a football match is about the closest thing I can find to soothe that sensation. It stills my head a touch. It simplifies life for that moment. Without a gig to play, the frustration of being cut out of people's lives taunts me. I feel a harsh, real sensation of how brutal it is to not be able to know what is really going on in other people's heads, to measure your own hurt against theirs, to judge whether everyone is fighting the exact same version of a battle or there is something actually seriously wrong with you. Somehow, crowds and football help with this. Everyone screaming blasphemy or hurt or celebration into the air, not a single feeling or thought or criticism going unvoiced. And then, whether the game is awful or exhilarating, meaningful or a dead rubber, a football match will always escalate, like a good gig should, accumulating unfolding of events and the haven of collective focus into being the only thing that matters as it reaches its conclusion.

In the immediate aftermath of the split of The Maccabees, feeling like I'd left a physical part of me behind at the last show at Alexandra Palace and returning bizarrely often to other bands' shows immediately afterwards, almost as if I was looking for it, I had a spell at sports events, blending into the crowds. I had suddenly become someone that people were referring to in the past tense, even in my company. And so I decided that I was going to say yes to everything. Yes was the only way out. Yes was the engine of survival. Yes was the seed of renewal. If someone asked me to do something, I'd say yes. And I set about building what felt like a completely new, a completely different person, stitched together by nothing else than a series of yeses.

I found in time that each little yes gave me a version of this adrenaline my body was craving. I came to understand how live radio gives you the same strange, disturbing sickness, the disorientation and internal interrogation of why you are choosing to put yourself through something so nerve-racking, so exposing, before giving you that endorphin kick just before going on air, that joint prospect of transcendence and communication. I then had to teach myself how to use that feeling in the exact opposite way I did at a gig – befriending it, accepting it, then calming it down, turning it into a warm, slow, throbbing confidence, asking it to grace me with the gift of calm and clarity of thought. I started recording the

Tailenders podcast, pitched to me by Greg James as a few episodes to talk loosely about cricket with Jimmy Anderson, only to find us still making it seven years later, teaching me that sometimes the honest, least pre-conceived thing is the thing that connects the most, us almost forming the spirit of a band between us. I found that writing books gave me a similar sense of having a long-term project as making an album – a mission to be completed, a pursuit in trying to unearth some truth under your skin and hoping it gets under the skin of a stranger. I don't know if it was better or worse, but I almost found it easier to write words than write music, with less internal expectation, excited at the prospect of using it like an intimate and close conversation, with no small talk or social anxiety to reckon with, just like a song. I learned that when you make music for film, there is a humbling dovetailing to the storytelling, the music only ever being right if it serves a purpose that is not its own. I liked the relief of that. Of feeling music fall out of me as a direct response to something I had seen on a screen, and how music could act simply as an empathic response to something.

As the jobs became more psychedelic, fuelled on a wave of a yes bringing more yeses, the more of an adrenaline rush I got, closer and closer to that first feeling. I cannot honestly tell you with a straight face the chain of events that led to me being in New York, at the Major League Baseball Network, about to present the baseball on TV. But there I was, a million thoughts racing through my head, why and what and how. Then it is too late to do anything and I am on live television, for hours, completely unrehearsed, and something about that – the simplicity of the interaction, the waiting for a turn to speak and then listening, the absolute electric vulnerability of the situation, and then surviving it – leaves me with a sensation somewhere close to those first shows, where something new had been presented to me, and I had not been spat out. Eventually, in the run I am currently in, I return to playing gigs with 86TVs. There is heavy nostalgia in starting again with my brothers, almost as if we are re-entering a world I left or that left me, I cannot work out which. All the feelings are still there. The absolute joy. The screaming. The sense of lovely, perfect completion. But we are starting again, excitedly and dutifully. So I continue to remind myself that I will have many, many experiences in life, I just might not have that one again, the one that really filled me up, of looking out across big stages, being in the middle of the prospect of total humiliation or total victory, no backing tracks, just The Maccabees, playing songs to a sea of people.

I have come to understand, rightly or wrongly, that a degree of necessary pain and searching and discomfort goes with everything worthwhile – that the moments in my life that stand out as memorable are usually those where I was being stretched, or was under pressure of some description that I was regularly telling myself I wanted to buckle to. I'm not sure whether it was some misplaced virtue, or a simple misunderstanding, but I have believed until now that part of the exploration of life is choosing to stretch yourself into uncomfortable places, to work out what your mind and body will allow you to do. I have learned, harshly and slowly, that happiness is something I have to work towards finding, almost but not quite a choice, that it is not handed to me, and that when I do find it, I will never have it in my hands for long. For whatever reason, whether it be unprocessed grief or just a human disposition, sadness and dissatisfaction crept much more readily into my system, ready to knock as soon as my guard was down, slipping through the door at any opportunity. I know that life has this unfair imbalance, even when everything points to everything being completely fine, with no tangible tragedy unfolding, and so when you find happiness, or something that makes you feel truly alive, you should take it in both hands and shake it if it needs it. And on the other side of The Maccabees, this always saying yes led to wildly positive things in my working life. It took me to many strange places, built me to be someone who felt they were not just a guitarist in a band. Sometimes I felt like I had been beamed out of space and could look back at The Maccabees from another solar system, showing me that it was all quite small and inconsequential from afar, actually, and that something is only as big as you decide it is.

The other side to saying yes, though, it slowly dawned on me over years, was saying yes because I had no idea who I was. Saying yes not because I wanted to, but because I needed to. Saying yes because I didn't know who I was if I didn't say yes, if I didn't try hard, or push myself to dizziness, or desperately try to stretch every aspect of feeling and reach out of everything I could do. Because, like happiness, the conundrum inside the adrenaline of all these little hits – chasing this feeling – is that the feeling does not last. I would pursue it for a long time, sometimes years and years, and when I got it, the moment I was anticipating – one of connection, or satisfaction, or adrenaline or achievement – would not be there for long. It might be an hour, or a few hours, or a day. And then the brain immediately starts coming off it, missing it, starting to work out new ways of finding that feeling again. The plotting starts. And the busier I got, the more of these moments I needed more regularly, the feeling each time giving me slightly less of a high for slightly less time, so I would immediately work out how to get back there. I begin to start hiding what I am taking on from people around me. It comes up in conversation and I say that things will change next month, I just need to get through this bit. I don't tell certain people certain things, because I know they will say I need to slow down. And before I know it, I am no longer really in control of anything. I am just saying yes because I need to, being dragged around by a hurt, manic version of myself who needs it, waking me up in the morning, forcing me bolt upright, saying come on, do better, keep going.

And as each return gives less, I convince myself to take on more, to hoard that feeling, to keep going. In these months, work piles up to the point that when I stop in the evenings, I feel literally woozy, literally seasick, as if I am on a boat. Sometimes, when I stop for a couple of hours, I feel extremely upset, upset like a child who is not sure why they are upset, they are just distressed. And I do what I have learned to do, I swallow this upset whole, stare into the distance, disassociate until the next thing is required of me, and wait for the feeling to return and the next goal to show itself to me, the promise of short-lived happiness keeping me running towards it.

At the end of each job, I start finding a way to criticise myself about something, to reflect on how I've failed. In the time I have promised myself I will stop, I find myself driven by jealousy or resentment or a sense that I am not as talented as other people, scrolling through Instagram, fixated on who is more successful than me, who is more popular, who is more worthy of people's love and attention. Comparison is the thief of joy, I say to myself, phone by my side, repeating it to try and kick the other voice out of my mind, the one that tells me to keep outrunning those footsteps, before forgetting all the positive reinforcement within minutes and scrolling again. I feel like there might be hours upon hours where I never put the phone down, picking up information upon information I am unable to process, just fizzing through it, building mazes inside my head that I will never leave. Sometimes I get so lost in my phone that I imagine that the rest of my flat could be pure rubble, or I could be sitting on a sofa in the middle of the desert, and it would make no difference, as long as there was enough charge on my phone, my thumb endlessly scrolling.

Occasionally, my body might show me what I am running from. It will tell me in sharp, strange physical alarms. I will have panic attacks while cooking. I will witness in my body an extremely unusual sensation, like a cold volt of electricity, every time I see a couple kiss on the street. Not passionately, but the sort of everyday kiss that says, we are secure and happy, and I'll see you tonight. Those little warning signs that might tell me, when I dig, that I am scared of domesticity, of a settled, normal life, of a family, and I am doing anything I can to move away from it, to find something else. I recognise it in brief lightbulb moments as the same exact feeling I would have before playing a show. The sudden sensation of being convinced I have made a mistake and don't want to do it, only to play the show and realise it is the only thing I want in the world. But there is no stage to walk on to, just a kind of work paralysis that keeps me stuck there. I have become obsessed with doing everything I possibly can, carrying this sensation that people don't quite understand how short life is, how much must be squeezed into it, and, as a result, I am trying to live about six different lives and careers at once, not compromising on any of them, unable to say no to anything at all, completely terrified of being left behind in any way whatsoever. And this has left me absolutely exhausted. The modern world encourages this. It tells you to never stop. It gives you the impression that you can be in five or six different places at once – putting something on social media that you did a week ago while on a Zoom meeting to an office somewhere else, as your brain tries to remember what it is you said again you would do tonight. I occasionally have this sense that I am fragmented, and that parts of me are in different places, as if the world is pulling me apart and dropping bits of me off in undisclosed, random places across England like a dismembered, spat-out toy. But to not be this is to be able to say no, which I cannot do. A no is an ending, and I can't do endings. I would rather run from unsolvable sadness towards adrenaline forever, baked into the procrastination, people-pleasing and perfectionism that comes with vulnerable self-worth.

There are only a few places that quell this feeling, sanctuaries from working or longing or being cut into pieces – bookshops and record shops and cinemas and football matches and cricket matches, whether on TV or in real life. All these places ask of you is that you love them, that you commit to them. And while I cannot commit to quite basic, constant, regular functions in life, I can commit wholeheartedly to these places. I lose myself here, melt into a blissful appreciation of something else. And, as the second and third qualifying rounds of the FA Cup take place in September, I am in a hectic, distracted spin, with project on project on project, and I turn forty. I do not want to celebrate. I don't want to see anyone. I take myself, inexplicably, to Bath, on my own, where I just want to be somewhere nothing can be asked of me.

During this strange, solitary fortieth birthday, sat wondering why I don't have children, unsure whether I should be proud or concerned or both, I think about those FA Cup rounds. I long for them. In my memory, they already appear like moments of calm, where I was not thinking about myself, but about something bigger. And, as cringe-laden as it can sometimes sound, I realise why football is talked about as a religion. It is a congregation, where you put yourself in a space and pray for something good to happen, where you acknowledge you have no control over your fate, and you all put your hands together, at the same time, in the same space.

I'd like to get back there, I think. To those little FA Cup games. I have to get to the next one. And, as I do, a message comes through. The Maccabees have had the offer to play some shows next year.

6

Fourth Qualifying Round

Saturday, 12 October 2024
Flamingo Park, Attendance: 1,222
Cray Wanderers vs Tonbridge Angels

I first met Jake Farey in 2006 – slightly older than me, a worn Second World War bomber jacket on, bloodshot eyes, blond hair standing on end. Jake had clearly watched a lot of videos of The Clash and, playing music itself not being his calling, had modelled himself as a kind of entrepreneurial, punk rock music manager. He had set up a record label and bumped into my younger brother Will's band, Talk Taxis, in South London pubs and asked if they wanted to put a record out with him. They pressed up vinyl together, released it and took themselves on tour in support of The Maccabees often, travelling in a black cab that Jake's mate Little Del owned and drove.

I remember him first just vaguely, images of him standing in the wings, very close to the actual stage, doubling up as a guitar tech, watching Talk Taxis playing their first-on slot in Academy venues. The way he watched them was as if he was a football manager – keenly and poised, as if the whole meaning of the universe relied upon what was spilling out in front of him and that only he could ensure its success. He always seemed seconds from waving his fingers around in formations to the band, having little words with the monitor engineers, an arm around their shoulder, part friend part enemy, as if they were a fourth official. He was impressively into it, the kind of into it where the pure spirit of boyish imagination in him sparked something in you too. With it, his management style on the road was, shall we say, hands-on. For example, I once saw him get on stage immediately after a show to less than a hundred people and punch the bass player of his band in the face because he had smashed up the band's drumkit, which they were borrowing. It was that sort of punk rock management.

Almost by osmosis, and not deterred by the punching in the face of bass players, years later Jake ended up on tour with The Maccabees. Technically he was the merch guy, selling T-shirts at the shows, but his role and unofficial job description became slightly more blurred and more general. As touring crew tend to with bands over stretches of time, he became a sort of extra member, whose answer to any question asked of him would always be yes. In winter, he dressed like an Eastern European soldier, occasionally adding a left-field flourish of a hat that looked like a massive crème brûlée. In summer, he dressed like a World War Two pilot, never with actual goggles pulled up over his head but, somehow, the attire was so loyal to the depiction, you felt like you could see them anyway. If spirits were low, he would occasionally do a flamenco-inspired tap dance, channelled through Sidcup suburbia, for everyone.

Me and Jake were friends then, but not great friends yet. On a night out in Lisbon on a European tour, we went back to the bus early, bailing on a night out, probably to get stoned. It was a long tour, opening for Editors in big, cold arenas in Europe that invariably were in the middle of nowhere, a long treacherous walk to McDonald's the only option for food. Our budget had not allowed catering for lunch, just one evening meal a day, so we shared crowded dressing rooms with Canadian band Wintersleep like alley cats, pawing at each other, constantly juggling the options of being within touching distance at every angle with at least three people or sitting alone in a parked bus on an abandoned motorway. Touring was always like this, veering wildly from "We are living the actual dream here, aren't we?" to "Wow, this is nothing like that dream I was sold", with nothing in between.

While everyone was out in a bar after a show, Jake and I spied a rare opportunity to have a sacred hour on a pitch-black tour bus, all power off, with something closer to just our own thoughts for company, and left together. Jake always had hash. As I burned it, sucking in the comfort of its smell, kneading tiny bits of dark brown blocks into long, thin pencil shapes, he rolled them. Hearing the lighter click and the occasional passing car, within minutes, maybe out of the shock of the sudden space, we began to engage in conversation as if we were the last people on earth, waiting for it to end, just with small talk to kill the time. We began to play a game, where one person names a sequence of football clubs and the other has to guess the player by their career path. Almost all these players were from the late nineties – most of them easy, giving the game a pleasing quickfire back and forth. He reeled off a list of Championship and League One clubs. Charlton, Barnet, Reading, Portsmouth, Charlton, Portsmouth. I didn't even need to think; it was there like a maths equation that had been rammed down my throat as a child until it was automatic. I knew who this was: Linvoy Primus. We were incredibly stoned by then, maybe a touch spun out and, it's hard to describe it now, like recounting a very boring in-joke about how you first met your partner, which no one else finds interesting but they smile along at the anecdote and say "No way!" but we found this incomprehensibly funny. I had guessed Linvoy Primus in sub one second. We spent the rest of the night giggling, occasionally on the floor, repeating the name Linvoy Primus again and again and then the list of teams – Charlton, Barnet, Reading, Portsmouth, Charlton, Portsmouth – before leaving a pause again and looking at each other and bursting again. Linvoy Primus. When everyone got back to the bus, we told them about Linvoy Primus. Nobody looked even the slightest bit interested and, maybe European night out induced, just looked back through us half disappointed, half confused, just wanting whatever was happening to go away.

From that point on, me and Jake were very close. Linvoy Primus and football had sealed the deal. We had moved in together within a year. We did not need to have anything else in common. We had Linvoy Primus and equivalent pointless levels of nineties footballer recall. We had football. We both understood what it could do to you, that it could take you back to some recollection of safety or childhood, that it was a life raft to ferry you between the crushing blah blah blahs of every day. We would never run out of things to say. We would never surf the nauseating small talk, or the terrifying introspection and interrogation other relationships would inevitably accumulate – we had football and The Clash and we had hash. We loved those things in the way children love stuff before it is necessary to communicate to any world outside of them. In our different ways, we had both been sold some sort of formative dream, an image of escape, a young impression of an adult world, and we both held them tight. There were flashpoints when it became quite clear that outside of football, our interests were going to spike in quite separate ways. I was reading books about therapy; he was going on retreats where you learned exactly what it was like to be a Second World War bomber pilot. But football was all that someone was required to understand in life to have an affinity.

Jake went to Everton away with Chelsea once and, just the same way everything about football at a certain age stuck to his everyday adult mind, he would sing their song every morning: "If you know about your history, iiiiit's enough to make your heart go . . ." Sometimes the chant would wake me up. I had never heard Goodison Park sing this, but through Jake, I felt like I did every day. Interjected into these morning chants, a roll-call of football phrases and chants just on loop and coming out at their own choosing, every morning he will randomly just shout "wouble-you" too, the Millwall supporters' chant where they spelled out Millwall and pronounced "double-u" with a "w". He drives to non-league football grounds on non-matchdays with a disposable camera and tries to sneak through railings to take photos of the grounds. Sometimes I go with him and just watch him dart around abandoned sites, running back and saying that he thinks he's found a good gap in a fence or a wall low enough to jump over. He is obsessed with football architecture – who has done what with which ground and what stands have been there since when and which team are doing a "pretty sad and fucked-up project" renovation of an old ground. When we are not talking about grounds or results or chants or guessing nineties footballers, we say things like "You've got to rest when you have the ball and hassle when you don't" to each other, about life events that have absolutely nothing to do with football and, even though it is a completely nonsensical and irrelevant analogy, somehow both understand exactly what we are talking about. I start seeing a girl and after a few months it ends, her telling me that she really liked Jake, but she didn't know why he had to come on every single date too.

Jake swears that his first footballing memory was Maradona – the Hand of God. He was four years old. He says he remembers it, or at least remembers it being a constant talking point everywhere he went. His first memory. By the time he was six or seven, he was at his first game, with his uncle. Charlton were homeless then, playing at Selhurst Park. Jake spent the majority of the game bored, pretending he could control the football with his mind, using his hands like a psychic remote control. When Charlton scored their first goal, the winner, Jake was held aloft by his uncle inside the celebration. Jake found the noise, all the sudden shouting, so alarming, so upsetting, that he cried his eyes out on impact. The noise. It was awful. Scary. Traumatising. And that was it. He was tied to football for ever.

It was unclear whether that exact moment spiked a conscious correlation between football and tears, that strange psychological loophole football opens that allows space for men to cry, but from then on, those two things were always close with Jake – football and intense, on the surface emotion. I understood that feeling. I willed it too through football. I wanted desperately for things to mean something, for the passing of time to be marked, for football to speak to something particular and personal and poignant. From the Charlton tears on, he could do nothing but find football incredibly emotional. He watched the Euro 96 semi-final at a family friend's house and when Gareth Southgate missed the penalty that ended England's hopes, he panicked at the surge of emotion and heartbreak running through him. Trying to think on his feet, he ran outside, got on his bike and intentionally crashed it into a wall. That's what the tears were about, he told everyone. It was the fall from the bike, not the football. Of course, no one believed him. His grandad had been going to Milllwall since the 1940s and couldn't bring himself to go to the last game at the Old Den, meaning Jake did not get to go either, giving him the first curious case of the way loss is too painful for some older people to even engage with.

In the halcyon days of his childhood in the nineties, Jake would go to any football he could find. Non-league club Cray Wanderers were local to his family, and he would often end up there. Even then, the ground looked outdated, the pitch on a massive slope. Jake would not watch any of the game in the early years, instead messing around with other kids until half-time when the players would leave and everyone was allowed to run on and boot balls into the goals until the players came back out and spoiled the fun again. One summer Sunday evening, Jake remembers with crystal clarity having a bath and his hair being washed before his grandad phoned his mum to say that England Ladies were playing at Cray's ground. Jake's grandad came to pick him up. He remembers thinking Marieanne Spacey looked so good she could definitely get into the men's Charlton team, and also a flicker of thinking it was weird that an England team were playing at Cray – a brief, youthful acknowledgement of the absolute gulf of opportunity between women and men. As he grew older, the club moved to a different ground with slightly more level terrain, and Jake started to go to training with friends he had met on Charlton summer camps. After training, they would set fire to things around the back of the pavilion, while the parents were on the beers. Cooper and Renshaw were the troublemakers, he would tell me. They convinced Chris Dodds to get into a shopping trolley, then pushed him down the concrete steps.

In the mid-nineties, when Charlton were back at The Valley, Jake was at the first game and many after that, his grandad being able to tell how shit the game was by how much Jake lay with his head on his arm. They were incredibly boring games of football that meant Jake would drift off and, like his first games, pretend that he could control the ball and the course of the game. The football could not compete with Chelsea when his dad started taking him to Stamford Bridge. They would go in through the Shed End terracing, then pay a little to sit on the concrete seats at the back. An old man once took a mechanic's pad that he had been sitting on and gave it to Jake, realising he was finding the concrete uncomfortable. Jake would recall this later with a tear in his eye, as if he was reciting some sort of profound poem on the kindness of strangers. Years later, in 1997, when Di Matteo scored the famous FA Cup final goal for Chelsea in the first seconds, Jake was at Wembley and, tears in his eyes of course, re-emerged from the bundle of celebrations seconds later to see tears in all his dad's friends' eyes too. It was enough to make any of the old school Chelsea nutters cry, all that time and history and failure that had led up until then. Jake returned with his grandad to see Charlton win their play-off final at Wembley too the next season, crying again at the final penalty before thinking, *Oh no, Chelsea and Charlton are going to play each other, and I'll have to choose.*

He chose Chelsea. His connection to his own life and Chelsea from that point on, in that nineties window of time, knows no bounds. Jake can tell you what was going on in his life when Tore André Flo did this or Eddie Newton did that. He remembers specific dates for absolutely everything. The slightest stat or image of football from the nineties would send him off, reflecting on exactly how he felt and exactly why and what the Chelsea score had been that day. It was always tenterhooks with Jake – unsure every time we got into rival teams whether he was about to cry with rushing empathy or call someone a fucking mug. Sometimes he would do both in the same sentence. He had dental surgery in 2011, after which he came round from general anaesthetic and said to his mum and the nurse, "I haven't felt this buzzing since Gianfranco Zola scored the winner in Stockholm, 1998," and then fell back asleep.

Jake went to Millwall plenty as a kid with a crew of friends he still knows. They once met a Millwall fan, Mad Uncle Gary, Little Del's uncle, who, when introduced to each of them ("This is Jake, this is Del, this is Steve"), just shook his head, said "Fuck that" and pointed at them one at a time, renaming them "Geez, geez, geez and geez". Jake still goes with the thousands of other "geez, geez and geezes".

There was a time I'd have loved to have been called geez. I really wanted to be geez. Not Felix White. Sometimes I still do. The idea of being part of one unthinking mass, unburdened from choice, where every decision against your team is the wrong one, where every decision for it is the right one, where there is no conversation to be had other than about what is playing out in front of you. The absolute relief of a total lack of nuance, the total focus of communal purpose. And yet, where I did find it, it would intimidate me, repel me, scare me, make me wonder why I chose to spend time in these packs. Jake used to talk about the thrill of pack mentality, of being in a herd, the adrenaline of thinking with one mind. I didn't want to do that stuff at all. I felt that strange impulse of being just as repelled by it as I was impressed, somehow, of how love and hate sit almost exactly next to one another, the dial continuously nudging between one and the other.

Sometimes, as The Maccabees' tours moved through the world, never-ending, our slightly different approaches and magnetic pulls would rub off against each other incongruently. On tour in Italy, we jumped off the bus to go to see Inter Milan at the San Siro. Despite me begging him not to, he asked for tickets in the "most mental bit" and we ended up in what felt like a borderline Mafia congregation, with packs of older men shuffling us over amid huge co-ordinated chanting. A man walked around with a hat, like an usher for a Catholic priest, that fans tipped notes into, and eventually a man with a tiny spliff and an espresso walked directly up to us and said something quite harsh and stern in Italian, shooing us away. Ranieri's Inter lost 1-0 and Jake spent his time excitedly bouncing around the end of the faithful, working out how the singing was being organised, conductors sitting with their back to play and counting everyone in. I smiled throughout, very sheepishly, hoping we were going to make it to the gig and not be absorbed into an Italian gangland syndicate.

But Jake's most famous, most football-managerish move in his time with The Maccabees did not come in Milan, where we made the gig just about unharmed, walking through the backstage door in Inter Milan scarves, but in Middlesbrough. He was appalled by our performance that night, discerning not incorrectly that it had lacked effort. His merch desk was in the venue itself, rather than the concourse or entry as usual, so he could watch the show, in disbelief at what he was seeing. He came back to the dressing room straight after the gig, us sitting there like deflated footballers, telling us that he hoped we were proud of ourselves and how did we expect him to sell T-shirts after we'd served up that shit. He then handed us a diagram he had drawn while on the desk – like a football tactics board, where he had drawn us as stick men, like a back four and goalkeeper, a circle drawn around me (sort of on the right wing) and an arrow pointing to the crowd and then an arrow going back towards the band. Nobody knew what he meant by it. Weirdly, but naturally, I did.

I've told Jake about Penrith, about Haywards Heath, about Dulwich Hamlet. That I am going to try and go to a game in every single round of this FA Cup campaign from now on. I don't need to explain why, as I do with other people, where a look of slight concern crosses their face that says, And you're sure you're all right and everything? Jake, by contrast, lights up. This does not need explaining. This is absolutely living the dream. This is the best idea he has ever heard. We have fantasised about versions of this kind of thing for years. He has been chiming in ever since he heard about the plan. What game am I going to next? Do I need a lift? He looks over the fixtures, calls me and tells me Cray Wanderers are at home. His son Rowan, two years old, has never been to a football match.

Jake ends up negotiating with his fiancée, Cat, that he can go to the football on Saturday if he has Rowan on the day too. It will be Rowan's first football match. It's strange to think of Jake's child not knowing football. It makes me realise that there was a time once when even Jake didn't know about football either. It's an even stranger idea, Jake without football. I'm not sure who either of us would be if we didn't have football. What would we have spent our time on? Jake did tell me that he once had a cowboy and Indians party and, when he was the only boy dressed as an Indian, suffered a severe sense of shame, had a total meltdown and started fights with the cowboys. He is not sure whether football came to the rescue or redelivered other versions of this forever since.

Jake is driving. I have never learned to drive. I sit in the front; Ro is in the back. Even though Rowan is two and unable to sit anywhere but the child's seat in the back of the car, I feel partly guilty to have the front seat, but Ro seems very happy making the odd sound, pointing out other cars and the colour of things he sees out of the window. While Ro does that, Jake and I talk about football, of course. Jake runs through the various "fucked-up projects" that are going on at various football teams and their transfer policies, me saying, "I can't believe that, that's mad," to everything. I tell him that I saw Blue Fleece the other day. Blue Fleece is a man who stands on the corner of a road I walk down every day, between my partner's and mine, exactly where Jake used to live. Blue Fleece always has a blue fleece on. He knows who everyone that passes him each day supports and, when their team has lost, without saying hi, he points at them, smiles and says "3-1!" or "4-0!" He supports Tottenham and Lincoln City. For years, the only conversation we ever had was him asking me, every day, "Do you think Harry Kane is leaving Spurs?" and I would give him an answer based on the latest I'd heard. I worried about what we would talk about when Harry Kane did eventually leave Spurs but, instead, there is always more football to talk about. He's obsessed with football programmes, so while I used to stash all my programmes, keeping them for the day when I would definitely want to read hundreds and hundreds of old football programmes, I now keep them just to give to him. He gets very excited on receiving them, like he is overheating, and does not say thank you, just takes the programmes and walks back to his wall, holding them like they are the first edition of the Bible. Jake has left that corner of South-east London, moving slightly further out to make a new home for the three of them. He says it's weird, because he used to begrudge all the time he wasted talking to Blue Fleece, talking about whether Harry Kane was going to leave Spurs, but the thing he misses most about the area now is talking to Blue Fleece about whether Harry Kane will leave Spurs.

When we arrive, there are signs to "the second oldest football club in the world". Jake wants to take me to the old ground first, the one on the slope. When we arrive, it appears to be basically just a barren space. For some reason, like an echo of the past, there are two men there, slightly overweight, in tight-fitting training gear, and a bag of balls. We do not speak to them, as if speaking to them would conjure up some sort of non-league footballing version of *Field of Dreams*. I'm fairly sure they are real. We don't check. Jake just points at places that he has memories of, before Rowan is bored to the point of distraction and we leave.

Flamingo Park has a car park on the grass, where mud slides mark cars pitching up on the laid-out parking area, which ended up running around the pitch. It might be the first time in the FA Cup I've felt an actual sense of occasion on arrival, with just the number of cars signalling that giddiness of an event. A feeling of a whole community being there for something. Among the cars is a Bentley. *It must be the chairman*, I think. It looks like Billy Williams's car.

When we enter, through turnstiles and up a slight pedestrianised incline, pavilion to the left, pitch to the right, there is a group of men singing. There are maybe twenty of them, dressed in yellow. They are singing Cray Wanderers songs – the usual songs all football fans sing, with a space for the name of your team, vowels and consonants often bent to fit and then sung as if it is your song alone. Standing thirty metres away from them, Rowan stares at them directly, unable to look anywhere but. It's as if he's in a zoo for the first time, and this is his first sighting of an animal. He studies them, head slightly to the side, looking as intrigued as a two-year-old can look intrigued. The look then leaves his face, becoming neutral, like he is looking into a potential future for himself, like he somehow recognises the chanting from somewhere. Slowly, as they sing into a football-less backdrop, kick-off not for half an hour, a smile slowly reaches his face. Jake goes to take him by the hand. Rowan rejects the hand. He does not want to leave. He just wants to watch them sing. It's kind of unnerving, kind of profound, to watch Jake's son have this first interaction with football like this.

In the clubhouse, adorned with a "the oldest club in London" sign, people are sheltering from a rain shower. There are Happy Birthday balloons up everywhere. One of the bar staff is running around, irritated, putting things back in place, taking balloons off children. Rowan has taken a particular liking to the silver streamers that hang from the pillars in the middle of the room. As Jake queues for the bar, I am set into sink or swim mode with Rowan, being the sole adult responsible for him for the next twenty minutes and, trying to keep his attention, we play with the streamers, tearing off odd chunks, wrapping ourselves in them. The barman walks up to me. "Please don't," he says. "We've got a birthday here and it was booked before we knew we were playing in the FA Cup today." He sighs and adds: "It starts an hour after kick-off." He has his work cut out for him, because the turnout is huge today. It is, in fact, the biggest attendance Cray have had since the 1960s. There is another kid with his hat pulled down over his head like a balaclava, running rings around the table towards the far side of the hall as Jake returns, looking over and saying he can't believe this is the same place he raved in "what feels like yesterday". It was handier than getting back from Leicester Square, he says, where a lot of Sidcup would travel from, but, looking back on it, it was scary, a threat in the air. While he looks over at the other side of the hall a bit, as if he is rolling back his own years, saying "fucking hell" a few times slowly, I look over to a tiny sectioned-off area. There is a table with biscuits and a sign that says "boardroom". Next to it is a man I can only assume to be the chairman, the only one in a suit and tie, his Bentley waiting outside.

As the rain relents outside, the concourse and stands are like a breeding ground of little geezers, lots and lots of little Jakes running around, ignoring the players warming up, all playing their own games. They are backgrounded by groups of men maybe twenty years their senior, some parents, some not, with plastic pints and cupped hands concealing the crafty smoking. The queue for the bar stretches out, everyone's back turned to the flying footballs that occasionally hurtle over from Cray's free-kick practice that is happening immediately behind them.

We walk along the touchline just before the game starts. Some sort of prize is being announced on the PA. When the announcer gets to the specifics of what you can win, he starts to speak slower: "The tickets will be in . . ." There is a deathly silence for thirty seconds. "I've forgotten what it's called now," he tells everyone down the microphone. It finally comes to him: "Oh yeah, that's it, hospitality." Jake's uncle joins us along the touchline. He went on holiday, "by mistake", to Lowestoft decades ago, and has followed them and Cray ever since. "Tonbridge are a mouthy lot," he says, rolling his eyes at the congregated away support at the opposite end to the bar. He tells me about the time Tonbridge beat Lowestoft 3-2 in 2017: "They got lucky that day and they knew it." He goes to Marc Bolan from T. Rex's grave every year on Bolan's birthday, and every year on the day of Bolan's death, he goes to the place where he died. Meanwhile, the rain begins again and, after ten minutes of the first half, we walk back for cover, Rowan under Jake's jacket. Out of the storm, I let Jake and his uncle and Rowan walk on a fraction, seeing them disappear in the mist in front of me, and take my phone out to film the game from the halfway line, between both managers. The Cray Wanderers manager is gesturing at his players, toes on the touchline, until, as if he has felt me filming him, he spins on his heels one hundred and eighty degrees to look at me. I stop filming, caught in the act, and then there's a bizarre moment of recognition. We both recognise each other. It's ex-Fulham midfielder Neil Smith. "No way," he says, and walks towards me and gives me a huge hug. When I release him, I hear myself saying, "Are you the manager?" He nods enthusiastically: "Yeah!" And with that, he turns back to the game, and I go in search of Jake, his uncle and Rowan, at his first football match. I find him back where we first walked in, staring at a bunch of men singing, a mischievous look on his face. Tonbridge Angels win 1-0, and knock Cray out of the FA Cup, agonisingly close to making the first round proper.

7

My best friend when I was growing up was called Billy Hunt. He told me once that the song "Billy Hunt" by The Jam was about him. I believed him without doubting him for a split second, even though it was released five years before either of us had been born. He supported Wimbledon Football Club in a very passionate if resigned it's-all-doomed-anyway-and-the-world-is-against-us-so-what's-the-point type of way. The school had been given free tickets to a game when he was eight and, going there with his dad, his mind was made up forever. His heart was here, with this team giving away free tickets and the ball quite regularly, even to an eight-year-old's eyes so clearly punching above their weight. The walk between mine and Billy's was ten minutes, alongside Wandsworth Common. It was the first walk in the world I had to myself, brief enough to be allowed to make it alone from a young age – passing the same houses, the same off-licence, the same roads, beginning to get a feel for the way the mood of the world changed at different times of day, seeing into people's houses and noticing how some families had breakfast all together at a table, how the same living rooms were turned into atmospheric glows by the TV in the evening, against the sound of silence outside at certain times – that really satisfying eeriness, when it felt like you had a tiny piece of South-west London to yourself. I picked up habits on this walk, little isolated routines, that I stuck to religiously. I walked over the same drains with the same stride, making sure it was my right foot that landed first. I counted how many footsteps it took between each section of road, always crossing at the same point, making sure the count was exactly the same each time, finding the way satisfying rhythm and routine and patterns are built into solitary behaviour.

Either side of these walks, me and Billy Hunt spent almost every weekend together for what must have been five or six years, almost exclusively at his house, between the ages of ten and sixteen. I knew the path to Billy's room with a similar learned routine and familiarity. I knew where the shoes were laid out, walking upstairs to find him, unless Billy was with me at the front door, in which case for some unspecified reason we would always run, holding onto the banisters, as if time were short and the window for hanging out would evaporate if it were not done immediately. Without exaggeration, we would spend the whole weekend on the top floor of his house playing *Championship Manager* on his computer, uninterrupted. We only ever broke off when we were called down for dinner or when we went to see Wimbledon on Saturday afternoons. The sessions at the computer were long, intense and wholly committed – an inconceivably addictive football manager game that tickled all those senses I had acquired from play-by-mail, my reign as Patrick Thistle boss only just finished. The game was built in essence for one person playing, so in multi-player format, each player took it in turns to play, the other patiently waiting. One turn – selecting your team, signing players, working out training, speaking to the press, asking the board for more money – could take at least half an hour. If you weren't in the chair and were waiting instead, sitting cross-legged on the floor, it required you to possess meditative acceptance and patience, staring off-centre of the screen, like a snooker player who had missed a shot and was watching his opponent clear up the balls, face shut down into telling, frustrated neutrality.

Championship Manager was definitely an acquired taste. The most high-octane part was watching the actual games via a bar in the middle of the screen which told you what was happening as the game unfolded. There was not yet the graphic capability to show you anything that resembled a realistic football match. Sentence by sentence, it spelled it out for you. It would say things like "It's hit the bar . . ." while you waited, clutching your seat too tight, before eventually telling you "IT'S A GOAL!" or ". . . and it's cleared". It's hard to imagine now, but it was genuinely exciting. It really felt like an incredible technological feat that you could be managing a football team like this, while text explained the goings-on inside matches minute by minute. It took a certain level of blind faith to believe that it was real, that it somehow was challenging you and really mattered but, for whatever reason, *Championship Manager* had a knack for getting this out of me and Billy. For big games in the season, we would set the speed of the games to "real time" and sit there like football managers on the touchline, chewing gum, arms crossed, as the words played out incredibly slowly for two halves of forty-five real-life minutes. This was tedious if you weren't the one involved in the game, but out of respect, you would sit there, trying to be supportive of the manager in the hot seat. We once took on a career mode of managing both rival Glasgow clubs – Celtic and Rangers. I was Celtic and, in an unbelievably ill-thought-out and reactionary piece of management, agreed to sell Billy my star striker Henrik Larsson before the first season began at asking price. I intended to strengthen the squad elsewhere, but Celtic had an unprecedently bad season. The fans were extremely unhappy at this decision I had rashly made, while I had to sit and suffer while Rangers won season after season. Statues were made of Billy Hunt – the one the Jam song was about – and I sat there watching his euphoric games in Europe set in real time, thinking that if I could change one thing in my life, just one thing, it would be clicking accept to that bid for Henrik Larsson.

Wimbledon, the real-life Wimbledon, were in the Premier League then and – in that horrible, human way you don't know that you're inside the good times until they're gone – were in their glory period of success. This success meant finishing inside the top half of the Premier League relatively regularly, occasionally reaching semi-finals of tournaments too, punching way above their weight against the country's heavyweights to do so. They did not do this at their own ground, playing instead at Selhurst Park, the home of Crystal Palace, who were in the division below. This displacement, the everyday longing that it built into this modest success, decorated the existence of Wimbledon in a romantic but relatable way. Whenever we were there, all you would hear was talk of the club's former ground, Plough Lane. "Show me the way to Plough Lane," they would sing, "I'm tired and I want to go home . . ." It was like they were aching for somewhere to belong, all these men and women. They belonged with each other but not exactly where they were. They were not home. There was something magnetic about this background which contextualised every experience they had, good or bad. They were somehow not where they were meant to be.

Everyone liked Wimbledon Football Club. Or, at least, I really did. There was nothing to dislike, really – they were, I assumed, how everyone would like to feel about themselves in some way – defeating the odds but self-deprecating, dosed up on perspective but enjoying themselves, hurt and homesick but on a mission against the bad guys. The takeaway around the corner, despite technically being a Chinese takeaway, did proper chip-shop chips, the sort that you would flood with salt and vinegar until your taste buds were gargling just looking at them. Billy would act continuously impressed that I knew to ask for battered sausage "even though it wasn't on the menu". To us both, that was real culture, a real getting to grips with the adult world, to order something not even on the menu and still get it served to you with a nod and a wink.

Wimbledon had a habit of conjuring wins that felt like righteous smash and grabs, every win a result from the football gods born from sheer force of will and community. On Billy's fourteenth birthday, we went away to Upton Park to see them for an evening game, where Wimbledon were losing 3-1 at half-time to West Ham. The Dons scored three goals in the second half, the winning breakaway goal coming from a Roy of the Rovers-style one-two over the length of the pitch, finished with a diving header from Efan Ekoku. When the goal went in, it was as close to real-life euphoria as we had ever seen first-hand, grown men falling over the seats into us in delirious celebration, as if the fabric that the world needed in order to make sense from day to day, to keep things ticking over, had been broken for forty-five minutes, and just for a fourteen-year-old's birthday.

Things like this, good and bad, tended to happen to Wimbledon more often than anyone else, for a reason no one ever seemed to exactly understand. Extraordinary goals tended to be scored against them, clipped up for ever with flailing Wimbledon players in the background: David Beckham's goal from inside his own half, for example, Neil Sullivan chasing the ball back into the goal. When Spurs knocked Wimbledon out of the League Cup the same season of the Upton Park miracle, heartbreakingly close to Wembley in the semi-final stage, we got back to Billy's room that night with him particularly dejected. He had not spoken all the way back; neither had his dad, Terry. I respected this silence, took a vow to not speak either out of respect for them and the pain they were feeling, bowing my head. When Billy got home and went back to his room, trudging up there when we would normally run, he remembered that for some inexplicable reason he had been given a Spurs ball, signed by the entire team, and a shirt signed by David Ginola, the team's French talisman, which were stowed in his room. When he found them in his wardrobe, throwing clothes everywhere in a bid to access them, unsure whether it was a bad dream, he held them in his hands for an extended period, like someone having an extremely dramatic realisation at the end of a feature-length thriller. In an embodiment of a detective realising just too late who the murderer was, he stared at the ball and shirt, holding them tighter and tighter until his hands and face were both bright red. In minutes, after this long theatrical moment had played out, I watched him become convinced that these bits of memorabilia in his room were the real reason that Wimbledon had been beaten, that they had been cursed, that he had betrayed them, and, as this shameful revelation turned to rage, he put both middle fingers up to these inanimate objects – a static ball and shirt – before he opened the window and threw them both out from the top floor, like he was exorcising satanic offerings back to the abyss.

Billy's house was a home from home. I loved his family, the back route between his and mine being a constantly made pilgrimage. I went on holidays with them, watching his nan tell waiters to "pour all the gravy on the roast, please, I've paid for it all" and spent Christmases with them and his little brother, Robbie, talking about *Star Wars* all day with him. And with that sense of extended family, Wimbledon too exactly merged. They were both brilliant, stable things I trusted, a gentle but assured sense of self to both. It sounds completely insane to say it, but I'm not sure it would have all fallen together in the same way had Billy supported Arsenal or Manchester United. Wimbledon and Billy and his family somehow all made sense. I'm not sure then, genuinely, what stopped me from pledging my life to Wimbledon too. Billy even asked me once or twice, "Why don't you just support Wimbledon, with me?" I would just shrug and dive back into the battered sausage and chips. I didn't really have an answer. I didn't know why not. It was one of those mysteries of the heart, where everything can feel totally right, every box ticked and, for whatever reason – maybe a lack of some unknowable spark inside you – you are not inclined to fall into it head first, and instead tell them that you would love it, really love it, honestly, if you could just be really good friends.

All the heart and goodwill and warmth of Wimbledon came almost directly from their displacement. It absolutely defined them. It pitted them against the world. It made them louder, prouder, their purpose deeper. In their own subliminal way, Wimbledon projected how people with a forced homesickness were often inclined to go more insistently into other shells of belonging. People without homes had to shout, just to try and find somewhere, to plead with the universe for some safety, for somewhere to be, to not send them under. I had not yet acknowledged it in myself – that unknowing of who exactly or what you are, that constant internal navigating for a place to be. Instead, I just thought they were a group of people who really, unapologetically, knew who they were. And for this, despite their homelessness, I was, in some small unvoiced adolescent way, envious of them.

Forming as an amateur side in 1889, even before "Billy Hunt" by The Jam was written, they existed in the non-leagues for their whole existence, before exploding into Technicolor blue and yellow in the seventies. The FA Cup suited the Dons, all the folklore that the competition promised – that anyone could achieve anything on their day – was manifested in the hands of Wimbledon. Arming themselves in all the underdog feelgood factor that would define them from then on, in 1975 they became the first non-league side to beat a First Division team away in the modern era – Burnley in the third round of the FA Cup. Thirteen years later they significantly outdid this when, in 1988, they wrote arguably the greatest version of the FA Cup story in the history of the tournament, beating all-conquering Liverpool in the FA Cup final. Calling themselves the Crazy Gang, they were pitched in a lumpy, partly accurate, media stereotype against "the Culture Club". It was a stark and contrasting clash of footballing philosophies and heritage. Wimbledon: the plucky underdogs playing unnuanced, impassioned and aggressive football. Liverpool: the most successful and coveted club in the country, with household names the world over; poetic, incisive, quick and classy. Everyone in England, bar Liverpool fans, wanted Wimbledon to win that day. It was reassuring to know that once, just once, it actually came true. These were images I did not experience first-hand – I was four at the time – but something about the constantly recalled footage of it made it feel like I had. Dave Beasant saving a penalty. Lawrie Sanchez's header. Vinnie Jones in the tunnel shouting "in the hole" while John Fashanu smiled. It was the only story you would need to tell if you were pitching the FA Cup to, say, an American sports fan. It was enough, just that one single incident, to believe every single year that despite all the laws of averages and form guides in the league, you really never did know.

By the time I was first taken to Wimbledon by Billy, the club's home, Plough Lane, had been abandoned. The Hillsborough Law and Taylor Report, designed to protect against any disasters supposedly brought about by standing football fans, meant football grounds in the top flight would no longer accommodate terracing. Plough Lane could not be turned from terracing into seats, and Wimbledon had moved to Selhurst Park in a ground share. Sometimes *Football Focus* or other TV shows would do little stories about Plough Lane – often cutting to images of it now, overgrown with weeds, the stands looking as if they had grown their own particular brand of moss, untended and unloved and left to wilt. After the success of the years we had seen, the team slipped away the following year and were relegated in 2000, on the last day of the season. Billy's life and mine started to diverge after this moment, our paths into our late teens taking us to different friendship groups in different schools, *Championship Manager* left in its box, unloved and abandoned for an adult world.

During Wimbledon's first years in the Championship, the Selhurst Park tenure reached its end and the future of the club become financially precarious. Various solutions were thrown around – all unthinkable to either the board or the fanbase. The club's then owner, Sam Hammam, said he would "rather die and have vultures eat his insides" than negotiate the proposed club share with Crystal Palace. He spoke about a move to Dublin. Wimbledon fans turned up to games with banners saying "Dublin = Death". Hammam eventually left for Cardiff City in 2000. Meanwhile, Pete Winkelman, a businessman with, in his own words, very little interest in football, had set his heart on a redevelopment project in Milton Keynes that included a stadium and saw his opportunity. He could take Wimbledon, rename them and relocate them. With Wimbledon struggling, and despite opposition in the press and across football, the FA-appointed commission eventually voted two to one in favour of the move after the Football League had rejected it. Wimbledon were to be relocated to Milton Keynes and called the Milton Keynes (commonly abbreviated to MK) Dons. It would be the first ever permanent relocation and renaming of a team in football history.

The displacement, stripping of history, the relocation of a home was met with the kind of ire and hurt and disbelief that football alone seems to specialise in. Somehow, football has a way of articulating something about loss and displacement and community that focuses people's minds much more than most other things. People in England can be told every day of wars and innocent people being killed across the world, and react with a helpless shrug, but if football is messed with, if someone's football team is taken away, or a breakaway league is put into motion, they will go to the very ends of the earth in outrage and protest. Its simplicity, the way football populates the emotional mind, turns indifference more actively into action against injustice. When or how it developed this emotional heft that connected more deeply with some than, for example, reports of genocide, is a mystery.

By 2002 – only three years after that night at West Ham and, unthinkably, just fifteen years after winning the FA Cup – Wimbledon football club as it had been was no more. Legally and physically, it was now MK Dons, even if the entire history still belonged to Wimbledon. Stricken by immediate grief, panicking about where they were going to go, four Wimbledon fans drank away their sorrows in the Fox & Grapes on Wimbledon Common – the same pub that the 1988 team had visited on the night before the FA Cup final. They tried to work out what they were all going to do without their beloved football team. What if there were a new club? One that could not be taken away from the fans? On 30 May 2002, in the local community centre, there was a wider call to arms. The heartbroken fanbase would start their own, self-owned club, one that stood against many of the values of the modern elite, beginning again at the very bottom of the football ladder. This dispossession and replacement, the stripping of one history and building of another, seemed like it was happening far away from me. By then I had moved away from that stage of my life and, in the way that it sometimes takes a moment after separating from someone to see them properly again, it just became something I read about, like everyone else.

I liked to think though, reading about it even then, that the men who had tumbled into us, over the seats, at Upton Park were also the ones that met at the Fox & Grapes and been part of the decision to start their own Wimbledon team from scratch. It had to be. With *Football Manager* on their shirts (the new brand of the *Championship Manager* games), AFC Wimbledon – a club with an even stronger sense of purpose and self than before – was an absolute success story to end all success stories. Beginning with squad trials on Wimbledon Common, in which Billy had to process the drop-down in quality by watching his mate George try out as goalkeeper, they rose through the ranks steadily, almost every year. They became the real feelgood story of English football. MK Dons, having inherited Wimbledon's league position, have struggled ever since, with one season in the Championship being the highest level they've reached. AFC Wimbledon, on the other hand, have been promoted six times, rising to League One where they enjoyed six seasons and to which they were promoted again in 2025, having finished fourteen places above MK Dons. In 2020, they even got themselves back home. They moved into Cherry Red Records Stadium on Plough Lane, close to the original site. A unique ill-feeling had been sown between the followers of AFC Wimbledon and MK Dons – one devoid of excitement or begrudging mutual respect. Many AFC fans cannot even bring themselves to refer to MK as Dons, instead calling them "Franchise FC".

Of course, as if it were preordained, the teams were drawn to play each other for the first time in the FA Cup, in the second round in 2012. AFC fans were divided on whether they should even turn up to the game. Many decided to boycott it, refusing to visit Stadium MK. Billy and his dad, Terry, decided to go. MK Dons won 2-1 with a winner in the last minute. Thirteen years later, when the teams are drawn in the first round of this season's competition, the studio is full of gasps and long, severe oooohs. I now have a little circle of friends who know I am on this footballing mission, that I am going to every round of this FA Cup if it kills me. Within minutes, I'm getting the messages. They all say the same thing: it's got to be MK–AFC this round. I can't imagine anyone better to do this trip with than Billy Hunt. We have begun to see each other again occasionally, having had decades apart, and we are due to catch up. He is not going to go to the game, he says. He regretted going there that first time and vowed never to go back. Meet me for a drink anyway this week, I say, hoping to convince him.

"It just felt like the right thing to do, to throw the season ticket away. There was no other choice," Billy says, about the last years of the old Wimbledon I remember. "Those early years, of me supporting them in the Premier League, I think now that was a bit of a charmed existence," he goes on. "But it's hard to not be sanctimonious about AFC, because I really don't think there are any purer stories than the way we've dealt with our club being stolen." It can be surreal seeing Billy now, sitting across the table in a pub by London Bridge.

Occasionally I can't help seeing him as a twelve-year-old, even though I am looking at a forty-year-old man, one who has just had his first child, Stan. "It all has really made me think, what is a football club?" Billy says. I'm about to try to answer the question, already floundering in my head for something semi-profound to say, before he does so himself, football manager-style. "It's the people, the place, the location. The players are almost just employees, the owners are custodians. It's not theirs. If you're a fan, it's yours." It has, incredibly, only taken AFC Wimbledon nine years to get back to the Football League. "We were told for decades that it wasn't economically viable; the FA deemed it eventually that football didn't need us, and here we are. With a stadium on the same road as Plough Lane, in the Football League again. It's incredible." It is incredible, I agree, feeling semi-inspired for a second to start my own football club from scratch.

"It's amazing how quickly you can reframe it all in your mind," says Billy, sitting on a high stool by the window of the pub, us tucked away in our own little corner, drinking Guinness. "Manchester United or Chelsea away became driving to Croydon Athletic." Billy realised that rather than being bleak, all it required was a simple internal choice: "Once you manage to put the same level of giving a shit into the game away at Croydon as into those games we grew up seeing, you're flying." Wimbledon would turn up at grounds completely unprepared for the amount of people that would come and see the games, with teams having to go and do quite left-field English things like fetching hay bales for people to stand on. "I remember one moment really clearly for whatever reason, where it all made sense to me," Billy says. Wimbledon were in the Isthmian League Premiership play-off final in May 2008. There were almost two and a half thousand people at the game against Staines Town, packed into Wheatsheaf Park. It had an energy, as those types of games tend to have, of being the most important thing happening on the planet, nothing else mattering outside of it. "We're all totally fixated, seventy minutes in, the game is so tense," Billy's eyes widen, as if he is watching it again. "And there's this bloke's garden that backs onto the stand." At the most dramatic part of the game, when everyone is "losing their shit", the man walks into his garden and starts mowing his lawn. "I thought it summed up our journey, and football really. He doesn't give a fuck what's going on the other side of his garden. We were all there, this huge back story behind and in front of us, everything depending on what happens in this very moment, but the most important thing for him in that moment was just to mow the lawn. The two things were happening right next to each other."

Billy, like most AFC fans, is a member of the Dons Trust, the not-for-profit, democratic organisation that owns and controls the club. He had the compulsion too, at one point, to be so immersed in the club to also make it his working life, joining as a marketing manager, but ended up running the monthly bingo competitions, doing the newsletters, mucking in on everything, opening the office cupboard every morning and getting a fright at the sight of the dismembered mascot, Haydon the Womble, with no body in it. There were maybe only eight staff working there full time, so "you didn't really have the luxury of a specific job".

"There's a great quote from one of the founding fathers of AFC Wimbledon, Marc Jones. He said to his son, 'I won't have anything really to pass on. I've poured all my money and time on working for free on this.' His son said, 'Dad, you left us a football club.'" This sense of a thread, of passing a hard-earned thing down, only for the younger generation to have to learn their own lessons before making their own conclusions, the mesh of changing values and virtues and tradition versus modernity, is where AFC sits now. A passing down of a sacred thing – should you deem it to be more sacred than mowing your lawn – so that it can last. "That first day back on Plough Lane, I don't think anything will ever top that," Billy says, with me thinking that it really must have been transcendent if it outdid Upton Park. "It didn't matter what the result was, it was about generations of work and fight to be home again. Wimbledon is just the attitude of, fuck it, whatever you say, we'll do it ourselves. It's always fun, there's always been gallows humour, there's always been these moments of magic, you revel in it. I think that's what we're built on and always have been. It's about protecting that and handing it down. I think it even manages to translate down to the players. There are obviously a few individuals that this would not have happened without, but essentially this is a huge community effort, a shared value and principle in action. The important thing for me is that, whatever happens, the fans have to stay in control."

I definitely can't tempt him to come to Milton Keynes? I'd love to watch Wimbledon with him one more time as part of this FA Cup journey, I tell Billy. "I can't do it," he says. "I can't pretend that I don't love it when we beat them, but I don't enjoy playing them. Essentially, they just stole a league position. I find it hard to call it a club. The MK Dons is just an unfortunate blip in the 136-year history of our club, but that's it. It's a rivalry that shouldn't exist, because they shouldn't exist."

I am still hoping for another AFC Wimbledon fan to go to this game with. I want to experience the complicated emotions of it vicariously through them, try to learn something from it. My next port of call, though, Katherine Hockley, a lifelong Wimbledon and AFC fan, will also not be going to the game, nor has she ever gone to see AFC Wimbledon vs MK Dons. When Wimbledon became MK, Katherine and her partner Jo had briefly considered going to Charlton, around the corner from where they lived. Everyone was doing their own version of it. Where were they going to call home now? Charlton? Millwall? Palace? Fulham? Panicked and desperately sad, she was at the famous community centre meeting in 2002. "Honestly, it was electric," she says. "Kris Stewart stood up and said, 'I just want to watch football.' And we realised, oh, that's what we all want, and we want to do that together, no matter what the level is. That's not really the point." There were various events to raise the money to begin with. Katherine found herself bidding on a massive signed picture of Lawrie Sanchez scoring the goal at Wembley in 1988. She could not afford it but leaned over to Jo and said, "We just won't do the bathroom." Fortunately, they were outbid at the last second. But she would have bought it, she insists, and she would not have regretted it.

Nobody in that meeting would have imagined the mirroring of history and the climbing of the leagues, without significant funding, that happened next. "I can't get it out of my head ever, honestly," she says. "Sometimes I sit at the games and just think, I can't believe we've done this. We had a ten-year plan to get back to the football league that I'm not sure anyone actually believed we'd achieve. We got there in nine."

For someone who has visited 151 football grounds across the country to watch Wimbledon, it is a statement of some magnitude never to have seen them play MK Dons. Katherine's dad took her to Wimbledon when she was small, in the early eighties. She was more interested in the chips and Coke on the way home than the football itself, but she was there with her dad and grandad and uncles, and slowly it began to penetrate her psyche. In 1993, she got herself a season ticket to Wimbledon, during the very same Selhurst Park years me and Billy were going for motivations semi-fuelled by battered sausage and chips ourselves.

Her dad had been going to Wimbledon since the 1950s and '60s, through the years where nothing was on the horizon for the club beyond non-league, purely local football. In 1988, having followed the club for decades, he refused to go to Wembley for the cup final because Katherine's usual ticket had been given away to someone else, the assumption then being that girls didn't *really* like football enough for it to matter. He was extremely offended on her behalf and boycotted the game, watching it on television with her instead. During the nineties, when she picked up the baton and started going to the games every week of her own free will, he stopped going to Wimbledon. He didn't like the atmosphere at games in the Premiership, combined with the fact that his dad had died and he now found being there difficult, his absence at the games accentuating the loss. He drifted away from the club, by choice, during what was easily their most successful period. "What's been really amazing about AFC on an emotional level is that my dad has come back to it," Katherine tells me. The games AFC began playing, the ones that might involve someone mowing the lawn in the background or hay bales and general miscellaneous idiosyncrasies, rang true to his original experience of Wimbledon. It was as if, miraculously, the thing he had loved had returned. He came back to the club, with Katherine, and they have followed the club the whole way ever since. "I'm thinking about this a lot," says Katherine, "because he is having a difficult time."

He was diagnosed with Alzheimer's a few years ago and, season by season, each one marking time in the way a football season so definitively does for us all, it has taken away much of his memory. "He can't remember a lot of things any more, but one thing that he absolutely remembers, one thing he has never forgotten, is that he's a Wimbledon supporter." As the Alzheimer's insisted and increased, he has not forgotten how to enjoy a game of football. "It's given football a whole new level of meaning to me," Katherine says, "because there's something very beautiful about how he engages still in a game." Although her father now struggles to remember most things that happened more than ten minutes ago, he will always stay present in a game of football, be aware and locked into how the game is going. "They say that about music, don't they, that it's on a different track in your brain, so people can still reach certain memories with it. It's been fascinating because football is like that for him," she says. In the last year, it has been things as simple as him at least knowing which team is which. He always knows who Wimbledon are. "I've bought him a season ticket for next season. I've still got this hope that even if he goes only once, I can take him. That will be enough. I don't think I can bring myself to have someone else sitting where he should be, even if that seat is empty." He is in a nursing home now, where he is likely to stay, and where they used to discuss old games and how the season was going. Now the football talk is purely in the moment, where he, like everyone else, is watching a game of football with all his attention. "I find it amazing that he still remembers the game at all, it's genuinely extraordinary." Sometimes, when she comes to pick him up on a Saturday, he'll be sitting there waiting, already having dressed himself in his Wimbledon scarf and hat because he knows he's going to the game. She tells me this as if she is still processing it, as if via football and AFC and her dad, Katherine is beginning to understand the complexities and peculiarities of how a mind works.

"I don't see AFC as a new club," says Katherine. "It's a continuation; it's the club my dad supported. There might have been some that went away, because it's a completely different experience, watching a non-league match compared to Premiership." But for Katherine, and her dad, there was a strange sense of not dispossession, but of AFC becoming the club Wimbledon always had been, almost as if someone had handed her an opportunity to see the club the way her father had seen it, almost like seeing history repeat itself exactly as the club climbed the leagues. It was just as her dad had remembered it too, the club getting promoted, strange echoes of the games he would always talk about where Eddie Reynolds scored four goals with his head, somehow coming true and playing out again. The club, as a result, has become an incredibly emotional thing to her of late – her dad recognising it, it distinctly and profoundly resembling home and family, but also the game itself, giving him the gift of enjoying the present moment, alongside everyone else. "That's half of it anyway, isn't it, enjoying the moment of just being at a football match with everyone else," she says, as if he is now teaching her this, even through his illness. Talking with Katherine is as clear and as poignant an expression of the meaning of football as you could find – its simultaneous ties between personal belonging, home, relationships, an individual and shared history, all inside a shared experience of the current moment.

When I ask Katherine about going to see MK Dons, I might as well be asking Billy. They say almost exactly the same thing – the same juxtaposition between vindication and hurt, acceptance and lack of forgiveness. "I just can't get over it, the stealing of the club," she says. "I mean, obviously set up a club in Milton Keynes. That's fine, but start from the beginning, don't steal someone else's." She insists she will never go to see AFC play against MK Dons. "I just feel like they shouldn't really exist," she says, as if she and Billy were reading from the same script. "It's almost like turning up validates what they did to us. It doesn't matter if we win, the hurt has already happened, it doesn't fix that."

"The thing for me," she continues, "it really has made me think about what a club is." Again, she answers her own question as Billy had done: "It's the fans, isn't it, it's a community. There's history that ties us all together, and there's a place, a space where we all come from, somewhere we call home. It's made me think about football in a much more philosophical way. Everyone that is going to AFC – or when it first started, at least – is making a conscious decision to be part of something. It's a statement of standing against something and standing for something."

The next big philosophical question for AFC is undeniably around the corner. The younger generation are coming into the fan-owned club with ambitions for the team to get bigger and bigger. "It's almost like history repeating itself," Katherine says, recognising her position now as her dad's, who did not care for the Premiership. "I think the younger generation get the story passed down to them, but they haven't lived the feeling, you know? So they might want the success at any cost. I think people like me have learned over time that there are more important things than that, that the reasons we go are not necessarily for that." She stops herself, almost embarrassed. "I'm making it feel very heavy, aren't I? It's not life, it's football." Then she pauses, corrects herself: "But it kind of is life, isn't it?" I nod. It kind of is, yeah.

So I will go to the game alone and, while I had once seen the draw with some rush of serendipity and excitement, a cosmic slice of luck that this piece of disturbed football history was put in front of me, off the back of the two conversations I've had the week previous, I'm now part dreading it. It's weird and unpleasant and not nice, I'm told by other AFC fans, who choose to not go. There is no sense of relish or joy that the arrow is pointing back at them in the footballing calendar. Neither club, it seems, is keen to be constantly reminded of how they came to be in this world.

8

First Round

Sunday, 3 November 2024
Stadium MK, Attendance: 10,419
Milton Keynes Dons vs AFC Wimbledon

It is the changing of the seasons, autumn turning into winter, and sickness and spluttering is everywhere. I've started to think of London Euston as the mouth of these lonely escapes, the dice before it is rolled. I stand with a sea of strangers in the middle of the wide-open space of the station concourse, among the sounds of hacking and coughing, Euston's gaping entrance like an open tent in a gale, everyone looking towards the huge electronic boards either side, waiting for a platform. One after another is announced. A train time, a dash, a platform number waiting to replace it. Then, in turn, like a form of abstract choreography, we split and go towards said platform, some in packs and some alone, each person's day unveiled. Most people remain, waiting for our number, until the platform for the 10.21 Northampton train via Bletchley is announced. Then, as one, the artery of the middle of Euston leaves, turning their backs to the wind and heading down the sloped descent to the platform that waits, AFC Wimbledon fans unbuttoning jackets as they go, revealing replica shirts in bright blues and yellows, and matching scarves.

The faces of those poor people, the people who don't know it's the "franchise" derby today, when they see the football lads with their train beers get on. They sit in sudden resigned acceptance, looking straight ahead, or at their phones, or their books, making themselves small against the piling in of the blue and yellow and the hard morning breath of alcohol that suddenly encompasses them. Everyone knows the drill. You stay still. You give them space. You do not engage. People nudge up, blessed free table upon free table becoming a two-hour journey to share with the boys, cracking open the cans. "That Sainsbury's saved my life," says the man who one woman has had to move up for, sitting her bag on her lap, "you could get three for two on cider." His friends make impressed if stern faces, eyebrows raised, arms folded, the kind of gesture that English people make when they say, "Not bad that, not bad at all."

Travelling football fans' faces tend to be quite worn these days; sort of blank, sort of vacant. You wouldn't tell them, but watching them in their rows lined up, in conversation, is a kind of observational seat for a very laddish iteration of trainspotting. *It's all the same really, all these tribes, we are all the same*, I think while wondering if there is any other clothing range in the world in which the shirts are manufactured to be as tight as possible for peak athletic performance, and then sold, almost exclusively, to men who appear to drink upwards of eight pints a day. On the way in, I am listening to them, a cross-section of chat from the replica shirts and a bunch of boys in very slightly different versions of the same Fred Perry shirt under very slightly different versions of the same haircut, talking about the best places for away days and package holiday resorts. One of them is a Fulham fan, on a trip with his AFC mates. "I don't think we'd take eight thousand to Chelsea, I really don't," he says, as if delivering grave family news. "We only took three thousand to United." A friend of his, his back to me, half listens while scrolling his phone. He is on Instagram, and he is preparing a post to his grid. On one slide is a photo of a pub, him outside the front, and on another is a close-up of a pint. He is flicking between the two very quickly with his thumb, working out which filter is best to really make that lager pop. He is quite painstaking about this, putting the post in drafts, returning to it, looking for other options of photos of pints that he should maybe post, his thumb hovering on "send post". It's interesting to observe this from outside, as if it's only really clear how addictive and how powerful Instagram is, keeping us all in our little numb loops, by watching it in action over someone else's shoulder. He and I cannot be the only people who spend days obsessing over copy and images that people will half-read, at best, in less than a couple of seconds. My loops with it now are particularly all-encompassing and mindless. The phone knows that I like football a lot. It knows that anything that looks remotely like passionate analysis, anything that looks remotely football-themed, on or off the pitch, I will wait and watch. I am starting to worry in the space between these scrolls that if I don't have children, all I will be left with in my spare time is watching Roy Keane and Jamie Carragher say the same things again and again, sometimes literally, until I die.

The Instagram-poster-in-waiting only looks up from his phone when his friends have begun discussing how shit some of the current players are. "He's so shit," he chimes in, agreeing, the accent firmly on the "shit". Then again, "He's so shit", accent on both the "so" and the "shit". Their faces are a collective shade of disgust, as if whoever this player is that they're talking about has disgusted them so much with his shitness that it makes them sick. They are taking this shitness as a personal affront. The man shakes his head and then, as if this topic is the push he needed to send the post, the little adrenaline before the adrenaline, he looks down at his phone, clicks "send post". Then he looks up, the journey halfway between London and the satellites that take it to Milton Keynes, and sees the name of the station we are pulling into. "Leighton Buzzard," he says, scrunching up his face, "*surely* cannot be a real place."

From the carriage immediately behind us, you can tell when we are getting closer, away from the land of "surely that can't be real" to another place unrecognised in the mental map of every AFC fan. There is laughter from the back of the train, occasionally male shrieking – we pass sheep as we approach the station, the fans breaking out into "Bletchley is a shit hole, Bletchley is a shit hole." There is clearly something very satisfying about saying this, as the train halts and the majority of the carriages stand up, meeting in the middle, ready to spill out at the station. They are laughing as if they are saying the funniest thing in the world, something no one else has ever thought to say, something unbelievably perceptive. But all I can hear is a bunch of men who likely were not born yet when the takeover happened, just again and again shouting "shit hole".

The walk from the station to the stadium is all dual carriageways and underpasses. One man, with one of the tighter-fitting tops hugging his chest, has a fist full of AFC Wimbledon stickers. Every time he sees anything that says "MK" or "Milton Keynes" on it, he plasters a sticker over it. He changes every "Milton Keynes" to "AFC Wimbledon". He is on a personal mission to reclaim everything, to tag it and say, "This is ours." The most challenging of these is a big " 'Milton Keynes' sign that points cars off the motorway. He crosses the road, not without a clear degree of risk, just about avoiding the onrushing traffic, meets the sign on its island and, to cheers of encouragement, plasters the entire thing with stickers. He returns jubilant, both hands free.

It's a strange off-road hike from here; a harsh and unloved way to get to a football ground, where deflated trees bend back between the road, only ever broken up by Lidl supermarkets or Costa Coffees or BP petrol stations. We walk past all the factories that make up this part of Milton Keynes too – all of it just space off main roads where businesses fill the gaps. One of them is the Marshall amp offices. Jake drove me there once, when they'd offered me a guitar amp. I played the Bluesbreaker so loud in their showroom that, when I turned around, it genuinely appeared to me as if Jake's hair had been electrocuted in the air. He said he needed a lie-down when we got home. Through another underpass, a mural reads "Future city", an old vision of what Milton Keynes was going to be. "Future city my arse," someone says. We stop at a crossing, where a car second-guesses whether to wait for the crowd to pass or not, before stopping but then being caught with supporters passing in front of and behind it. "You better move, franchise, or I'll smash your car up," says another AFC fan. There is an abandoned child's scooter in the middle of the path up ahead. "The average Milton Keynes mode of transport," someone else says, pointing at it like a badly written sitcom bully, hyenas laughing. Another fan walks past it, drags it for a second as if it's roadkill, tells the pack to his left, "That's getting smashed over someone's head, mate." He carries it for a bit before realising that the only thing moving in the opposite direction is the traffic and a man with a ponytail, walking with a Zimmer frame, stopping every twenty yards for a break, puffing, camouflaging into nothing while fans pass, then making his way again.

Although I cannot really be any less suited to being in a pack of people behaving like this, I reflect on the walk about how at some point in my teens, I would have found this more scary but also more impressive and exhilarating, collecting little vignettes and anecdotes to embellish for everyone when I got back to school. Now, it just feels a bit sad and humiliating to be walking among it. You keep your head down, you pretend to be one and the same, you walk on. There are many truths about football fans, many things, loving and loveless, all at once. The AFC Wimbledon fans on this trip are no different to any other football fans I have seen on away trips – no sweeter, no kinder, no harsher, no worse. There are no actual altercations that I can see. It's just, somehow, on some level, a shock to me. I have built such a firm idea about what Wimbledon is – where it is from, what it stands for, its opposition to football, a nostalgic warmth for it – that I'm caught off-guard to witness something I do not like. I want to speak to each of them about this, ask them about how genuine injustice and hurt and rational fighting for what is right can be handed down from generation to generation until it is just a twisted, inherited hatred that is carried as a belief, how one person is the enemy for no reason other than they just are, and how when they see someone like that, they are going to smash them over the head with this abandoned child's scooter.

MK Dons' stadium – Stadium MK – appears next to an Asda supermarket the size of an airport. The MK Dons fans line up next to a shopping complex row of restaurants, Wagamama, Bella Italia and Nando's; they are singing "franchise get battered everywhere they go". I am walking past them, beyond the complex, when I bump into two friends of Jake's fiancée, Cat. They are a married couple, Chloe and Pedro. I am only walking past them for a second but catch them just in time to say hi, when the "yooouuuu Dons" begin from the snaking queue. Chloe hears the first one and, like a rallying call, answers it, a huge grin on her face. I hear her in the background, just after I have said goodbye, "yoooouuu Doooonnnss".

I get into the stand minutes before kick-off, climbing the stairs and entering a concourse that is by far the most "sports stadium" of anywhere I have been so far. It's all so proper, so purpose-built. I find my seat on the halfway line. The ground is impressive but maybe a third full, the empty black seats giving it the feeling of an abandoned Death Star. There is happiness and relief in me when the game starts. Here is something we can all understand, something we all came for, a game of football. For the first time in the FA Cup this season, the vastness and sparseness of the attendance remind me of how football can feel like something far away, somehow in a parallel universe to you while you sit and watch it. I have not had that sensation yet in this FA Cup. Everything up until now has been so close, so reachable. Wimbledon are wearing a blue and yellow kit very close to that of the FA Cup winners in 1988. It does a canny trick of consolidating exactly who Wimbledon are – that the entirety of the club, the history of it, even though it was technically bought and sold and moved – belongs to them. The kit has a slightly oily reflective quality in the light, the way the colours are so bright against the white and black of Milton Keynes that it's almost as if you can see Dennis Wise, John Fashanu, Vinnie Jones, Lawrie Sanchez and Dave Beasant on the pitch. Joe Lewis even wears his shorts so tight and high that he genuinely looks like he is playing in 1988, when everything looked at least a size too small on footballers.

I am technically watching the game in the press box – the ticket for the match sorted via an email I sent that week that had at least two too many "absolutely no worries at all if not" variants in it, asking whether there was space in the press section. Joe Thompson, the press guy, as luck would have it, likes The Maccabees and 86TVs and *Tailenders*. As I have arrived late, I have not seen the press section itself, but do have the privilege of seats, part of the stands but paired off into tiny little tables with power sockets for reporters or scouts writing notes. Taking up these seats gives me equal parts a thrill and a feeling of guilt – for not having a laptop or a scouting report, for not really having a genuine capacity in which to be using these seats, but using them nonetheless. I find Joe, a row behind and to the left, to thank him. We break into a conversation about what brought us both here but also, more keenly on my part as I sidestep questions about why exactly I am choosing to go to every round of the FA Cup, about what made him an MK Dons fan. "When the club first came to Milton Keynes, I was seven or eight, and they were really active in schools," he tells me. Eight-year-old Billy found his allegiance to Wimbledon via free tickets to Selhurst Park, and Joe had the exact same experience: "I remember it really well. The mascots, Donny and Mooie, came in and did an assembly and gave out free tickets. It was really simple, really exciting; I was immediately in." From that moment on, Joe and his mum and dad took to the team. "I think, generally with Milton Keynes, there are a lot of people that don't come from here but moved here, so we are the adopted town and adopted team of many people. But, for people like me, growing up here, they're my only team." It didn't matter then to Joe that the club he had fallen for had one or two years of history versus the many, many decades other teams had. He fell in exactly the same way everyone does – instinctively, unconditionally and deeply.

"It's not quite worked here how we wanted it to," he says, veering from fan to press guy every few minutes, eyes keenly flickering with the play in front of us. "I think a sustained period in the Championship, for example, and people would really come, but it hasn't come together that way yet." Instead of the bigger clubs regularly coming to Stadium MK, as had clearly been planned – it's a place that looks built for big games – they have more regularly entertained Accrington Stanley, Morecambe and Grimsby.

"I'm living proof that the way in is through young people. I pestered my parents for a long time. We still do kids for a quid," Joe says. As we watch AFC Wimbledon vs Milton Keynes Dons, the game close and tense, not yet telling us where it is headed, I can sense that Joe knows what I am going to ask him. How does it feel to have inherited something that broke up another club? "I understand where AFC are coming from, I really do. But they formed AFC in 2002, we formed MK Dons in 2004. They had some real problems with Selhurst Park that left them in the lurch, which was nothing to do with us, obviously. Milton Keynes was actually the nearest move available. This whole area, it was a consortium deal with Ikea and Asda built to sustain, and it does." He catches himself, maybe worried about making excuses or toeing a party line. "I know people turn their noses up at it. I know that it's not traditional and there's much less history here. But I think there are so many good things about MK Dons." The ball is put out for a throw-in on the far side, score still 0-0. "It was twenty years ago, and the only person around from either club that was involved in any of that, even on the board, is that guy." He points to a red-haired man in the distance who has the ball in his hands. "That's our left back, Dean Lewington." Lewington was a young player in the original Wimbledon squad when they were moved, and now the elder statesman and captain of MK Dons. He takes the throw-in. "Look, I understand it, we're the only people left that they can get angry at now. But the previous ownership that did it are long gone. We are just a visible reminder of what happened. It's not nice for either of us."

AFC refuse to recognise MK Dons as a team at all, not putting their name on the scoreboard when they come to Plough Lane, and initially not using their name or the word Dons in that context anywhere. When the teams started to play each other more regularly, the league ruled that AFC had to make mention of MK Dons at least once in the programme. "There were a number of years where the scoreboard was mysteriously broken, but it worked for every other game that season," Joe tells me. "We do try these days. We invite them into the directors' box; they refuse the invitation. For our new CEO, Neil Hart, it was the first time he'd ever experienced that. We're all trying to navigate it the best way we can."

As the game pulls and contracts, with neither side managing to get a firm grip on it yet, Joe says: "For me, the lazy soundbite can be: MK Dons are bad, AFC are good. Often, TV or radio have got thirty seconds to tell the story, and people just want a very brief summary. But, as with everything in life, it's not all black and white." I don't point out that MK Dons do, in fact, literally wear black and white. Joe continues: "There is a lot of grey, a lot of nuance, but that doesn't make a great digestible story, does it? So when these games happen, we've grown happy to play the pantomime villain. We're the franchise. We always will be. We've had to grow to embrace it. It's tribalism, isn't it?" – he nods towards our right, where families take up rows and rows of seats, watching the game – "those kids are going to find and fall in love with Milton Keynes the same way anyone else is with any football club, the same way I did. Surely, we're allowed that." As he finishes, I hear the Milton Keynes fans behind the goal to our right sing, "No one likes us, no one likes us, we don't care."

Right at the end of the first half, the ball breaks free and then goes loose again, fatefully falling to Mathew Stevens of AFC, who squares it into the far corner. There's a fraction of a second between the goal going in where time is elasticated – the ripple of the net first, then the sound of the AFC fans in the away end only happening a moment later, the way a goal in bigger grounds can clarify the difference between the speed of light and the speed of sound.

It's 1-0 to AFC. With the goal going in just before the first half ends, Joe is shaking his head, writing something down, and I separate myself from the game, realising this is the time to beat the queues, to find a burger. In the big empty concourse, some screens are showing the match and, strangely, a few older men sit watching it there, rather than the actual thing occurring five metres away. There is no queue for the burgers, which gives me a childlike thrill. I am starting to love this about my FA Cup days out. For the rest of the week, I worry about my weight, I stand on the scales in my flat. I leave them disappointed, saying, "Come on, do better, lose weight." I hate not being able to eat junk food at will like I used to. I feel like life has robbed me of an essential coping mechanism. Instead of allowing me a moment with Domino's pizza or KFC, flooding comfort and gravity through my system without revealing itself in my appearance, now that I'm older it shows itself, telling me that every private sin can no longer be private. But I have given myself a pass for these FA Cup days out. I square with myself that a burger at the ground is like an anthropological experiment – it's part of what I'm doing. It's part of the experience. The weekdays are for part starving myself to try and lose some weight, the FA Cup days are the free pass for this. The burgers are all waiting for the half-time whistle, stacked in a transparent cabinet that keeps the heat in. It's the sort you are more likely to see at baseball than football – the presentation a sign that the competition is flexing its muscles, moving towards a world where profit fuels all motivations. The burgers are covered in silver foil and, even from here, look like they are sweating. That does not put me off. I buy one and find the sachets of ketchup on the side, unwrapping it and taking in its heat, letting it hit my face when I open the bun, as if it is life-giving steam. I squeeze sachets, those impossible Heinz sachets where you never get as much out as you want, in there. Under no time pressure, no queue behind me, I take more sachets. Two, three, four. I fill that thing up with ketchup. I become giddy with what is next, that sensation of being soothed, excited about the moment, up to but no longer than a minute, where I will feel sated and calm before the inevitable guilt and heaviness and itchiness through my skin will attack. It's as good as I'd hoped. I hear a roar. More time has passed than I thought, half-time somehow flowing through while I have been oblivious. The game restarted. AFC have scored again. The men watching the TV tut and shake their heads. "Well, that's that then," they say and skulk off, now choosing to watch the actual game, or maybe more likely, to leave.

By the time MK have a player sent off to add to their misery, I leave, ready to trace back the motorways to the station ahead of the travelling support back to London. As I am walking the lonely outskirts of the stadium, a bleach-haired man, similar age, is walking towards me in the opposite direction. I am about to pass him when he stops me. He likes The Maccabees. He listens to *Tailenders.* "What are you doing here?" he asks. "You don't support AFC, do you?" I tell him that I don't, that I'm going to every round of this competition, that I'm not sure how it started, I just can't stop it now. "I had to leave when that sending-off happened," he tells me. "I need to get back to London before the rush." Milton Keynes Dons fan from London, then? I ask. He nods. "It's a long story. I'm Andy, good to meet you."

Usually I revel in the solitude of the walks back from these games, but I'm glad to have some company for this one, especially one with a footballing story attached. I am learning that most of us have a footballing story of some description. "I'm part of the England Supporters Travel Club," Andy says. "So I've told this story quite a lot, because you bump into Barnsley or Leeds fans or whatever that are interested in it." Andy, it turns out, is one of an extremely, extremely small group of people – someone who was a Wimbledon fan and now supports MK Dons. "The thing that happened over time is that younger fans, people new to it, felt like the switch happened overnight," he says, as we walk away from Stadium MK, falling into step. "The story they know is that Wimbledon had some financial trouble and were wearing blue on the first of August, and were moved to Milton Keynes and wearing black and white on the second. It was so much more protracted than that."

We walk past the bent-back trees, now bent towards us, and along the people-less, factory-laden path back to Bletchley station. Like my story, like Billy's story, like Joe's story and like Katherine's story, Andy's story begins at the age of eight. "I started supporting Wimbledon because they were the closest Premier League team. I grew up in Kent. My old man used to work at a factory there, which meant you could get cheap tickets to Selhurst Park, so we'd be there with my older brother a lot." We reel off players from that Wimbledon team, one at a time, legendary players with names that stick with you like footballers from a certain period of your life do in an undetachable way: Jason Euell, Neil Ardley, Chris Perry, Kenny Cunningham. It goes on. If you meet another football fan the same age as you, just say the names of footballers from when you were both young. It is all you'll need to do to have a good time. We go through most of the squad, each repeating the name that the other has just said as if they were old school friends. We end on Neil Ardley. Andy begged his dad for a Wimbledon shirt when he was eight, he tells me. He came through. "So, by the time all the MK stuff came about, I'd been a proper Wimbledon fan for ten years."

In 2002–03, when it was confirmed that Wimbledon would be moving to Milton Keynes, there were mass protests outside the games at Selhurst Park. Andy and his brother had grown attached to the Wimbledon team of the time, David Connolly and Neil Shipperley up front, those players as close to their hearts as all those we have just listed. They were heavily invested in the team's plight. On the first day of the season, they sheepishly sidestepped the protests and decided to go through the turnstile to see the game. "We'd been supporting those players for a good few seasons and, I don't know, we didn't want to go to Wimbledon Common to watch non-league football. With all due respect, it was a really steep drop down. I guess we just wanted to watch our team still." Wimbledon were, strangely, brilliant that year, Connolly and Shipperley scoring forty goals between them, just missing out on the play-offs back to the Premier League. A largely undocumented microcosm inside the explosion happened, where Andy and his brother found themselves as two of only a thousand fans who followed this transient team everywhere. "It was almost like there was this cohort of a thousand people that grew this really close, strange understanding," Andy says, walking back past the same scooter that was going to get smashed over someone's head, still lying on the ground. "It was like we had this very big club all to ourselves, it was sort of intoxicating. We all shared feelings really closely. It was just spot on, almost secret, and extremely special."

We keep walking, the game long behind us, AFC Wimbledon stickers plastered over every sign that says Milton Keynes. "There was this one guy, that had just had a newborn baby. He was bringing it to these forbidden games at Selhurst Park." Because there were so few people at these games, a sense of trust and closeness was formed, almost on a name-to-name basis, between the fans. Andy is describing a turgid game, at home to Portsmouth on a midweek evening. "This man said to me, 'Can you hold the baby while I go to the toilet?' So, I'd be there, an eighteen-year-old, holding this stranger's newborn baby at the football, protecting it until his dad came back." Andy looks at me for a second, as if he is about to share a secret: "You know what?" I shake my head. "I saw the man today, he comes to Milton Keynes still, like me. His twenty-year-old son is there with him. The same baby I held."

I receive this story like an undercover message of warmth and community in a time of war, to hear of a baby born at the same time as MK Dons, shepherded from Wimbledon to Milton Keynes against the grain, but still going. "It's weird because that season, I could tell you everything about every game. It's all so vivid to me. The goalscorers, the half-time scores, I could tell you about the blades of grass that season." This is the first time I've ever heard of a Wimbledon fan that moved with Milton Keynes Dons, I tell him. He nods. I won't be the first person to have said that to him. I ask him, trying not to sound presumptuous or alienating or disapproving or suddenly journalistic, are there many of you? Andy searches for a second, as we approach the station, taking the sweeping right that the AFC fan crossed to plaster stickers to wild applause earlier today. "If I had to give you a number, I reckon there's maybe a maximum of eight people that still go from that thousand in that season." Do you still speak to them, I ask. Andy takes a second to answer, as if this bit is maybe private. "We do a bit of the acknowledging from a distance type of thing, but there's a couple where, if you were to say, 'I remember you from Selhurst', they wouldn't want to discuss it. It would be slightly embarrassing. It's almost a bit, 'I know and you know', but let's not talk about it.' "

It is an interesting place to land, on nearing the station. The idea of an underbelly of low-level shame in adult male football fans, trying to fit in, leaving it unarticulated, just nodding across a crowd at each other. The simmering discomfort of being from somewhere different, of having something to hide. I resonate with this, the sensation of being half in and half out of a crowd, wishing you felt some truer sense of purity with your tribe. "I think, subconsciously, I probably missed that real launch of AFC, that heartbeat moment at the start," he goes on. "It was so ahead of its time, that maybe I missed the point of it, I'm not sure." By the time the team relocated, Andy had made his decision, almost without knowing it. He belonged to the team that was moving, and not AFC. To begin with, he could have sworn the thousand or so moved too, but the numbers quickly dwindled. "When we changed the colour of the kit, that was heartbreaking. It's like it suddenly all dawned on me then. But I'd made my decision, my momentum just took me a different way and it never relented." The way Andy talks about it, it's as if I can see a football fanbase splintered in a freezing, inhospitable landscape, shards of ice breaking off with different people on them, floating them out to unspecified parts of the sea, at the mercy of the tide, him ending on the other side of a great divide from most he had gone to games with. "This fixture brings something horrible out of both sets of fans, to be honest," he says. "I feel like there's almost a forced anger, a falseness, that younger people are carrying because they feel they should be angry and hateful rather than because they have a reason to. It's like the hurt gets indoctrinated into you."

We are about to part ways at the station, the conversation feeling like it could unfold for ever, me wanting to get Billy and Katherine and Joe and Andy together somehow, to see what would happen. I think they'd all like each other a lot. They all seem to like football for the same reasons, separated only by pure circumstance and coincidence. "I think it was, dare I say it, a real sliding doors moment in my life," Andy says. "Going into Selhurst to be part of that thousand that season. It was an amazing year but, of course, sometimes I see AFC celebrating these promotions and think, did I make the right decision?" In time though, a certain type of fan identity has developed in Milton Keynes, which has become part of Andy too. "I think we've learned to accept that everyone is going to hate us. You can't control that. We are having to learn to take that and find pride in what our football team is."

There is an eeriness leaving it all behind on the train, back through the bent trees, the very surface of a story much more complicated than the one I had left with in the morning swirling around in my mind. As I board the train, two men at the station are asking for money. They see a man walking onto the train with a football hat on. "What was the score, lad?" one of them says to him, trying to butter him up. He throws up his hands as if to say, don't ask me, I've got no idea who won.

9

I don't know how it did this to me or what exactly would give it the right to do this to anyone, but football, on finding it, gave me the impression that everyone else had been born with a team – an innate sense of unquestionable belonging – and I was the only person in the world looking for one. I don't know whether this is in some way how every young person in the world feels about themselves, but football undeniably sharpened this for me. On first sight of it, amid all my instincts to plunge head first through the television towards it, football also unlocked in me a dormant sense of displacement, maybe a transgenerational one that had been handed to me from somewhere else, and shone an internal spotlight on it like a bedside light that refuses to dim, no matter how hard you try to sleep.

Before I had seen those first FA Cup semi-finals, before I'd imagined then seen that Chris Waddle free-kick faithfully play out, before I had envisaged play-by-mail as a genuine route into professional management, I felt I must have had heard the phrase "you don't choose your club" a thousand times. "It", football incessantly told me, "chooses you." This essential truth about football haunted me, the sense that life was something that had to be handed to you and that was that. You had no choice. This was particularly alarming for me because I had not been given a club to not choose from. Football may have barged its way into my life, meeting my enthusiasm and filling up all the space in my reaching brain with numbers and names and places and dreams, but with it, it also opened up a longing in me that could never be put back in the hole it came from.

My dad did not have a team. He did not even like football. I asked him who he supported once, because everyone supported someone, and his only memory was watching Ryde United on the Isle of Wight as a child with his friend Johnny Holton, whose father ran the tea hut and weekly bingo with "Auntie" Phyllis. There was a boy who moved from London to his school on the island and always wore a West Ham shirt – claret with blue sleeves – to remind everyone of this. To all the classmates on the Isle of Wight, this simple top symbolised something impossibly glamorous – a tiny picture of another world they had not seen. My dad, days spent by the sea in various summer jobs – on the canoe lake or collecting money or grabbing hold of boats while people got on and off – would look across the Solent, imagining the lip of the shore and Portsmouth to be like Broadway because of the twinkling lights. He first left the island in 1971, at the age of seventeen, realising only then that those lights were just ordinary streetlights, not a new frontier. Moving to London, he first met my mum that same year at the ICA with some friends. They met once or twice again before, in 1978, he moved into room three of number 49 Northside, a block of bedsits. My mum had room seven. By late October, they were a couple, and, in that room my mum, struggling to know what to do with her life, said she might like to be a carpenter. He suggested they started making things with wood and they built a wooden box together in the evenings, with very few tools, in which they would eventually keep toys for their three children. It now sits in the house of their youngest son, and Will keeps toys in it for his daughter, who shares our mum's name, Lana.

In that summer of 1978, they listened to Ian Dury's *New Boots and Panties!!*, Joan Armatrading, Van Morrison, Leonard Cohen and anything from Dylan's most recent prolific period – *Blood On The Tracks*, *Desire* and *Street-Legal*. I love those albums, always carrying a fondness for them that sometimes makes me feel as if I had known them when they first came out too. Those original vinyl records are in my flat, blending with mine in one huge, alphabetised collection. That summer of 1978, my parents would go and watch blues bands on Electric Avenue in Brixton, before sometimes ending up in a West Indian club called the Blue Lagoon, in a basement on the Brixton side of Railton Road, that played reggae music and served Jamaican lager they had not seen before, called Red Stripe.

But as far as football ties went, that was it. All too often back then, street violence was an everyday occurrence to navigate and football became an extended shorthand for this – not a magical thing to run towards, but something to avoid as much as possible, reinforced by the constant news reports on football fan violence. My dad's main thought on the game itself was that it was ridiculous – crazy how much they fell on the floor, how much they complained about everything – and his main focus, when it was on television, was on how much footballers were paid, especially after every mistake any of them ever made. His cousin Roger Holmes, who I knew from his job of playing house piano in hotels, supported Portsmouth in the kind of fanatical way that meant he made unofficial fanzine books with a record of every Portsmouth player that had ever played, which he sent to our house along with a tape of his latest recordings of piano standards, with a little note to say where he was in the background of some of the photos of the players (a torn piece of paper inserted inside: *Kit Symons, pg 127, you might notice me behind him, third row, slightly blurred, second to left*). That was all I had to go on from my dad's side – no Portsmouth or West Ham or Ryde United telling me that I had no choice but to choose them.

My mum, Lana Odell, was born in Lebanon. Her mother, Abla Assily, was born in Palestine, and had been forced to flee during the Nakba of 1948. My mum and her younger brother Paul were sent to boarding school in England at a very young age, after an early life spent moving around the Middle East. Paul loved football. He, no doubt more urgently than me, because of their constant displacement and moving from one place to another, had a sharper, more pronounced desire to attach himself to a place in the world through football. He had almost nothing at all to go on, and, on a left-field whim, chose Wolverhampton Wanderers. He had never even been to the West Midlands. He did not know anyone from there, nor even particularly where it was. He chose Wolves as randomly as closing your eyes and pinning a tail on a donkey. It was as good an imaginary home as any. My mum had decided she supported West Brom. This was not to align herself in some sort of inexplicable Black Country rivalry with her brother, but because she had heard that her parents lived in Bromley West now, in the London suburbs, where my English grandfather, Harry Odell, who had met Abla while working in telecommunications in the Middle East, had eventually provided a leafy and safe place for his wife and family to call home. My mum had not seen this home yet and had just assumed Bromley West and West Brom to be the same thing. West Brom, she ascertained on very little information, was where her new home was. The football teams they chose were, in their own small way, as telling a description of their sense of disorientation as anything was.

The days I would spend at my grandparents' decades later, in what felt like a world away, through to the outskirts of London in Purley, would be littered with me overhearing my grandmother talking about friends and relatives that she had not seen since fleeing Palestine, who were scattered as far and wide as Egypt and Canada, or wherever they could find home or work or refuge. Maryse, my mum's cousin, was forced to flee twice, firstly from Palestine to Lebanon, and then from Lebanon to Paris when civil war broke out there too. The driver of the car she fled in had told her to stick her head out of the window when they left, because there would be slightly less chance of being shot at if they saw a woman was in the car. If my mum had not been diagnosed with multiple sclerosis when I was the same age she was when she was sent off to boarding school in a foreign country, completely alone, I'm sure I would have been told similar stories of her own experience. As it was, the disease would take from her, year on year, parts of her sight, then her ability to walk, then her ability to talk, then her ability to do anything but shake in pain. I always think of her upbringing and imagine her as I remember her, always smiling, but younger, never complaining, an incredibly kind and sociable and naturally caring person, and I cannot help but theorise from time to time that her body might have found a way of eventually expressing all the hurt and stress and pain and abandonment that she must have buried somewhere inside all that love and generosity.

I can still hear my grandmother talking about Palestine if I reach for it. I hear it now as almost pixelated sentences from another room, the way a child overhears everything without anyone around them knowing about it, absorbing and ingesting it as information into their skin. You mustn't tell anyone where you're from, she would sometimes tell me, earnestly. She had learned to keep this information as secret as she could, at first out of pure necessity, fearing for her life simply because of where she was from – her first job in Lebanon depended on her not being Palestinian, which she had told them she wasn't – then as a learned self-defence mechanism for the rest of her life, which only relented for the games of cards she would have with her friends in the darkened back room of her house, all of them hunching over a dimly lit table, shuffling and redealing the deck, hoping the cards landed in their favour. On display in the room, among the miscellany picked up from the shores of the Middle East, was a key, almost mythical in its size, appearing to be half the size of a cricket bat. It was the key to her home in 1948. She had kept it. They all had. They were their homes, and they were going to keep the keys, even if they would never return. She looked obviously Arabic, so her Palestinian blood must have been a complicated thing to hide, especially for a woman as bullish and proud as her, the way she would shoo us up to bed shouting "Yala! Yala!" still in my head on recall if I need to hear it. My grandfather had not known his father, who had left home when he was young, and had never heard his mother speak of him. She herself was a mildly terrifying figure to me, sitting in a corner of that dimly lit back room at my grandparents' house at Christmases. When she died in very old age, she was holding a photograph of a man that no one could identify, that my grandfather had never seen before. He didn't know whether it was his father or not.

It was as if I had a feeling that did not even begin in me, but instead in the people that had made me – a collected, inherited sense of displacement that, in the way these kinds of things silently grow feelings inside, had turned into a present-tense reaching for roots. And out of this smattering of history, of known and unknown DNA strands, football called to me like a conduit in which to colour in an awakening soul, saying *Find yourself a home, make certain you that you can define yourself clearly, then everything will be OK*. Before I knew home could only ever really belong inside you, and not in crowds of people who supposedly felt the same, I looked for one inside football. And the search began.

It is March 1992. Oasis won't even put out their debut album for a couple of years and so I am yet to be sold music and the guitar like a unconditional commitment. Graham Taylor's England have not yet failed to qualify for the World Cup or been knocked out of the Euros at the first stage. I am yet to feel the first specific sting of how football can hurt more than real life. My mum has not yet been diagnosed with multiple sclerosis. My uncle Paul, still a Wolves fan, is going to take me to my first game of football. In a few years, he will find a family home in Reading, which will feel, as much as anywhere, like it is finally a place to be from, and he will start to support Reading, tying him to his new, permanent home. But for now, he is a Wolves fan, taking me to see Chelsea at Stamford Bridge for the first time. They are playing Sunderland of Division 2 at home in the quarter-final of the FA Cup on a Monday night. I have been asking about going to see a game and, for whatever reason, this is the game that has been negotiated between the adults and chosen for me.

We are high up, in the East Stand, looking down from a side-on angle, when I first see the pitch. It reveals itself out of the evening chaos, an impossibly bright green, neon lit from the floodlights, brown mud running through the pitch, deepening in the penalty areas. It is like a glistening light in a solar system, almost too blinding to look at, the first magical thing I have witnessed with my own eyes. Paul has the match programme and he listens to the announcement of the teams, while I watch him very diligently. He turns the programme to its back page, where the teams' first elevens are printed, and crosses out some changes in the starting eleven, adding the three substitutes to the empty spaces provided. The build-up to this game feels like it has taken a very long time, the way that events you are told about when you are young feel like they take decades to arrive. You will them closer every day, only to find when you are older that everything moves too fast, everything slips through your fingers, and you wish that anything at all retained a similar depth of suspense or duration. For now, I can take it in as if we are hovering above earth, just looking back down on human life for an eternity, thinking for the first time, *Look at all those people, all living their own lives, outside of mine.* The peculiar, heartbreaking giddiness of that first glimpse of the pitch lasts throughout the entire game. I ask a lot of questions, have things explained to me, and, with stoppage time at the end of the game dying out and the game 1-1, plead with Paul that we don't leave before the final whistle, just in case something happens. "It won't, trust me," he says, doing a good impression of someone who knows that, and we leave early, to beat the traffic. He is right. It ends all square.

From that evening, for maybe three seasons, I felt like I had found my football team. I supported Chelsea. Chelsea, then, had a nice, scruffy, shell-shocked underdog feeling to them. They lost the FA Cup quarter-final replay at Roker Park 2-1, Sunderland going on to reach the final that year. I convinced my dad that we should go to Stamford Bridge more, him taking us to games despite his apathy towards it, and still bending to entertain this itch I had. If he was from the Isle of Wight, but didn't like football, and Paul supported Wolves, and my mum was from Lebanon via Palestine but for some reason had supported West Brom, it was hard to attach a familial connection to Chelsea. I felt keen, very keen. Part of me wanted to reach back inside my history, twist it a little, fabricate some things, stick a little badge on, one that said this is who I was, then take it with me to football where everything in life was crystallised and simplified into "this is who I need to win today", and I am standing with people who feel the same. I tried to make it Chelsea.

In the few years that unfolded since that night in March, Chelsea began their escalation back into the high echelons of English football. I was engaged in this at first, going to games occasionally. But, as the club became bigger and more successful again, something in my young bones began to disconnect. Almost like a growing, twitching discomfort, I started to get a disturbing sixth sense that supporting Chelsea was not going to suit me. I worried that supporting Chelsea from afar, being one of a mass, not going to games, was going to feel unsatisfying, like a connection that had nowhere near enough of the sustenance and sense of belonging that I was after. I wanted what Billy had – a home from home, a place that somehow filled in all the parts of me I had not yet coloured in. With it ringing in my ears that you can never change the team you support, that once it chose you, that was it, I sensed that my moment to find something else, something that suited me more, was going to come very soon or I would forever have to hold my peace.

It has been a season since I have gone to Chelsea, who are signing big-name players like Ruud Gullit and Mark Hughes, beginning their rise to becoming one of the glamorous clubs in the country again. It is harder and harder to get tickets. As Chelsea continue to become bigger and bigger, this itch to find something that will fit me becomes unignorable. The survivalistic way you begin to shape-shift into different possible versions of yourself at the age of eleven is taking place inside me, and I tell my dad that it would be good to go to more football, if that was OK. "Fulham is a nice club," he says. I hadn't ever even heard of Fulham Football Club, in the bottom division of English football. I wasn't sure that nice was *exactly* what I was after, but it was worth a try.

My dad takes me to Fulham the first time on the train. It's like most of the world is just a blurred, undiscovered mass to me, like a map of places that have not been explored. It isn't like going to Chelsea, where there was my house, a car I was in, then suddenly the pitch. This requires thought and process to reach. He explains each part of the journey as we do it. It's one straight line from our house to

Clapham Junction, a fifteen-minute walk in an exact, unmessupable straight line. You get a child off-peak day return ticket from the machine. £1.75. It spits two tickets out at you. The machine at the station sucks the ticket out of your hand, like it's snatching it from you, then presents it back in a different place, as if it's a slightly annoying magician doing the same trick again and again. Then it's a train to Putney, from platform five, two stops. Once you get out at Putney station, it's another ten minutes' walk, down the high street. We can just make out the floodlights of a football ground over the trees to our left as we reach Putney Bridge. I stop to look at the gently looped bridge for a moment, pedestrian pavements bordering ongoing traffic, waiting at lights, before it crosses. I have not yet built a Londoner's rhythm for the Thames, how crossing it somehow marks something definitive in your day, tethers you between your universe and another and back again. I take it on, a feeling of mild vertigo running through me, one small step for a man, one giant leap for mankind, then an immediate left through Bishops Park. The park is gentle and fairytale-ish, a Gothic church and small graveyard on the right-hand side ushering you into another straight-line walk, swept either side by tall, proud trees, the river now parallel on our left hand, before the park opens out into a concrete square, giving way to a long road out of the gates, towards Craven Cottage.

There doesn't seem to be any football really happening at first. It's like those early rounds of the FA Cup, where just over the lip of the journey people seem to gently appear from everywhere, as if they hadn't existed before, making their way to the game from an unspecified surrounding point. With them, Craven Cottage reveals itself like an old relic. It does not glow phosphorescent or feel like

I am hovering above the world's axis, like at Chelsea. It is more like I am stepping into an internal world that had already existed inside me. As if everything is familiar but ancient, everything showing itself in that strange way you sometimes meet someone and develop an immediate, unspoken feeling somewhere between infatuation and affinity without knowing anything about them. It's not overwhelming. Instead, I just have an innate sense I might have known this place for a long time. I seem to understand what it is about almost immediately and, oddly, perhaps psychotically and a little desperately, that it might understand me. "The Fulham Football Club" is written across the actual cottage, sat behind gates on the left-hand side, in block capitals, in black and white. The bricks on the ground are red – warm and old. The tickets are £5 on the gate, through iron turnstiles that have to be pushed hard to get through. When I put my hands on them for the first time, they are cold and textured. I can feel where paint has hardened and formed small lumps, again and again over years. It feels like I am putting my hands back in time, onto an archaeological discovery like excavated bones, now connected to everyone who has touched them before.

When the pitch reveals itself, two and a half sides of the ground are terraced standing. I have not seen terraced standing before. It is lump-in-throat, gulp-inducingly beautiful. I have never seen a place that actually looks like I am inside the 1960s. It is very simple, very still, very grounding, very beautiful. It is all these things in the same way that someone might tell you that the Moors or the Highlands are beautiful. It tells you that life is hundreds of different things, and that you should not expect anything of this than a place to be. It does not promise you things it can't deliver.

I sit there quietly for most of the game, almost mute, letting it whisper its thing to me, and as I do, take in the chants coming from the back of the stand on the left, the Hammersmith End behind the goal, and the conversations happening around me. It is like I'm quietly in an interview with it, in a sort of silent, privately arranged affair, working out whether this is going to be worth jumping for. It finds a way, through these oddly intense ninety minutes of introspective interrogation, of articulating to me that its history has been one of loss and disappointment, that the foundations of the place are built on an acceptance that they will not win, that things will not fall for them, and if it could be any expression, it would be one long sigh. This place could take my hurt, it would accept it, it would embrace it. Five thousand others see Micky Adams's Fulham beat Barnet 2-0, but it might as well have been just me, no football match, and an empty ground. I don't remember a single detail of the game, as if it were completely inconsequential to anything. If I want to go again, my dad says, I know the way now.

From that day on, my heart unreservedly and unconditionally belonged with Fulham Football Club. It had offered me something that no other place had – solace, understanding, unfussy connection. It was a perfect place to start. And to add to that walk alongside Wandsworth Common, I now had a second journey of independent life, in the exact opposite direction to the walk to Billy's – the one to Craven Cottage. With games never even close to sold out and tickets very cheap, it became an incredibly simple, almost meditative thing to do to go to Craven Cottage. I liked getting there as early as possible, two hours before kick-off if I could. There was a very sensorily pleasing routine to watching the ground half-fill up from completely empty, watching the players warm up, asking them to sign autographs, which they did every week, the same players to the same me. I took to it with a passion, straight into school, singing the songs that I had heard and not participated in as if I had actually sung them in the games very rowdily, exaggerating the fervour of the atmosphere (the atmosphere could not be described, with any semblance of reality, as fervent).

I enjoyed and took pride in supporting a team that not many people did. It was as if, in the confusion of potential belonging, a part of me had chosen to begin anew, to find something that felt like I could become what I wanted with it. I liked the people at Fulham too, who seemed like almost exclusively old men to me, all gallows humour and collective rolling of eyes. I liked how on bumping into each other, these grown men would say "alright mate" instead of sorry, but shorten it until it became "o-wa-may", said very quickly, and both parties knew that all they needed to say to each other was "owamay" and then walk away. I liked learning these tiny little rules of male football engagement. There was also no conversation in the world that I wanted to overhear more than "What shall we do with Fulham Football Club, then?" I loved that conversation, just standing on the terraces nestled within earshot of people talking in these defeatist tones. I would tut with them occasionally when leaving, tell them that it was a joke really, wasn't it, that we were terrible today, weren't we. It was only a few years later that I realised, very privately, and quite shamefully, that, like my total commitment and connection to the nineties English cricket team, or even Damon Hill's plight in attempting to win the Formula One World Championship, although I was desperate for these people to do well, I stayed with them because they lost. They lost beautifully and tragically. I would have never said it, for fear of being exiled, but I found myself wanting the only thing everyone is invested in not wanting. There were often times that, very secretly, very guiltily, I really wished Fulham would lose. I would be stood there, secretly hoping the ball to go into our own net. When Fulham did lose, I felt something align within me. Suddenly, physical contact was acceptable, everyone wrapped together in a momentary funereal feeling. I would not unpack until decades later, with long and slow work in therapy, that while my mum was dying, and I was young, I was looking for places where the world momentarily aligned with my unarticulated loss. I did not want to celebrate. I wanted to find some ways to express pain – safer ways that did not involve watching your own mother's life end as yours was just beginning. Initially, in some strange childhood pact with a place, I was going to Craven Cottage for the way it did loss. The way it told you it was OK. That it was natural. I wanted to suck that in, be just one of thousands of people feeling sad about something more negotiable than death or disease, momentarily sensing that the dark part of my mind was aligned with the people around it, even for those few minutes before we left the ground, and I did the walk back into my actual life again.

By the time I was thirteen, I had a season ticket to Fulham. I was very proud of the thick, handsome wad of paper with the club logo on it. I would take it with me everywhere I went, put it on the table at the school hall, leave it on top of my books in class, wave it around pretending it was a red card at lunchtime. I began to find too, with self-perception creating itself some space in these solitary, routine walks to and from the ground, that during that walk over Putney

Bridge to Craven Cottage, that little ledge between one world and another, I would have to fight a compulsion to take my season ticket and then the rest of the contents of my pockets and throw them into the River Thames. Sometimes I almost sensed myself straitjacketing my hands from doing this. It was as if the sudden expression of nature in London, the break between high streets and greyness via the huge mass of water suddenly under us, and the evergreen, ancient trees of Bishops Park waiting, would activate some primal sense in me, some deep recognition of anger or pain or feeling. I could do it if I wanted. I could throw this all away, then I'd be free. It was like the feeling at Dulwich Hamlet in that early round, leaning over that rail at the pitch, for a second giving way to a feeling of reaching out. Like that day, I have never once given into the sensation, I only contemplate it and, as if re-entering the physical world and not the one made of fantasy, merge back into my own body to get closer to the football.

How could I find ways to be here all the time, I started to ask myself by the age of fifteen. How could I make Fulham Football Club the only thing in my life? I devised an idea one weekend on that same walk to the ground, with total sincerity, of inventing and running an official fish and chip van for the club. The magical thinking at play was that because vans were portable, I could drive to the away games too. Everyone would know that it was the only fish and chip van worth going to, the official one endorsed by the club. I'd park outside the ground, do my work, meet my people, talk about "what we were going to do with Fulham Football club, then", then go to the games. I would technically be working, but I'd be watching Fulham every week. I had not done any groundwork on the logistics of this job, though, except telling people enthusiastically about it. I also could not cook or drive, and the fish and chip van didn't come to life.

As this new routine at Craven Cottage took hold of my life, I began going to the football more regularly with the same friends, building a habit and set of rituals between us before each game. We listened to the men shouting stuff, learned all their catchphrases, how a big guy called Cliff liked to shout "what a pile of mack" or another whose name we never learned constantly shouted "come on, my team", or we spared a moment to gaze curiously at the man with a monocle who looked like he'd been stuck in his seat since 1920. We tried different places to stand at Craven Cottage, spending chunks of a season standing in one area or another, almost like they were permanent residencies that, when left, could not be returned to. We followed the play in the Stevenage Road to whatever end Fulham attacked, stood next to the drummer, absorbing all his and his friends' chants and shtick to repeat at school that week as if we had been part of it ourselves (we hadn't). The big end point for us, though, was the Hammersmith End behind the goal. The noise at Fulham came from the back of the Hammersmith End. I would hear this sound and imagined it to be where the real men came from, where one day I might be from, too. I thought of it like a hierarchical system, beginning at the very front of the stand, leaning over the barrier, before moving slowly back towards the back of the Hammersmith End with the passing of time, each season moving a few slabs of concrete back, as if it were a loyalty programme and I was earning stripes. It was only when eventually reaching the back that I would realise the noise was all coming from mouthy teenagers, younger than me, in the same clothes as each other. It was like walking into the end of *The Wizard of Oz*, as if the prophecy had been completely imaginary.

For me, the silent problem with supporting Fulham became apparent quite quickly. Everyone loved Fulham and usually, Fulham liked everyone else. It was that sort of club, for better or worse. It defined itself on being reasonable, on its comparative lack of tribalism. Except, that is, for Chelsea. Fulham hated Chelsea. Most of the songs were tailored to hating Chelsea or fuck Chelsea or stand up if you hate Chelsea. This, for obvious reasons, activated sharp, dormant shame in me. In my mad scrap for home, I'd once belonged to that thing, the thing that everyone hated, and I had decided to switch. In footballing laws, there was no bigger or greater sin. It left me often internally tormented at games, almost concerned that my cover was somehow going to be blown, that someone would see on my face that I was not of pure stock, and the whole of the Cottage would turn as one and point me out and chase me back into the cold of Stevenage Road halfway through a game. Whereas lots of other Fulham fans of my age then seemed to have family ties to the club – let's be honest, why else would you have chosen to support then Third Division Fulham – I had no such connection. I had just made a decision, a calculated one, based on my intuitive emotional response, that this was going to be me now.

As Fulham climbed the leagues, and Chelsea dominated English football for a period, the hatred increased, and I learned to push down that old version of myself, making it so small that I barely accepted its existence. I can't imagine how my grandmother or my mother felt, forced to flee where they were from for safety. Because even that was, unironically and genuinely, a source of actual torment for me. It would be far from the last time, but it would be the first, most pointed example of how life contrives to point you in the direction of the exact thing you were hoping to avoid. This residual sense of uncertainty and displacement, twisting itself through all the time it was left unspoken and turning into a shame, planted itself inside me too via football. It was a little voice that, left to circle inside my head like a rat in a cage, gathered momentum and became pronounced in an entirely internalised way, using the exact fuel that shame needs to survive – a misunderstanding about where the feeling was from, and an inability to say any of it out loud for fear of being ostracised. You mustn't tell anyone where you're from, I heard my grandmother Abla say again.

Regardless, I loved Fulham Football Club very, very deeply. I did not fall out of love with it despite this internal balancing act. I moved closer towards it. I planted my flag there even deeper. I continued to genuinely feel that it understood me, and I understood it. I developed a habit in time of saying "Come on Fulham Football Club" out loud about almost anything. Going to school. Just before playing a show. Waking up in the morning. In the gym trying to lose weight. "Come on Fulham Football Club" wrapped itself into my life, starting to mean, *Let's make this happen now, come on, switch on, make life work for you.* In time, in decades and decades of slow unfolding, I came to realise that all people, if you ever had the time to sit them down and discuss it with them, would have a history more complicated than when they were blurred into a crowd, wearing the same colour as everyone else. During the beautiful periods of Fulham's highest achievements – travelling to see them eventually lose Europa League finals and achieve seventh place Premier League finishes – I started to think of everyone as complicated shards, and about the circumstances and consequences that had led to us all being in the same place, bending ourselves into shared truths. And I also began to learn that anyone could be from anywhere at all, and how opposites sat directly next to each other, ready to tip to the other side of the axis – pride and shame, joy and despair, the familiar and the foreign.

This constant reaching to identify with a group of people, finding itself precariously inside Fulham Football Club, I can see now as a sort of natural human instinct at play. It is not something to criticise myself for, but sometimes it blurs with a vision of watching my mum, me not knowing her history then, and seeing how trauma does its work – not mine, but hers and her mother's, turning itself into me. I was seventeen and not in the room when she died, but when I arrived to find her there, part of me still felt as if I would be there for ever, promising to bring the world back.

Fulham didn't ask anything of me. It was just a place to go, its players and squad transient, all moving through, a place I could channel whatever I wanted into. And I channelled it all. Unarticulated loss, home, shame, longing, yearning, community, euphoria, happiness and sweet, sweet, consolatory sadness. It felt like I was being recognised and called by Fulham Football Club, and whether it required it or not, that place was so valuable to me that I would be indebted to repay it for ever, with however much losing or disappointment or boredom or destroyed hope, because it had already given me the thing I needed most – a welcome, and a world to move into with it.

10

Second Round

Saturday, 30 November 2024
Broadfield Stadium, Attendance: 2,831
Crawley Town vs Lincoln City

There appears to be no one else travelling from London Victoria station to watch Crawley Town vs Lincoln City in the second round of the FA Cup. At first that's a surprise. But actually, as I suddenly remember that it is only me on this self-made footballing pilgrimage, why would there be? In the days between these rounds that are now signposting time, it has become an entirely internal conversation with myself. Which game should I go to next? Where have I not been in England? What do I have time to do? What will be the best game? I throw these questions around silently all day, even when I am engaged in some other conversation or activity or job. Here is another goal suddenly set in the conversation of my mind that, with no other voice of reason to witness it, I decide I must rigidly stick to. Go to every round of the FA Cup.

I am in an odd, melancholic mood today and, Victoria being the regular departure point for trains out of London going south, I am there again, having chosen Crawley Town vs Lincoln City for the next round. *One more small ground*, I think, *before the Premier League sidestep into the competition and mine-sweep all before them.*

I like the comparative silence of this train – the lack this time of dodging the eyes of groups of lads on the morning beers going to the football. After the journey with the AFC fans, I have realised that this is likely to be the recurring occupational hazard of these journeys, every path coming with *Super Mario*-style obstacles to get to the football, usually in the form of huge groups of lads on their way too, looking for some sort of altercation to fill the time. It's an especially challenging aspect for when the part of me that decides, as it has today, that I would like to make these journeys without communication, without interference, without anything I can't control shoving its nose in my face, telling me football can actually be alienating and isolating and aggressive. So, in the silence, today's unprovoked, unspecified sadness allowed to pool with the space made for it, I sit.

I have always liked travelling, moving somewhere, staring out of the window. I have been thinking about it since Haywards Heath – that maybe something is dragging me to the in-between, no commitment or responsibility, nothing demanding my time, no guilt for not working that needs to be thrown around. Maybe I have sought that out here. Maybe everyone on tour and in circuses or on constant business trips is in their own way doing this? Maybe that is where

I am trying to be? In the responsibility-free nothingness, light and detached? Most people I know will complain about travelling, or they seriously dislike airports. I've always felt extremely relieved in them. I like when a flight is delayed, being left with nothing to do but drift around abandoned shopping centres. It has always calmed me down, mock-complaining about the delay but secretly revelling in it, getting some perspective on the life I am leaving, the life I'm arriving at, being able to see home or friends or friendships clearer when I am outside them, outside myself, stuck somewhere. On these trains, I miss touring the world. I miss the drift of it, the way it dials down the volume of a panic to make something happen in my own life. On tour, everyone is confused about where home is. No one has a home apart from the hotel or bus or dressing room or airport. I liked that levelling out. It suited me then, I consider while looking out of this window, to never have to make any commitment to anything apart from weightlessness.

There is a woman in a pink jumper on the train, knitting. She looks very at peace with her Beats by Dre headphones on. Over her shoulder, all the back gardens of the outskirts of London go by. Each home looks so appealing to me from here. Even the kitchen sink pictures of an England sixty years ago that rush past the woman, the washing line back garden suburbia from the view of a train, make me tingle with jealousy. *That would be nice*, I think, *to be packed that tight together with people. Maybe I'd feel less tired if I had that?* Just out of sight, a man is muttering, cursing the world. Fuck this and fuck that and fuck this again. As I stand up to leave the train, disappointed to have arrived at the station and the daydreaming over for now, I reach the voice that has been muttering by the doors in the strange single seat that trains provide next to the big circular toilets. He looks like an extremely down on his luck Father Christmas, sitting almost in the foetal position, head bent over his knees, a can of Guinness in one hand, and scrolling on his phone below his knees on the other, saying fuck this and then fuck that out loud at every passing image.

It is so still off the train, the fuck this and fuck that disappearing towards the south coast. I am entering an absolute greyness peppered by birdsong. The walk towards the ground gives way into Barley House Estate, where green moss grows on windowsills and an elderly woman with two crutches walks alone. There is seemingly nothing else for more than a moment, the only noticeable landmarks a funeral director's building and a Tesco delivery van. When I do stumble across anything, the very lifeblood of Crawley appears to be hearing aids and hearing aids alone. You can hear them ringing, feedback in pensioners' ears as they pass you. A small hill incline challenges my knees and my asthma, feeling that I am lugging excess weight, more than I would like to admit, sensing myself as a retching forty-something with a brewery on his back and in his hips. I thought weight would never get me. As a skinny teen, I would provoke it. Eat all the burgers. Drink all the Coke. Smoke all the cigarettes. Now it feels like they have all arrived in me for the first time at exactly the same time, in physicality, on this very hill, Crawley bending me to its will, walking the same pace as all those I have just passed. Maybe it was that one at MK at half-time? Was that the one burger too far? I pass a teenager with his hood up. He does not look up, just continues to roll his spliff, the sugary smell of factory skunk for a brief second setting my taste buds to tingle. As I am walking back down Ditchling Hill, at first there appears to be nothing, then the New Moon pub suggests itself, emerging from behind bracken. It looks like the Narnia adaptations I remember from when I was young, an entire civilisation hidden behind lazily placed leaves.

At the bottom of Ditchling Hill, there is the first sign of football people, some of them coming out from behind the bracken of the New Moon. They just appear in the exact same way I am learning all football people do, out of nowhere in these satellite towns. There are kids jostling and talking about the Premier League out of the silence. A huge red and white football marks the ground we walk towards, a Poundlandish deity, as we collectively begin to merge, bodies getting closer, reaching the underpass. As we pass, the fabric and architecture of the giant-sized football become clearer, sitting alone in the middle of a roundabout.

I get into Broadfield Stadium, but for some reason I would rather still be on that train, ploughing on idly into the middle of nothing, than at this game of football. I feel like my feet have taken me here out of some other ancient, unproductive programming, not my own desire or will. In the spot of terracing that I choose to take up, there is a group of men, maybe ten years older than me, who are trying to impress each other, cackling. Sean Roughan of Lincoln places the ball at the corner near us. He does the thing footballers do sometimes when they check the bottom of their boots, flicking them up like a horse. "Got shit on your shoe, have ya?" one of the men shouts at him. I feel myself disassociate. The corner is snuffed out, but an unthreatening goalmouth bundle means Lincoln win another corner. The exact sequence takes place again; one of the less imaginative of the older men shouts, "Don't do a grass cutter," which gets less cackling, before he adds, realising that he needs a good line that plays to his crowd, "Now the shit's on your arse." There is louder cackling. He is encouraged and adds, "Whatever you do, don't miss." He has won the cackling of his friends over again. They all look at each other, extremely proud, like they have achieved something. It's these days, when you are not in the mood for it, when you are standing close to people you don't really want to be with, that I begin to understand other people's world view on the pointlessness, or worse, the nastiness of football.

More entertainingly, behind the goal, a bald, small man with a Crawley Town shirt and camo vest on does windmills, punching the air across the terrace when the home team open the scoring. A second goes in and he runs the length of the terrace again, this time followed by two kids who are semi-mocking him and semi-worshipping him. The man eventually falls to the ground, theatrically holding his knees for an extended duration before a sympathetic man leans down from the barrier to check if he's OK. Receiving the attention he was after, the man ignores the helping hand and sets off again down the terrace.

The mood sours in the Crawley end as Lincoln get back into the game. I walk across the front of the northern terrace in search of the largely vacated red seats on the opposite side. Someone shouts "Too predictable!" and then "You're shit!" at everything at once as the second goal goes in. In the red seats, as the game nears the end of an extremely eventful first half, the Crawley goalkeeper, Matthew Cox, makes an incredible double save. When the ball miraculously ends up not in the goal, parents with hairdos brushed over like children at a wedding shush their kids with very salty crisps, before they too scream swear words out into the sky at no one in particular.

At half-time, the lights go off completely. The stands suddenly are in darkness. I sit in there, cold. Are they saving electricity? They must be – not long after the lights are back on, the players run back out. With the score at 2-2, the second half is not much older, the lights have not been back on for too long, when it happens. It suddenly feels very neon-lit, and very focused. I am starting to forget the melancholy I have floated with here now as that special gift football has is happening again. It is dragging me towards it, a situation intensifying, suddenly giving me the gift of the present moment. Lincoln have a long throw, the ball looped into the penalty area like a grenade with the pin pulled out. Crawley half deal with it, a scuffed clearance leaving the ball to bounce once on its way out of the area. Erik Ring of Lincoln City is waiting, unmarked, on the D of the penalty area. The ball could not fall more perfectly to him, as if someone has underarm thrown it in a training drill. Like all those famous FA Cup goals, like Waddle's in that semi-final, there is a moment of universal inevitability, as if everyone's breath slows, everyone knowing what is about to happen. Erik Ring waits for the ball and then, in an explosive, quick, sharp action, almost like a golf swing, closes his hips on the ball, connecting so perfectly that the sound is just a gentle thump, like he's kicked a comic cloud. It travels so rapidly, so directly, that no one has time to react, bar the Crawley goalkeeper, who can only jump directly upwards and punch it up into his own net. It's a beautiful thing. Swift and deadly and magical in the floodlights, as poetic as anything you will see at the highest level. *That's why I've come here*, I think. Because there's always a chance you might see something like that. The same reason you go to a gig or a gallery – to leave having been shown something different to re-enter the world with.

There's worse to come for Crawley fans: only a minute later Lincoln's Jack Moylan scores from close range. The away side have turned the game around completely and lead 4-2. Now a restlessness in the home crowd sets in, and the attention drifts as a group of men try, not aggressively, to get the attention of a female security person standing with her back to the play. One waves his hands enough to catch her eye. She raises her eyebrows as if to say, *Yes, what is it then?* "I'm sorry about him," the man says, half putting his friend in a headlock. "He just wanted to know if you're single, he wants to take you to Nando's." She half glazes over, half smiles. "Ah, bless," she says, sarcastically, before turning her head as if she has just swished a fly.

Eight minutes from time Crawley score a third, giving themselves a lifeline. It has been a real classic, actually, and I have left behind the sadness I arrived with. It has shaken it from me, as if football has ruffled my hair, picked me up from the floor, told me that there's nothing to worry about really, is there. The lads are already up to leave when the third goes in. "Shall we stay?" one of them says. "They're not going to score again, are they," the guy who did the headlock says. The man who wanted the date at Nando's but is not going to get it shrugs and they both leave.

As I walk back into the darkness, back towards the station, past the football on the roundabout, out of the football portal and back into my real life, following their lead and leaving before full time, it is hard to distinguish whether we can hear the motorway or an equalising goal behind us. Even though I've been grumpy all day, I'm for some reason manically checking my phone as I walk away, refreshing the score, hoping they've equalised. It's suddenly unbearable to me that I don't know the score to this game. It sounds like a battle in the distance – the drama and energy of whatever I cannot identify exactly, motorways or goalmouth scrambles.

It ends 4-3 to Lincoln.

11

Third Round

Saturday, 11 January 2025
Etihad Stadium, Attendance: 52,056
Manchester City vs Salford City

The third round of the FA Cup signals the inclusion of all the Premier League clubs to the world's oldest football competition. They waltz in, disrupting the pleasing way every round is halving the teams with dreams intact, ready to stomp all over the thing. With them comes a sudden wider focus on this year's tournament that I am choosing, by this kind of weird, pleasing gravity, to spend my precious days off at, up and down the country. For this weekend, where the other rounds have passed without much mainstream glare, everything else suddenly appears to be on hold in the world of football. The third round is the heartbeat on which the entire famed magic of the FA Cup exists, one of the best weekends in sport. This weekend is that little storm where any of the teams from the beginning of the journey, to use football parlance – your Penriths, your Haywards Heaths, your Dulwich Hamlets, your Cray Wanderers – could find themselves drawn against the giants of the game – your Liverpools, your Chelseas, your Manchester Cities or your Arsenals. It is from this possibility alone, this serendipity, that the phrase the "magic of the FA Cup" has been kindled. These games – drawn at random on television by footballing celebrities taking numbered balls out of a bag, trying not to drop them while reeling off anecdotes about their FA Cup memories, as teams sit at home and beg them for a home draw – are what separate it from everything else. The very, very unlikely but tangible possibility, that drawable thread, is alive and with us today, as the arm that reaches out and takes a club with a regular attendance of under a hundred and brings it to the doorstep of the biggest clubs in the world of football, takes its pick.

The history of the third round has seen endless mismatches like this, some of which have turned into giant-killing miracles. In 1933, almost a hundred years ago, Walsall beat Arsenal in the third round, 2-0 at home. The leather used to manufacture Arsenal's boots, £87 in total, was £18 more expensive than the cost of the entire Walsall squad. Non-league Hereford United took Newcastle United to extra time in 1972, through a Ronnie Radford strike from distance, an immediate pitch invasion in its wake. They won 2-1 eventually in bad weather and on an inconsistent pitch, setting a template for all cup upsets to come. In 1989, FA Cup holders Coventry City were sent south to Surrey and beaten by non-league Sutton United, managed by an English teacher, 2-1. In 1992, Wrexham knocked out cup specialists Arsenal, a free-kick twenty-five yards out from a thirty-seven-year-old Mickey Thomas writing itself into the book of magic.

Shrewsbury Town, at the bottom of the Football League, beat an Everton team chasing Europe with Wayne Rooney in 2003 through a last-minute header at their place, Gay Meadow. In 2005, new Liverpool boss Rafa Benítez was beaten 1-0 at Burnley's Turf Moor via a Djimi Traoré own goal – the defender spinning 360 degrees as if disorientated by the cold, unaccommodating conditions, and putting the ball in his own net. Liverpool would become European champions that season, AC Milan failing to do what Burnley could in the final. Leeds, finding themselves disturbingly drowning in League One, beat historic rivals Manchester United at Old Trafford – an afternoon of nostalgia having been starved of what they had been so used to up until a decade earlier. The years at this stage have been largely magicless, though, since 2011, when Newcastle were beaten at Stevenage, a 3-1 loss confounding the four divisions that separated the sides.

This season's draw has thrown up some good ones. Tamworth have got themselves a tie at home to Spurs. There are ninety-four places between them in the football pyramid. Tamworth are a part-time team made up of accountants, a zip salesman, bricklayers, teachers, retail workers and a personal trainer. Tom Tonks in midfield works for a catering company and has a long throw that causes havoc at non-league level, measured at 44 yards. "Tottenham players are probably having recovery massages, while I'm delivering food," he tells the *Guardian* in the build-up. Tottenham players are warned that they are "going to hate it", that all they will have is a tiny dressing room and an electric heater. I try to get tickets for this game. It is completely impossible. Tamworth has never known demand like it – television are coming to the game, rigging up cameras and lights in a place not built for lights and cameras, the kind Tom Cullen once marshalled at Hamlet – strange logistical challenges suddenly arising of an entire heavyweight broadcast infrastructure being squeezed into a non-league club, them welcoming household names like startled competition winners. Tottenham are taken to extra time by Tamworth but eventually win 3-0. I am silently relieved at this, worried at a distance that I might miss something truly special, wincing and checking the scores while nodding and smiling at a lunch obligation I have tried to get out of but absolutely cannot, I am told, under any circumstances. Elsewhere, Accrington Stanley have got themselves a tie at Liverpool. Josh Woods, Accrington Stanley's number 39, has gone viral weeks earlier, filmed jumping around his living room, his brother shouting "Oh my god, oh my fucking god", when his side have drawn the team they support and love passionately. When they are beaten at Anfield by the champions-to-be, an even more wholesome video goes around with Liverpool manager Arne Slot talking to Josh, their arms around each other.

Generally, though, along with the satisfying titbits and these nice little anecdotes to tell each other about how beautiful football is, the way the big clubs roll in now, distracted and weary, gives a growing sense of the football world stretching itself, morphing away from tradition, and taking it somewhere you don't remember. The singular romance of the competition has been eaten away over time for the bigger names in English football. There are other, more financially pressing motivations. The clubs sometimes appear to treat it, in part, like I am treating the obligation I am at during the Tamworth–Spurs game. I'm there in body, smiling. I am somewhere else in my head, checking the score under the table.

The arrival of these great yawning behemoths at this stage can feel like watching an old film, those little scenes I half remember where a character has been lost at sea and finds refuge on a featureless rock, but just when they are feeling safe enough to relax, the grey inanimate mass they have arrived on begins to move, a shape shifting in the water, a huge tail suddenly snapping. In a sequence of denial then shock, they suddenly realise they are sitting on the belly of a whale or a great white shark or Godzilla. The monster, without even noticing, irritated slightly by this itch, opens its mouth, and, taking with it all flotsam and jetsam in its wake, consumes them and all their petty little dreams.

In this case, with my chosen game today, the monster is Manchester City, the stranded protagonist is Salford City, and I am on my way out to sea to meet them. It is icy cold leaving London on the way to the belly of the beast. There are train delays – those little blessed ones I secretly love – and then white sheets of snow on the way to Manchester. We are passing frosted-over stations and iced trees, appearing to me like diagrams of lungs and bronchitis after a winter I've spent on hold to the doctor's, trying to get inhalers. Eventually, as the train picks up speed, it is pure whiteness.

The first Maccabees rehearsals will start in two days' time. It will be the first time the five of us have been in the same room with instruments since walking off that stage at Alexandra Palace in 2017. We are going in for no other reason than just to play, just to see what it sounds like, to work out how it all feels. I am in part excited about this – as excited as I will allow myself to get – the other part apprehensive. There was a time, for years, that I longed very deeply to be back inside those songs again, the only place where everything felt safe and soft. In time, as my life stretched and grew and changed, I began to think of it as if the band was a sequence of events that happened to someone else entirely. Now it is around the corner, all I can think of is a scene in *Girls*, when Hannah and Adam have got back together and are excitedly planning their lives together again, sitting opposite each other in a diner. Then Hannah looks into Adam's eyes and, tears forming, no words said, they have a moment of silent recognition, before asking each other what they are doing that night, and they spell out their evenings, apart. They did not need to say anything. It just wasn't going to work, in the real world. I worry about that a lot. About it not feeling right, about being stranded in the wanting something to happen and it not working. About having to walk away from it all again. Because, with all the things we have loved and have lost, we are never walking away from them once, we are walking away from them again and again, in myriad ways, each time a history of hurt rising in us that we thought we had left behind.

Just beyond Stoke, the houses are punctuated differently against the white backdrop, each suddenly now noticeably a different pastel colour, like a perfect Raymond Briggs illustration. England, from this moving train, is sad and ancient and wounded and beautiful and magical. It is as if a real, hidden warmth reveals itself in the freezing whiteness, as if a myth is manifesting inside it. The cold accentuates the age and resilience of everything. It is truly beautiful to see England like this, in the snow, completely still.

As we near Manchester, two couples join the train carriage,

drinking beers. A child is with them, maybe early teens. It's very early weekend in their energy, all kinds of unpacking of the week's stresses and excitable plans being thrown around. They have the enviable confidence of people who have had two drinks – the absolute sweet spot where we all wish we could stay – and are lightly teasing each other about washing duties and who does and does not do what around the house. Eventually one of the women looks down at her phone, apropos of nothing, and says, "Oh wow", a deep intake of breath. "It says that all planets are aligned on the twenty-first of January." The men are silenced by this for a second, maybe unsure whether to ask what this means or make fun of her. They don't need to. The kid, completely silent until now, looks up from his computer game and says, "Oh yeah, and what about Uranus?" He does not say another thing for the rest of the journey and they discuss the planets aligning no further.

On arriving at Manchester Piccadilly there are some warnings of trains back being cancelled, England being completely frozen over. I go to the ticket office, ask the man what happens if my train, the last one back, gets cancelled. He looks to his left and right, checks no one is listening, looks again, then leans over the desk. "If the last train back to London gets cancelled," he whispers, before quietening his voice further, "they'll get you a taxi all the way back to London." He then does a face at me that looks like he is hoping now, on my behalf, that all trains get cancelled too. I have often found this to be the difference between Manchester and London – the *I'm on your side too*, the slightly more discernible patience, less of a feeling that if you collapsed, people would just walk over you. I collect these little interactions; they privately keep me afloat. It's as if, without one or two of these a day, I begin to feel a tired, peculiar heaviness that I am unable to really describe. A primitive but profound, tribal safety swell meets me after I receive the wink. It must do, because I am inconceivably moved a second later, when I come across a single glove once belonging to a pair, left stranded across the station floor, people walking over it.

Outside the Etihad is a kind of open, nondescript vastness. A child in full kit with their hair done up into a ponytail – à la whichever continental midfielder that has just been signed – stands in the growing crowd, an Oreo in each hand. A group of teenagers walk past, their gelled hair brushed forward so that their fringes resemble the teeth of combs, one of them repeating "I didn't know that, to be fair" about the player stats his friend is reeling off. An older man is just in their line of sight, none of them acknowledging him, as he waves a booklet called *30 Years Later: The Kippax Revisited*, his unofficial fanzine, high in the air, trying to sell it among the endless throng of Erling Haaland scarves while they walk past. The screens outside and the walk that appears to be nothing but a car park is like the first time the FA Cup has opened up into vast, purpose-built space. For the first time, in the freezing evening air, the show turns itself into a drab kind of awesome. The walk into the stadium is via brutal, concrete, spiral inclines. It speaks of the Italian stadiums I once visited on tour with Jake – in their own way disturbing, not homely at all. Everything here is saying, *This is an inhospitable place where winning is everything*. As I walk up and around, up and around, up and around, the walk never-ending, it feels like I am being chased by a group of voices singing "Hello, hello, we are the City boys." It's hard to work out whether they are behind or in front of me, the sound bouncing around the winding structure. The voices disappear when it opens onto the concourses, but the harshness doesn't. There is a crazy steepness to it, an austere ambition in it all, making it feel a sort of madness to call somewhere like this home. I think of the cover of *There and Then* that I would stare into as a child, Noel Gallagher with his arms crucifix wide, Manchester City's previous home Maine Road looking back at him, the video that once appeared to me as if it were a place to reach towards. Beyond the faces in that crowd, every detail of every face focused on Noel, the council houses in the background explained something too. It said he'd come from one place, and he had arrived here. It all said, this is what Manchester City is. But seeing this entry of the Etihad, it's hard to recalibrate that, to feel that this is home to the same people.

Walking up into the stand, half an hour before kick-off, I realise how high up I am. I have an odd sense of vertigo, holding onto a rail and cautiously walking further and further up to my seat, exactly on the halfway line. Ominous stats for Salford City are projected across the digiboard walls: Manchester City first entered the FA Cup in 1890. They beat Liverpool Stanley 12-0. A banner is held aloft, huge, spanning almost the entire north section of the ground. It says, "We'll see things they'll never see." Everything here is an Oasis quote, an Oasis line, both City and Oasis now huge, universally celebrated, where they were once small, raw underdogs. An Oasis remix is on too, merging their classics with the strange club music that for some reason accompanies all football at every level – just four to the floor programmed kick drums pumping into your veins, making it hard to talk or do anything but concede to it, everything designed to make it extremely clear to you that this is a big deal, check this out, honestly, it's a really big deal.

From here, it is almost the same perspective you get coming in to land on a plane, where people look so small that you are momentarily gifted the perspective that we are all just little ants tunnelling our own little burrows, living our own weird lives. From here, there is almost no difference between managers Pep Guardiola and Karl Robinson really, or Salford and Manchester City, no differences between lifestyles or fame or success or bank balances or trophies, anything; they are all just dots, running around after a football, in warm-ups before the game begins.

There is *almost* no difference. Once I acclimatise, bowing to the slightly unconvincing sense of occasion, even from up here, from what feels like outer space, watching the shapes of Erling Haaland and Phil Foden disappear into the tunnels, I suddenly realise how distinguishable they are to me, for how much time I must have been exposed to these people, cameras tight on their faces, their unguarded mannerisms broadcast every week into the living room or the pub. I do not, of course, have anything resembling an affinity with the Salford team, who are in the FA Cup third round for the first time. Jack Grealish is starting the game and, for the first five minutes, I find myself watching nothing but him. The way he skips sideways, out of tackles, the way his shorts tug tight to his thighs, the flicking of his hair. It becomes like a sighting of a cheetah or something you've seen on a wildlife programme, so far away that it still seems slightly unreal, watching it in its natural habitat. Next to me, a dad brings food in for his two children, who have been sitting there with their mum, dangling their legs, staring blankly at the football. "It's an absolute farce," he says. He's referring to the queue.

The Salford away support, so secluded, such a minority in here, begin singing "Big cheating bastards, we know what you are", as their team hang tough for the first ten minutes. They are referring to the 115 alleged breaches of financial regulations that still hang over Manchester City and their dominance of English football in modern times. The little patches of crowd menace and nark that popped out like jack-in-the-boxes in the round previous are sucked out of the air in a ground like this, where everything is obliterated by the wide openness of it. There's no point screaming too much into the air, no one will hear it. And with the drift, the lack of occasion this understandably holds for City fans who have won the Premier League four times in a row, that beautiful thing happens again, my favourite part of these trips. A game of football is happening now and everything is fine. I am grinning to myself, hardly paying attention to the football specifically, but just letting it do its thing, staring at the technical areas, just enjoying that one of those men is Pep Guardiola and another is Karl Robinson. I think about Karl Robinson, standing there, wondering if he has anything resembling imposter syndrome or, maybe just as likely, a sense of finally being where he is meant to be.

When Manchester City inevitably score their first goal, the ripple of the net happening a fraction of a second before the sound, an exaggerated version of the first AFC Wimbledon goal in Milton Keynes, I stand up with the home fans and look around. There is genuine celebration and punching the air. For a second, it is confusing – how could anyone in any sane state of mind be pumped up for Manchester City to win this game of football? Who would want to celebrate it like an achievement? That is part of the allure sometimes of a big club; the safety of it, knowing the odds are stacked in your favour and that you are very likely to go home happy. If it were anything else – music, art, film – this would be an acknowledged, fundamental transaction between performer and crowd. People want to go home satisfied, not sad. It is maybe why so many people choose bigger teams. There is more risk-free satisfaction. Especially when you are Manchester City in the third round of the FA Cup playing Salford.

The referee lets a tackle go from a Salford defender, the City fan dad folds his arms and sniffs, "That's an absolute joke." He is now talking about the referee. To be clear, the referee is an absolute joke, and the queue is an absolute farce. City's Mubama settles this performative injustice seconds later, scoring on his debut, a tidy finish with his instep into an open goal. Pep, like the ground around him, claps with verve as if it's a massive goal. As if the universe were conspiring against Manchester City beating Salford but against all odds, they're beating them anyway. I look at him down there, the sheer urgency emanating from his tiny, tiny figure, and think, *Do I care about anything in the world like he cares about this? Maybe playing music? Maybe a gig feels like this to me, however small?*

At half-time, I queue for hotdogs, head down, listening to Manc conversation all around me. There is something quite piercingly lonely about eating fast food on my own here, something that illuminates that I am eating for a small sense of a buzz, as if the endorphins will momentarily lessen this loneliness only for the inevitable crushing low to follow, like reaching the peak of a rollercoaster. It's just as well that, as I'm balancing my hotdog and Coke, in the almost entirely light-blue-and-grey concrete concourse, a man spies me, moving to his left to reveal a little ledge. "Do you want to sit down, mate?" It's nothing to him, a tiny gesture, and yet I get that little caveman community kick again, like at the station. Thank you so much, I say. "Yeah," he shrugs. "Crack on, mate." I sit down, head down, giving in to the feeling of plasticky, lovely, cheap football food, the tastelessness so pleasing, as a woman tells a seven-year-old child, "You're old before your time, you," and next to that a man shouts at his son from point-blank range for spilling his drink. The soft and the hard, they are all here.

The Etihad becomes like sinking sand for Salford, two becomes three becomes four, notably then a woman nearby does a fantastic impression of stress and nerves as Jack Grealish waits to take a fifth, a completely inconsequential penalty. Football fans like to pretend they're suffering even when they're not suffering at all. It legitimises the whole experience somehow. Maybe Manchester City fans would like to suffer more. Maybe it would tie them back to their past again. It's eventually eight, as Manchester City fans leave in a shrugged celebration. The closest Salford get to any threat is when Savinho is spilled out into the photographer's pit chasing a ball, crashing into the boards. When he emerges, he looks like I do when I wake up – ruffled, confused, aching, tentatively learning to walk again. It's like the whale again, it's got its daily feed, swallowing up an entire universe and decades of meaning in a non-league team's struggle. The remaining City fans are singing, "Fuck off back to London, this city is ours", as I leave early, hoping the trains are cancelled and they put on a free cab for me all the way home.

I am waiting for the train back from the Etihad to Piccadilly, a few others having a similar idea to me and darting back, pretty safe in the knowledge the game will not end eight-all. A family is walking towards me, and then I realise that I recognise them. It's Adam Horan, one of the first people who wasn't immediate family or a close friend to come to Maccabees shows. "Bloody hell," he says, laughing, "what are you doing here?" I explain my mission this year. For some reason I tell him, this being the first time the sentence has left my mouth, that I am "looking for the magic of the FA Cup". His wife and boys are with him, all the boys dressed in City shirts, very excited about the number of goals they have just seen their team score. The first time Adam saw The Maccabees, we had driven to Manchester to support the Mystery Jets, only to be told that there had been a mistake and we weren't even on the bill that night. After sheepishly pleading, we were squeezed onto the line-up at Jabez Clegg and allowed to play four songs, literally when doors opened. There wasn't really enough time for us to play to anyone, and so we played to the first two people in, both hovering at the back, one of whom happened to be Adam. The same way adversity tends to bond football fans, this little exposing experience sparked something in Adam, and his affinity for us. He has seen us fifty-three times since, taking his kids to 86TVs soundchecks too, our initial meeting as chance an encounter as meeting outside Manchester City vs Salford. He has seen The Maccabees news, just announced. We are going to play a couple of gigs. He makes a face as if he's not sure he's allowed to ask, but then asks nonetheless if there are any other dates, other than Glastonbury and the one just announced at All Points East at Victoria Park. I hand him the dates we've just signed off on, but haven't yet announced. He puts them in his diary and says, "I won't be going to work on these days, then." And I say I'll see him there.

There are no cancelled trains, no secret direct cabs back to London, instead an extremely packed, freezing-cold train with drunk people heading home. A man next to me, sitting on the aisle seat so as to pin me against the window, is swaying back and forth in his seat, occasionally burping. I'm so annoyed to be penned into a window seat with this man, developing a simmering irritation with the whole thing, building quite complicated narrative plots about who this man is and why he has come to ruin my evening and everything that is wrong with England. He has no idea, of course, that I am doing any of this in my brain and as he, fortunately, gets up to leave halfway through the journey, he turns to me to say bye. I realise how gentle his face is, how sweet he suddenly seems, and how some tiny action from a stranger – the way they sit next to you or the way they look at you – can set off an entire, completely incorrect, surging rollercoaster in your head.

Two days later, the first Maccabees rehearsal begins. I remember every single part of every song, without needing to even think about any of it. My hands just move through the songs by themselves, remembering how they've played them so many times in a distant past. All the information is buried there ready to be used, the very definition of muscle memory. *Where did I put all this information when I wasn't doing this? Where does it pack itself away to?* I can do all the pedal changes too without thinking, sort of like driving a car, not that I can drive a car. The band are all the same. We are all playing as if Alexandra Palace was yesterday. As if those skins were left there for us to step back into. There's a very nice familiarity in it all, a memory of when my whole life was this one thing, every tiny dynamic of a song all-important, like spending a lap as a Formula One driver, going through gears and turns, somewhere between deep concentration and total thoughtlessness but, most pleasingly of all, not disappearing into a phone, not thinking about the next day, or the day after that, or some unresolved wish. Just playing, with no one else there to watch it, and playing being enough.

12

In January 2012, *Given to the Wild*, The Maccabees' third album, came out. I was twenty-eight years old. As I was beginning to accept, it was as difficult as seeing anything worthwhile to a finishing point is. It was a record that we made, for the first time, outside a rehearsal room, an untried discipline – trading real-time hashing out and constant replaying of pieces of music until they formed something for piecing music together through various home recordings, made in bedrooms and living rooms and makeshift studios. Eventually we went to the famous Rockfield Studios in the Wye Valley, filming ourselves playing the piano from 'Bohemian Rhapsody', inhaling the stories the owners told about the Gallagher brothers fighting with cricket bats, before aborting the process and going back to Elephant and Castle and our new studio – The Jesus and Mary Chain's old and abandoned studio, The Drugstore – to make the album on our own.

After what felt like a lot of time – never-ending days in different darkened spaces, a low-level sleepiness in my bones – we emerged with our album. During the build-up to its release, Lisa Ward, the label manager at Fiction Records, asked if any of us had any other interests. It would be helpful, she said, for the band to appear in some places other than the obvious music sites and papers. We sat there, half looking at the floor, completely polite and completely unwilling. "What about, for example," she said, looking at me, "you and sport and football and cricket?" I didn't want to do any of that, I said. I didn't think it was particularly cool. We'd just made this record, more atmospheric, more grown-up and conceptual than anything we'd done before, and it probably didn't suit the tone to be turning up in football and cricket magazines promoting it. Just try it, she said. See if you like it.

I was quietly, below the surface, excited about this idea, thinking that I could talk more naturally and animatedly about sport than I probably could about music, to be perfectly honest, and that I'd like to meet all the people from that world who were part of my daily intake. And so it began – a cricket magazine, *All Out Cricket*, asked me to write something for them. I interviewed England spinner Graeme Swann for them and wrote a piece about the nineties. There were little guest appearances on things – going on *Test Match Special* in a leather jacket, feeling completely out of my depth, saying hello before I was introduced, desperately aware that Jonathan Agnew had absolutely no idea who I was, asking vague and broad questions about rock and roll bands that I stuttered through. It was picked up somewhere at Fulham Football Club that I supported them. I went to be interviewed for the club magazine and walked around the empty Cottage with a photographer, half trying to look cool, half dumbstruck, eventually giving in to goofiness and kicking a water bottle across the touchline as Mark Hughes had that year when we conceded a late goal. I tell them a story about how I managed to acquire Eddie Lewis's e-mail address as a child and started e-mailing him, sending him messages of consolation when the crowd had been on his back, and he would write back confiding in me about how difficult it was to hear the abuse sometimes. They invited me to games. I took the band. I felt very emotional to be asked to go to Fulham by Fulham, that they wanted me, and it was a source of extreme pride to bring people there and say, this is the thing I chose, this is what I call home, this is where I do loads of my feeling.

That year, Fulham had started doing charity games at the end of the season. A celebrity ex-pro's eleven would play against a Fulham eleven, and they would sell tickets and host it at Craven Cottage. I'm not sure whose idea specifically it was, but I was invited to play and, because they thought I would really like it, I was asked to play in the Fulham team. I was the only player in the Fulham squad, they told me, who hadn't actually played for Fulham.

The game at Craven Cottage lands the day after the Ivor Novellos, where we won the award for best song. I got so drunk that there are only some very faint memories the next morning – waving the bronze statuette out of a taxi window; repeatedly calling Oasis's manager, Marcus Russell, Alan; some extremely heavy conversations that were had very publicly in a bar. The normal sort of stuff. I hadn't considered until the morning that the game is real – I'd just been telling everyone about it like it was a funny story happening to someone else. It's only as I am crossing Putney Bridge – the Putney Bridge that first appeared in my life as a walk over the River Thames into a new world – carrying a bag with football boots I have never played in (I haven't played football in football boots for about fifteen years) that it suddenly hits home that this might not be that funny, actually. It might be awful.

The bridge draws me towards it, the greyness and the tide and the unseeable depths of the Thames below having their usual gravitational pull. I think it again: *Shall I throw everything overboard into the Thames? Shall I just sack this off? What would be in front of me if I did?* Some sort of new beginning into adult imaginings, cruel and dark, or a rewilding liberated from everything before it.

It's strange walking to the ground without a crowd of any description. Not in a panic, running late, hoping to make kick-off. Not early, alongside the odd man in a tight-hugging replica shirt. I think about throwing in the drawstring bag, about turning and running, about taking myself and the hangover from Middle Earth and the adrenaline from winning something that says you did a good thing, taking it all to the pub, saying, *I don't want any of this, actually, I hate all of this, I want to be alone.* As always, I do not do that. I do what I always do. The feeling stays, unprocessed, rattling around inside me, taking me to the Cottage like an imposter syndrome-fuelled rattling bag of bones.

When I get to the ground, everyone is very friendly. I've learned this about Fulham already. The staff, the people who work there, almost exactly mirror what I hoped the club would be. Extremely welcoming, very open, slightly gallows humour like in the stands in those early years. I am ushered through the gates into the cottage that has been in part a mythical thing to me: a story, a piece of history, a thing to look at, not an actual building. I can't get a read on the actual size of it when I walk in, sensing my body tripping a little, wearing my nervousness so clearly on my face.

They are all already in the dressing room. All the players I have grown up idolising in Fulham's teams, players whose autographs I spent every weekend getting as a child – Paul Peschisolido, Chris Coleman, Kit Symons, Simon Morgan, Neil Smith, Barry Hayles, Louis Saha, Sean Davis, Andy Melville. I feel like I know them, but they do not know me. I am rolling through the events of how I am in this dressing room. There is so much about this situation that I haven't done the maths on. Our names are up on the wall. The kit is laid out. White – 9. I sit there, slightly stunned, next to Gordon Davies, Fulham's all-time-record goalscorer, and Brian Greenaway, who turned pro the day Fulham reached their only FA Cup final. I sheepishly take my boots out of their bag and Gordon Davies says, "They look new." He looks at me and winks, kindly. It's a wink that says, *I know you don't play football* and then, *Don't worry, it's all going to be OK*.

Except, it isn't going to be OK, is it. I am literally inside the Craven Cottage dressing room, with all the greats from the recent and not so recent past, all bantering with each other, telling stories, laughing loudly. I have no stories to share with them from my time in the dressing room. I only have cartoonish impressions of them as footballers, as adopted friends, whom boyish projections had endlessly been thrown onto. I am sitting very close to Paul Peschisolido, one of my very first Fulham heroes. I tell him about how much I loved watching him play, how much he meant to me, that goal against Liverpool where he turned from about fifty-five yards out and chipped the goalkeeper in a League Cup game, falling back into the arms of Simon Morgan in disbelieving joy.

I am asked if I would like to see the physio room (of course I would like to see the physio room), but when I return I discover that my bag is no longer underneath my shirt. At first, I think I must have taken it to the physio room and left it there. I go back and check. I haven't. I go back into the dressing room, looking around while trying not to cause a scene. As I do, it slowly becomes clear to me that someone has hidden my bag. It's a very light sort of football dressing room initiation, but even so, with the hangover and the general surreal nature of what is unfolding, with the team I have somehow ended up being a part of, the trip starts to turn bad. I've had this before, when we took mushrooms in Amsterdam and walked up and down the canals. For a second, everything was very good and then, in an indescribable and intangible moment, everything was very bad. I feel the walls turn in, my bottom lip starts to wobble, the general rules of sports dressing rooms come flooding back to me as a complete nightmare, until I catch the eye of Kit Symons, who is sitting exactly opposite me. The conversation elsewhere, me still not having announced that I've lost my bag, he mouths, "Felix." I nod. "It's over there," and he tilts his head a little to the left, indicating one of the small benches below the hanging kits. I scamper over, like a haphazard teenager just conscripted into war, flapping, trying to fit in, retrieve my bag from underneath the bench and go back to my spot.

There is an extreme kindness to the footballers in the dressing room that sits alongside a par-for-the-course ribbing of everyone. I can see that they are all enjoying being in each other's company again, those glory years now gone, the first of their two lives now lived, being allowed to dip back into it here. What I am not prepared for, though, is that when footballers get changed, they get completely naked in front of each other. They walk around with nothing on but slippers, towels over their shoulders, letting themselves be seen wholly and fully. Indie bands do not do this. We have never sat around naked before or after a gig. We do not have showers together or whip each other with towels while wearing only slippers. And so, as this could-be-mushroom-trip turns inwards again, I try to find spots in the room to look at that aren't the body parts of my naked footballing heroes, suddenly finding the ceiling really interesting, or studying the kits, as, sweating, I put my shirt on by taking off one half of my jacket and shirt, then putting on one half of the football kit, in a bid to reveal no part of my unfinessed physique.

Tony Gale walks into the dressing room and writes a team on the blackboard. It is all extremely light-hearted, extremely male and extremely loud. I am trying to laugh along with jokes I do not understand, doing my best. To my extreme surprise, he puts my name in right midfield. I am starting, he says, due to pressure from the sponsors. I look up and see the entire dressing room looking at me expectantly, waiting for me to say something. I look at all of them, my eyebrows raised as if on puppet strings, eyes wide and bloodshot, half wearing a kit and half my jeans and jacket, and say, "Don't pass me the ball, don't pass me the ball, don't pass me the ball." I say it three times. The room pauses for a moment. Silence. And then they all laugh. I look to my right and Neil Smith is giggling. "Don't pass me the ball," he is saying again and again. "I should have tried that one in my day."

*

When the game starts, I am genuinely beginning to zone out. Before I technically know what disassociating is, I am disassociating on the football pitch of Craven Cottage. Everything is moving far too quickly for me, the touches, depth perception. It's hell. Wales international Mark Pembridge keeps telling me to keep moving. He's taking it more seriously than I thought anyone would be. I want to tell him to please leave it out, Mark, that I'm the guitarist in The Maccabees, not Fulham's actual right winger, that I don't want to keep moving, that I'm really hungover and haven't played football since school, and that I was really out of my depth even then. Chris Coleman keeps telling me that I'm doing absolutely fine, which I take as a sign that I am absolutely not doing absolutely fine.

For my first touch, I receive the ball, Fulham attacking the Putney end as is custom for the first half, roughly where Paul Peschisolido scored that goal at Anfield. John Scales – ex-Liverpool and Wimbledon defender – is about ten yards from me, closing down space. I stop the ball dead under one foot and then, out of the corner of my eye, I see Andrejs Štolcers, Latvian international, gesturing that he wants the ball fed through on the right wing. He's making a run. It suddenly occurs to me what I should do. I should up-and-under dink-chip this ball over John Scales's head and into the path of Andrejs Štolcers. That would be pretty heroic. Especially for a second touch at Craven Cottage, the first being the one I have just taken. Even to me, it feels like it takes ages, like my body has the speed and scope of an industrial digger getting into position, to wedge my ball under my foot. And, with time standing still, John Scales stops his advancing to the ball out of pure curiosity at what I am trying. I scoop the ball with my right foot, into the air. The ball's trajectory is not the intended one. As Andrejs Štolcers moves into the distance, the ball just travels upwards, only upwards, into the sky, as if controlled by the opposite of the gravity. It journeys very slowly too, as if someone with soft invisible gloves is comically guiding it far into the sky and then down again. When it eventually lands, John Scales is standing in front of me. He stops the ball, looks directly at me, quizzically. Everyone looks at me. And then, as if play has been stopped and then restarted, he turns and passes the ball where the game begins again.

I will never live this down. From this moment on, all my friends who gathered into the Riverside Stand to watch this game will text me whenever a footballer gets "the dink" out. I invented it.

I run up and down the touchline, begging to be taken off, and am eventually allowed to by Simon Morgan, my Fulham hero. I give Neil Smith a hug as I go and he is substituted on. I told them to not pass me the ball, I tell him, and he smiles at me and says, "You did great." Thirteen years later, he will be on the touchline at Cray, turning round to see me at that FA Cup tie.

13

Fourth Round

Saturday, 8 February 2025
Goodison Park, Attendance: 38,909
Everton vs Bournemouth

I have been doing *Tailenders* – the loosely cricket-based BBC podcast – for seven years. Which means, in some form, I have been in contact with Everton fan and *Tailenders* producer Mark 'Sharky' Sharman once a week at least for all of those years. To know Sharky is to know Everton. What I mean by this is, I could tell you when they have lost without already knowing, because Sharky will come in wearing all black. At first, I thought it must be pure coincidence, or that maybe he only ever wears black, but then I started to notice that when they won or were on a prolonged slight upturn of form, he would be in increasingly bright shades of blue. People do dress, after all, the way they feel. As anyone who loves the game enough will know, a football result has the power to affect everything else for the rest of your week. Sharky, unwittingly, is a walking exhibit of both these theories. Just like someone will put their finger in the air and tell you a storm is brewing, a sight of Sharky is to know Everton's league table position. If you ask him who Everton are playing next week, Sharky will respond, usually dressed as if going to a funeral, "We're losing to [insert club's name] next week."

Sharky tends to attune his attitude to life in general with Everton FC. His very essence says Everton. Just short of three decades in which Everton, a historically big club, have won absolutely nothing have taken their toll on Sharky's world view. The years of constant underachievement. The years of trophyless relegation battle after relegation battle. The years of developing an understanding that good stuff happens to everyone else but them. Most pointedly, the years of being in the shadow of next-door neighbours Liverpool. He refuses to wear anything red. He will not touch, purchase, or be affiliated with anything that has ever sponsored Liverpool FC. This extends to the, quite frankly, ludicrous. In the early nineties, he made sure his washing machine was not Candy. He has never drunk Carlsberg since they landed on the front of the Liverpool shirt. He will try not to watch a Hitachi television. And don't start him on Crown Paints. Not if it were the last paint brand in the world would he ever use Crown Paints. When I am meeting Sharky somewhere, usually at a busy train station or in a packed pub, there is one certain way of knowing that it is him even from a distance. His Everton scarf, royal blue with yellow outlines, popping out of his jacket. Sometimes I swear that I can actually see a little Charlie Brown cloud following him around at those stations or in those pubs, hovering over him, always raining on only him.

*

For the fourth round of the FA Cup, Everton have been drawn at home to Bournemouth. This is the last season before they relocate from Goodison Park, their famous old ground, and, recognising it as the last chance I will likely ever have to get there, I ask Sharky if he can take me. I imagine it like a sort of no-thrills, it-is-what-it-is, stripped-back-and-raw tour of Everton history.

I am proudly and excitedly taking to these days, and with each game I feel a momentum building in me. These are daily escapes from the world, little adventures out of my real life, into football. I am on the usual tip of travelling by train, from Euston. I've booked the ticket late this time, so my window seat is essentially a wall, with no view. I've heard that some seats at Goodison Park have pillars blocking half the pitch or, in some cases, have almost no visibility of the pitch because of the upper tier. When Everton fans tell you this, they say it as if sitting there is some sort of rite of passage. It's like, if you haven't seen a game of football at Everton with a restricted view, you haven't seen a game of football at all. Literally. So I have, accidentally but fittingly, a window seat with no window en route. A couple of women in the row in front have their feet up against the windowpanes, sitting side on, looking straight out at the passing view and not at each other, talking about undercuts and dying their hair ginger. One of their faces suddenly lights up. "Hold on," she says, turning to look at her friend for the first time in the journey, "have you got Dan's credit card on you?" They both pause. She does. The silence after, the muted giggling, suggests some telepathic plotting, like they both know that today they will use Dan's credit card and there is nothing Dan can do about it.

There is something about another journey into the heart of

footballing heritage and the effect travelling has for whatever reason that is making me feel very emotional. I'm seeing my own life back in London with a short, sharp focus of gratitude when, as I drift down the train, I bump into the Fulham press team. They are on their way to Wigan, where Fulham are away in their fourth-round FA Cup tie. I have been lovingly doing the official Fulham podcast, *Fulham Fix*, for them for the last few years and feel guilty for a second that I am not going where they assume I'm going, not going to follow my team. I tell them about this adventure I'm on. That I am going to every round of the FA Cup. That I am not going to see Fulham this week. I tell them about Goodison, how I've never been, how I need to before it's gone. They all half swoon. It's brilliant, they all say as one. It's almost as brilliant as the Cottage. Proper. Old. The real deal. Carmelo Mifsud tells me, as I leave them to it, sensing work happening on the laptops that they look over politely, that I should go to Stanley Park, from where you can see both grounds – Anfield and Goodison. This excites me, the idea of standing on the tectonic plates of the Merseyside derby, looking at both stadiums as if I'm on a footballing equator. I text Sharky. Is this true? Sharky's text back is immediate: "Don't know." He always writes back quickly. It is always blunt, two or three words max. He always leaves a full stop. Then, there are three little bubbles, little dots, telling me he's typing again: "I never look at that cesspool." I'm not sure why I expected anything else. Stanley Park will evidently not be part of the Sharky tour today.

I am struck on entry to the station that I cannot identify Sharky immediately. Whereas there is usually one Sharky alone, the station is full of them. It is as if every single person waiting is the same. Late forties, early fifties, black jacket zipped up tight, Everton scarf around the neck, poking through stubbornly and unapologetically. It's like seeing all the Sharkies out of the factory, in their spiritual homes, little clouds above all of them. Outside the station at St George's Hall is the first Sharky landmark tour. "Right there" – he points at the steps at St George's Hall – "is where I got the biggest bollocking of my life." Sharky and his local radio team had made a mock announcement implying that the then-huge pop group Steps were playing on the steps at St George's Hall as an April Fool's joke. They thought it would be funny if people turned up to see Steps and they hadn't technically lied. Thousands of people turned up. Sharky had to try and announce to them all that it was a bit of a prank gone wrong and they should turn around and go home.

It turns out, I realise quite quickly, that the Sharky tour of Goodison Park is quite Sharky-based. Our second stop is Shenanigans on Tithebarn Street, where he proudly points me to a plaque dedicated to him by Radio City, where he used to work, that makes it "look like I'm dead". It reads, "The Sharky Settee – presented to Sharky to commemorate his 2,000th pint of Guinness – drank here." This plaque-worthy status, he thinks, might have been secured when he went to cover the Grand National with them and, after the coverage, got so drunk that he did his own version of the horse racing over an assault course of parked cars outside.

The route to Goodison Park is a continuous conveyor belt of what feels like closed-down pubs on Scottie Road – The Eagle Vaults, The Throstles Nest baring their remaining shells, pointing to a world that's been and gone. It is enough, just driving past them, to make you feel homesick for a thing that you haven't ever seen. There used to be twenty-six, a pub on almost every single corner, in the sixties – The Foot Hospital, The Parrot, The Honky Tonk, The Corner House, The Clifford Arms, The Hamlet, The Holy House. There are now only 700,000 people and decreasing in Liverpool. When Sharky talks me through it, he conjures up gently mythological visions of post-war slums that are "just a dual carriageway now", before driving on through the stories of his life. "This used to be the second city of the empire," he says, before pointing to a football cage where there was a "massive scrap" when he was twenty-two. Sharky chose to run away. It was the right decision, he tells me. Everything seems to take its name from fighting here. We pass Uppercut Barbers as he conjures constant pictures of more fights and scraps and rumbles.

Eventually, we reach Stanley Park, Sharky modifying his earlier stance of not wanting to show it to me, at least acknowledging that Anfield is "over there", in the begrudging way that a man might talk about his ex and her new partner, before Goodison appears in front of us, with its big blue suspended letters. Sharky makes sure he tattoos in my head all the small victories Goodison Park has had over Anfield – it had undersoil heating first, for example. He heads into a car park outside a Sri Lankan beauty studio where a man in his early twenties is waiting with a slightly resigned demeanour. "They probably make more using this as a car park," Sharky says, before being incredibly half-heartedly waved into a space on the corner that looks like it will be very difficult to get out of. This is a site of significant historical importance in the mind map of Sharky, where he had decided, after the third-round win over Derby County in the 1995 FA Cup, there was a "lucky bush" he had touched on his way to the ground. He continued to touch it before every cup tie that season at Goodison, Everton reaching the next round every time. A superstition developed in Sharky, in that strange way football will tease this out of very non-cosmic-thinking people, that the bush was responsible for this run. When they got to the final at Wembley, Sharky broke off a piece of the bush and took it there with him. It worked, Everton beating Manchester United 1-0, Paul Rideout's header probably just as responsible for it, but not quite, as the twigs that Sharky had in his jacket pocket.

Metres from the lucky bush of 1995 is the Top House pub. The pub literally looks like a house, with a kid on the stairs up to the first floor playing a handheld computer game. He seems unaware that the bottom floor of his house has been turned into a heaving working men's club. The stairs he sits on are packed with bags, as if someone is either about to take the contents of this place and leave, or has just realised it's matchday and stuffed the contents of their home into bags and squeezed them onto the steps. There is a piece of paper by the bar, saying it's "great value, £3 pint", where middle-aged Scouse men with heavy, thick accents line up as if forming a moat between them, anyone else and the bar.

There are two televisions showing the early game on BBC, where Leyton Orient are, unbelievably, beating Manchester City. There has just been a goal, the sort of goal where news spreads quickly. Have you seen the goal? What a strike! Even though it only happened ten minutes ago and I have not seen it, it's the kind of goal that I have already imagined, have had described to me a handful of times – on various messages on the phone, in the pub – and that is already being turned into legend. There are goals like this, particularly in the FA Cup, where for the period of time it looks as if it will affect the outcome, everyone will be saying or writing the name of the player who scored it. That this kind of thing can happen, that someone from a League One team can score a goal out of nothing against Manchester City, plugs back in a sort of mass footballing belief system that at all other hours, at all other times, especially with age, dwindles. Anything can really happen. That moment of magic might be inside anyone, any player from any league, waiting to move through your system, just a simple kick or moment of inspired poise sending your surroundings into rapture. When the replay eventually shows it back, it's better, more wild, than even I could have imagined. Jamie Donley has picked up the ball, loose and somewhere between the halfway line and penalty area, and expertly chipped it from this distance over Manchester City goalkeeper Stefan Ortega. The ball has backspin on it, awe inspiring and artful, like the world on its axis, set to spin in fast forward while everything else is still. Ortega runs backwards, flailing, only managing to bundle the ball over the line off his back as it bounces off the crossbar. The pub is full of a kind of low-key giddiness, that Manchester City are losing to Leyton Orient in the pouring rain in East London. Former Manchester City full-back and now beloved pundit Micah Richards is on TV, his glasses heavy with dew, the kind of smile on his face where you can almost sense his back teeth clenching, the score 1-0 at half-time.

Of course, Manchester City eventually win. And as we leave the Top House, sunken into the boring laws of football rationale, we pass the next stop on Sharky tours, a William Hill bookies where Sharky put £1 on David Weir to score at 40/1 every week. The only week he didn't do this, "the fucker went and scored". Goodison Park now emerges from a heavily residential area. It's reassuring to find it here, all the history and the real life informing it, hugging it, contextualising it. It's like a bit of seventies England has been chopped out and hung in real life.

In the mid to late nineties, Sharky worked for Radio City, who had the Liverpool and Everton games. In the job that would eventually earn him that plaque in the pub, he would turn up with an old-school tape recorder and go and talk to people about the game at Goodison. Because of the time constraints, he would then have to take the interviews back to edit them on tape with a chinagraph pencil and a razor blade, this being pre-digital, when even small radio stings were done by hand, with love. He would get to Goodison Park at midday. At Liverpool, it was very difficult to find people because it was all tourists – "and I'm not just saying that" – but at Goodison, he would often be interviewing the only people there – the programme and fanzine sellers. The old Everton fanzine *When Skies Are Grey* could not be more aptly titled. Seagulls circle. Skies are grey. His questions were always the same: What will the score be? Who will be the first scorer? Why are Everton so shite? Eventually these people would be so bored of getting interviewed that they didn't want to do it any more, point blank refusing him no matter how much he begged. So Sharky would take himself into town, where taxi drivers initially did it happily, but like the fanzine sellers before them, would grow so sick of him and his microphone that they would drive off in the opposite direction when they saw him. In the end, he had to resort to finding mates to do these vox pops, putting on slightly different accents for him; someone who could do St Helens, for example, as well as your standard Scouse, was "two for the price of one", he tells me, that "saved me even more headaches".

There is a queue on the corner at the ground, which reveals the entrance to a church. St Luke's, hemmed in on two sides by the football ground, has the FA Cup on show in there and people are waiting to meet it. The church and the grey skies and the shut pubs and UTFT (Up The Fucking Toffees) graffitied on the wall, all accumulate around Goodison to spell something about the football club, something that Sharky carries around with him everywhere he goes. A kind of pessimism, a rugged and weary way of looking at the world, but a softness too, a humility and generally the relief of an energy to be in the company of. There is a precarious, miraculous way the soft and the hard rub up against each other, both eyeing each other warily, knowing they are one and the same if tipped over either way. There is a Dixie Dean statue, with wreaths next to it, and beside it a boy with a flag that says "Kopites are gob shites". He's how I would draw a little Sharky, with that speech bubble popping out of his mouth. Sharky did, in fact, go to his first Everton game in full kit, including shin pads, and an Everton tracksuit on top as well. His son Will, naturally, supports Everton too. When England got knocked out of the World Cup in 2022, Harry Kane missed a penalty, and Sharky walked home with Will. Will was upset. Sharky turned to him and said, "Mate, when I was growing up, England didn't do *anything*, and you've seen them get to a Euros final and a semi-final." Will turned back and replied, "Yeah, but you've seen Everton win something, and I'll never see Everton fucking win anything." Sharky paused, their footsteps still moving amid heavy silence. He turned to his son, said "Fair point, well made", before softening his tone into commiseration that Will hadn't had his own lucky bush moment yet. "If you want to bail out, loads of your mates are Spurs fans, your grandad is an Arsenal fan, I will understand." "No, Dad," Will sighed, equal parts proud and dejected, "I'm an Evertonian." "Fair play, fella," said Sharky, relieved, before patting him on the back and saying, "Welcome to a life of misery."

Next to the church, there are statues of the holy trinity: Kendall, Harvey and Ball. Beyond them, outside the ground, outdoor bars house what feels like thousands of Everton fans, young and old. Its history meets itself here, in 2025, with a world that you can imagine looking almost exactly the same as it did in 1970, as if it has been preserved both for and against everyone's benefit, rubbing up against modernity. There is a "developmental ebar" for Guinness, where Toffees are served self-pouring pints of Guinness by a machine, tapping their cards, while in the background a big screen shows replays of Kevin Campbell scoring goals. Goodison is the kind of place, Sharky says, that needs a good strong tackle to get the crowd going. A good thunderous, crunching tackle. There is something, culturally speaking, that tells you everything you need to know about a certain type of English football psyche and Everton. A tackle is when you don't have the ball. A tackle is an expression of a kind of resilience, a kind of hope, a kind of fight, but it also betrays a lack of control, a desperation, a jumping into harm's way, a last gasp, putting your health and wellbeing under a list of priorities for the sake of your team. That's the kind of thing the beating heart of English football, despite all the modernisation, still likes, still craves, in all its uselessness: that and corners, which these days rarely if ever come to anything, but are still cheered as if they are a certain window into an equaliser.

The commentators at Goodison Park are faced with intrepid levels of exploration just to find their viewing point. Steve Bower, of *Match of the Day*, has a fear of heights that is tested with every trip to the ground. Through the away fans, onto the concourse, up the stairs, down the stairs, back to the furthest row against the end of the stand, revealing a small door to walk through. He is then exposed to the roof of Goodison, Anfield just in the distance, a treacherous walk across the roof of the stadium, down through a small hatch as if dropping into the bomb-aimer's perch in a Second World War aircraft, exposed and stuck in position, before finding the view, high and rickety, but in its own way, absolutely breathtaking, overlooking the halfway line. In 1998 Everton were relying on Bolton losing to Chelsea to stay up during the last game of the season. Chelsea scored and Sharky fed the news to the commentator. A few seconds later, he heard the crowd cheer as the news reached them via radios they had taken to the ground. "That gave me a massive buzz," Sharky says. "I was thinking, I did that." He doesn't tell me whether the lucky bush was still in his pocket then.

From my perspective, walking into the ground, through the turnstile, up concrete steps, into the concourse, kicks up that memory of my first football match. All the smells and the sounds, the implied history, the way these entrances are still part-intimidation and part-warmth, breathing into you a foreign type of exhilaration. When we find the seats, they are blue and wooden, laid out almost as if for people hundreds of years ago who were half the size, like being inside a little house where the door is too small for your head, your knees scrunched tight against the row in front. It's beautiful, exciting, beaten up. The first sense of the FA Cup waking up as a tournament of big, visceral, historical, emotional meaning is here when the roar meets the teams walking out to the *Z-Cars* theme tune, all marching band and musical patterns from another time.

Bournemouth are on an unexpected run of untamed, attacking football, winning games as is their habit. They almost score in the first minute. Sharky turns to me, Everton immediately unsettled in the game, "That was nearly worse than last week." Watching Everton play with Sharky is like having a little gloomy man on your shoulder, dooming everything before it happens. "We won't score here," he says, when Everton win a free-kick. "Welcome to my world," he says, when a chance is scuffed. "Nothing will come from this," he says as they break with the ball. He is, of course, right each time too. It's almost as if it dawns on the whole crowd at the same time – the inevitable tide of this game, that it is likely to be all Bournemouth, that there will be no FA Cup magic today for Everton. It becomes incredibly quiet. Funereal quiet. I say to Sharky, almost whispering for not wanting to be heard, that I hadn't expected it to be quiet. He shrugs. "People are just worn out from all the shit football," he says. It is partly that, and also possibly partly the slow, mass acceptance that this will be the last game of FA Cup football at Goodison Park. By half-time, with the game out of reach, 2-0 down, the little girl to the right of us, her bright blue eyes full of hope at first, has pulled her hat right over her head, covering her eyes. She sits there like that for the duration of the second half, until the final whistle is blown and she can finally go home.

It is hard to explain, but even though I am leaving Goodison for the first time, I feel incredibly sad about it. I feel heavy and melancholic. I wonder how life would feel if we knew every time we were leaving places for the last time, or seeing faces for the last time, whether life would be more unbearable or more precious? It feels both – especially with an Everton defeat to help make it as authentic an experience as possible. I put both palms on the wooden seat – mine for the first and last time, seat 186, row 6, Main Stand. Goodison. I let my hands rest there for a second, giving in to the compulsion I have had since I was a child on seeing beautiful things from the natural world, the need to put my hands on trees, making sure that both hands and both sides of both hands have had equal contact there, before leaving.

In May, months later, Goodison will host its final ever game of football. Blue smoke fills the sky and the surrounding area, the sun splitting the stands in half horizontally as if it is a religious moment. The television cutaways I watch from home reveal the bird's-eye view of Goodison I have just walked, looking almost the same as it did when, for example, it hosted a World Cup game in 1966 and Pelé's opening goal of the tournament, and shows the surrounding area packed against it, giving it the impression of being a house itself, with that church on its corner. The camera will cut away often to fan Tommy Griffin, who looks on, holding the bar tight. He's eighty years old and first came in 1945. The latticework, designed by Archibald Leitch in 1908, looks brighter, more vivid than it ever has appeared before. Man upon man and woman upon woman are on camera saying things like they've been here for sixty years, seventy years, holding season tickets from 1965 aloft to the camera, people bringing their dad's ashes. Ally McCoist enthuses that he saw a baby too, maybe weeks old. Football is obsessed with these sorts of things – a mushiness about generations being alongside each other that is only occasionally cheesy because it's absolutely true. Sharky is in there somewhere too, slightly drunk and almost definitely crying. It's a melody that dreams of Everton. It's a melody that brings us all together. The bomb-warning siren goes off and the players run out for the last time.

On my journey home to London that evening, the train will calamitously ingest various different football fans, packing the train and the poor unsuspecting families and miscellany face to face, shoulder to shoulder, tight together for the next four hours. A group stuck in a carriage, squashed into each other after running for the train and then forcing an already full waiting bay to squash up further to accommodate them, spot a man in glasses wedged between the seats. They cannot see that he has bags either side of him, that he cannot move. They start calling him Harry Potter. That the next stop is Dumbledore. That he is taking up all the space. The poor man looks blankly at the floor. He looks nothing like Harry Potter, he just has glasses on, but this is an unwinnable fight, and he knows it. Everyone is packed so tight that we are in close physical contact with each other, belly on belly, thighs next to thighs, breath on breath. It's hard to know whether I'd rather be here, right next to all this singing, or Harry Potter over there, just beyond the glass, his eyebrows slightly raised, waiting for his stop, Dumbledore.

14

There was a time when the big Fulham away days used to really matter to me. I couldn't conceive of being anywhere else. As a sixteen-year-old, I consoled a man three times my age, his fingers across his face, as he repeated, "I just really thought it was going to happen this year." I know, I said, patting him on the back. I know. Liverpool had just dumped us out of the League Cup in extra time on a late weekday evening at Anfield. The following season, I gave into that private loss-manifesting I was doing and secretly willed the ball into our own net at Villa Park against Chelsea, the feeling perfectly painful. It was the only FA Cup semi-final the club had been in since 1975 and I privately relished the loss, locking in the sickly sweetness of suffering that I had by then come to know to be Fulham-ish.

A whole two decades have passed since those heartbreaks. I really thought, amid the actual life that crushed itself between then and now, flashing by as if it might have been ten days, bringing with it actual losses, actual deaths and actual sadnesses, that I was beyond it. Even when Fulham were relegated for the second time in three seasons in 2021, it didn't feel the way it used to feel. There was no dissociative trigger, no performative pain, no wishing to go back to when this had not happened. I received sympathies from people on WhatsApp. I smirked as I read each of them. In what universe does a man in his late thirties need consoling because of a football team? Not me, I thought.

And yet, the same way I have learned grief to be like an elastic band being stretched further and further before the inevitable snap back to its original shape, there it is on Sunday afternoon. There it is, with seventeen minutes left of an FA Cup quarter-final away at Manchester United.

I'm not there. I rarely go away any more. I'm in one of the spells where I drift away from it, only checking scores, not making the trips. I'm making soup in front of it on the TV. Butternut squash and fucking sweet potato soup. I am in a phase of enjoying doing this a lot. This is probably because the first time I did it, it wasn't a complete disaster. I felt such satisfaction that I'd turned raw ingredients into a passable meal that I had bounced around for a day or two on a gentle high before remembering that life rarely rewards you in any actual tangible way for making soup once.

Regardless, now I make it almost weekly, repeating the exact process of the first time – the time that was not a complete disaster – without ever thinking to hone the recipe even slightly. Better to stay completely safe. It is just for me, but I make enough for twelve people. That's what the initial recipe said and so that's what I still do. Soup for twelve. Chopping all the raw ingredients up for this far-bigger-soup-than-necessary gifts me the calm of simple control. I treasure these kinds of moments. I have grown to enjoy anything and everything being in order, all in their own homes, little piles of specified categories, all the vinyl alphabetically arranged and the books compartmentalised by genre on the far wall. I watch in the background as I chop. Fulham are dominating this game of football. I take a moment to look at the ingredients as it plays out in the background, each in its neat, stacked compartment on the chopping board – the ginger and the onions and the garlic and the carrots and the rosemary and the chilli. They will soon make something, marginally, better than the sum of their parts. *Like that Fulham team in the final in Hamburg that lost with four minutes of extra time to go*, I think.

I chuck the ingredients into the pan on a medium heat. I boil the kettle. I find the stock. Fulham are still controlling this game, unintimidated by Old Trafford, with a remarkable, new-found commitment and confidence. The base of the soup begins to lightly cook away, throwing back that smell of onions and garlic that make you feel like a genius chef just by heating them up. Fulham now lead 1-0, an Aleksandar Mitrović poach at the back stick. I watch the celebrations unfold as I peel sweet potatoes. I'm making fucking soup while this momentous thing is happening and Fulham players are wheeling away celebrating as the camera cuts to an away end of travelling supporters' limbs being thrown around. This must be a symbol of adulthood, a reward for some hard-earned perspective – growing up and letting go. They are there and I am here.

As I marvel at my sense of calm and detachment, from some unguarded place the daydream slips in. I'll definitely go to Wembley when we play Brighton in the semi-final, actually. I'll maybe cry a little bit when we win. Chops the sweet potatoes, now ready to add. Then I'll write a really passionate paragraph on my Instagram about how much I love Fulham Football Club. Puts chicken stock into boiling water and adds it to the pan. The words will supplement a real-time video of the full-time whistle that I'll have to credit someone else for – as I'm in it myself celebrating – and a second photo of me, age fourteen, holding the Second Division trophy. That will be really nice, actually. Quite good content too that might get decent likes. Deseeds the butternut squash.

As the stock and the squash go in, I have forgotten about the safety of my zen-like detachment. Fulham are still playing liquid football, winning every tackle, stringing Manchester United along at their own pace. Mitrović comes close to making it two a couple of times and I begin to crystallise the picture of what Wembley will be like this year. It'll probably be a warm day. I should make sure that I've had no less than two pints and no more than three by kick-off. That way I'll take it all in when we win.

There are fifteen minutes left when, in the space of ninety brutal, unthinkably catastrophic seconds, a breakaway Manchester United counterattack, a handball on the line and a few overenthusiastic protestations (Mitrović pushes the referee), Fulham have gone from 1-0 up to 2-1 down with nine men and a sent-off manager. The events are so self-implosive, so quick-moving, that they don't allow any opportunity for guarding yourself against them. I am too exposed, too vulnerable to it – all of that horrible feeling. *This could only happen to us*, I tell myself. All football fans, regardless of club, tell themselves this with no sense of it being anything but a localised universal truth. All teams think their sides are doomed in some specific way. Typical *us*. It's who I am too. There is no door back to retain the person who was making satisfactory soup with a sense of superiority only minutes ago. That person no longer exists. This person needs to communicate injustice to the world. I'm messaging people saying I will be offline for the foreseeable. Then checking my phone again to make sure they've seen it. I'm posting on social media announcing a blackout until I am able to process what has just happened. I'm staring at the wall, fingers spread over my face, saying to no one at all that I just really, really thought it was our year this time.

Fulham lose 3-1.

In the hopeless final minutes, thinking of ways that what is happening can't be happening, I remember all the people I have been in all those moments in the past. As I am experiencing it, remembering what it feels like to be eight years old, football delivering its first heartbreak, that elastic band pulled back, I realise for a moment why it stings so bad. Football has a specific habit of telling us, so unforgivingly, so distinctly and so dramatically, that things in life can just happen without any warning whatsoever. That everything you've fought so hard to contain and control and decorate into your own little mounds can be destroyed without even any of your own doing. People can die and relationships can end and wars can start and disease can barge itself into your life. You may have had the big stuff happen to you already, or maybe not yet, but either way, the small stuff will get you. It can all happen, just as easily as football teams can concede goals and, oh for fuck's sake, I realise an hour later, as the living room phases back into being, a toasted smell suddenly engulfing the flat, simple soup can be burned.

15

Fifth Round

Sunday, 2 March 2025
Old Trafford, Attendance: 67,614
Manchester United vs Fulham

It's two years later and the same tie has come up in the FA Cup. Fulham away at Manchester United, this time in the fifth round. With it, I am sucked from this FA Cup adventure feeling like I am experiencing everything out of my body, like an observer witnessing it somehow all for the first time, feeling like the entire ocean of football is suddenly inside me. I know that this does not matter really, in the grand scheme of things. I know that two years ago, burned soup excepted, everyone survived and everyone moved on. I now collect it in my memory of Fulham heartbreaks and tell this story with an almost delighted conviction. As if the pain I felt is my proof of love, of having cared. I know that whatever happens in this game too, the world will likely not stop. And still, I pray to a god I do not believe in. *Please, lord, after last time. Let us win this time.* All the football myths and superstitions and rituals and curses and karma are suddenly deep parts of my belief system. The universe must not be fucked with. I must put every single step right from here until the game at Old Trafford in order for a delicate balance to be restored after two years ago.

Hating Manchester United was one of the first things I learned about football. It was the absolute prerequisite of getting into the game. Before I discovered them also to be likable people with beating hearts, Manchester United players, like the Australian cricket team, like Michael Schumacher, were herded into a net of winning villains in my mind, alongside Darth Vader and WWE wrestling tag team the Nasty Boys. They were all one and the same, their only desire on this planet to wreak injustice and smug, ruthless victory on the world. In the nineties, it was the amount of winning. The way they would do it, in the last seconds of games. A decision that went their way again. The continuous gloating and affirmation that it was all because they were Manchester United and that's what Manchester United did – they won. I could not unlearn that hatred, no matter how long it's been since they've actually won the Premier League. I still resent them now, in a completely irrational way, for the amount of football coverage that is committed to talking about them, the amount ex-players talk about current players not being fit to wear the shirts, the amount of time that I have to hear that "this is Manchester United we're talking about here".

I have never heard anyone say that this is "Fulham we are talking about here" when a team has under-performed. So travelling to Manchester United, witnessing my desperate want, my need even, for us to win, breaks me like a minor revelation. Maybe the cost of losing doesn't suit me anymore, when it finds me as a forty-year-old man. Maybe we all need to learn to outgrow old versions of ourselves at some stage, and it only comes by asking the universe for it, saying "I choose to change this story about me that I tell myself, that protected me once, that propped me up once, that now keeps me curled up like an emotionally stunted man-child." Football, as ever, is my soft-landing vehicle into this. I do not secretly wish loss upon Fulham today. Not here, not anywhere. I want us to come to Manchester United and go through to the quarter-finals of the FA Cup. I want that, now I think about it, so desperately that it scares me. God forbid that I think about other things in my life where I could also change my story and open a new portal. Love, relationships, family. I could stop saying yes to every single job that comes my way, ween myself off this ragged habit of looking for gold stars and accept that, like everyone else, I probably just want love, and, like everyone else in football, I desperately want my team to win today. Football, in the wake of this opening up of vulnerable hope, has become almost completely unwatchable for me. My need for us to win, it turns out, is maybe so big that it is unbearable. I learn to understand, slowly, that this is some kind of coming face to face with pain, acknowledging want and hurt and desire, accepting that you do not always want to be frozen in hurt and realising how close success is to sabotage. Ridding this secret addiction to hurt and defeat and playing the martyred victim is a very disturbing place to put myself. It's as if I suddenly see what that little thing that feels like a knot in my throat actually is, that constant feeling of tightness that I presumed had been nerves or tiredness, spitting it into the air and seeing it in all its ugliness, all its scarred and naked want. Suddenly I understand how and why people run naked in the streets or move to the wilderness. I see my life, how some of it has been, and how the rest of it could be, all this safeguarding against any sort of loss, making everything small and contained, all the deep temptation I feel to go that way, to get in the hole. I will try to choose something else. I will try to open myself up. And maybe there is no better place to start than in the fifth round of the FA Cup, away at Old Trafford, against the current holders, Manchester United.

There are a couple opposite me on the train from London in their Manchester United shirts. They are very sweet, very much not from Manchester. They giggle and finish each other's crosswords. I sit there silently, avoiding eye contact, hoping that they are going to go home less happy than they are now. As we arrive at Manchester Piccadilly, the train driver announces that "Manchester will be always red". The walk to the ground at Old Trafford is long and unusually empty. It reminds me of the walks out of Glasgow, where there appear to be huge stretches of nothing immediately outside the city centre. It is not like the Etihad, where purpose-built trains take you to a Manc light blue amid grey. The walk towards Old Trafford appears to be built almost entirely with the red brick that characterises the ground, that I am so familiar with from television, framing Alex Ferguson pointing to his watch for added time. Birds circle as Railway Road turns off into small residential streets. It is here, and only here, only now, that it finally lands with me that Manchester United is actually the smallest, biggest club in the world.

The stuff about community, the regurgitation of its history, feels in some way eye-roll-y until you are walking up to the ground. I am with Joel Porter, a close friend since school. He is a Millwall fan with little allegiance to Fulham, but happens to be in Manchester. He hates Manchester United too. He is here mostly in opposition to Manchester United, and we have based large parts of the last thirty years of friendship on hoping they lose together. In his mind, the away end at Manchester United is his end too, whoever it is. And yet, somehow, in the same way that hoping to lose is needing to win, there is something charming and oddly small, oddly real we both see in turning the corner. Maybe it is because everything is so familiar, like turning up in New York for the first time and seeing yellow taxis, feeling like you're inside all the films you watched on repeat as a child. Old Trafford is the same. Somehow, despite all my predisposed opposition, it is friendly and reassuring and could only be one place. It is undeniable.

The Fulham fans are in the left-hand corner, ushered away. When we walk out of the concourses, opening up to see the pitch, it is quite overwhelming. It's hard to focus on a game of football to begin with, a tension built into the game that is being punctuated by a Fulham team that give the ball away regularly. I know this feeling from gigs, where you want something so badly that you make more mistakes than you knew you had in you, just through nerves. This results in a tense, stressful, over-eager first half.

I have floated through every round of the FA Cup so far like a football tourist, like someone observing human life for the first time, but now it is all undeniably in me. I cannot explain why it means so much. My bank balance will not be affected by this result, there will be no work promotion, it will not affect my life in any real way, and yet it feels as if the entire future of my wellbeing is completely dependent on it. Marco Silva, the Fulham manager, who has successfully steered Fulham into the Premier League, has to walk up a steep ledge from his dugout to the pitch, to the little boxed-off technical area. When he stands next to Manchester United coach Ruben Amorim, they look like two rattled, tiny men in a cage. I love watching Marco Silva. Sometimes I will watch nothing but him, watch him plead with his players and with referees. I think, *Maybe I should write a song called "The Unending Sadness of Marco Silva".* He is almost always frustrated and when he isn't, he looks sad the way a child looks sad, huffing at the injustice of the world for the very first time. I love this about him. I find it funny and heartwarming and reassuring.

Andreas Pereira has a corner in front of us, just before half-time. The ball is skimmed into the penalty area, where Antonee Robinson meets it on the edge of the box. He heads the ball down and Calvin Bassey is running towards it. *He's going to get there first,* I think, pulling myself up on the railing, gesturing as if to head it myself. Bassey makes it there and, turning his head to guide the ball, heads it decisively and confidently. There's the ripple of the net. Then the thing only football can do for you – totally unplanned, spontaneous chaos. I am jumping up and down, feeling the state of my knees as I do, each bounce a dose of pain that I will receive when the endorphins wear off, each one worth it.

Then, back into the concourse at half-time, with adrenaline surging through my body, I am one of those men who I have been wary about. All inhibitions are gone. I am shouting "Yyyooouuuu

Whhhiiiiittteees" in a tone, low and guttural, that I never affect anywhere else.

The second half plays out exactly as I know it will – an extremely, extremely heart-racing series of not particularly high-quality scraps. It's the way every tense game of football of real consequence tends to play out – nothing is fluid, there is very little graceful expression, it's just a never-ending sequence of panic and trying not to fuck something up.

Manchester United level through Bruno Fernandes with nineteen minutes left. Of course they do. From that point I am holding onto Joel like he is a banister on a very, very steep flight of stairs. I have a distinct sense of vertigo. Manchester United have a couple of gilt-edged chances at the end, which somehow they miss. From there, it worsens – the sickening, sickening hell of nothing else mattering, of readying myself for the inevitability of being extremely disappointed, talking myself down already, as if I'm speaking to a child. *It's OK if we don't win. There's nothing I can do to affect this.* It's the panicked sensation of being trapped in a tank; by extra time, I have my fingers in my ears, blocking out any conversation around me about the game. I don't want to hear anyone's thoughts on anything. I don't want anybody focusing on anything but that ball being anywhere but the Fulham goal. I think I need to cry. Maybe I should leave? I am finding this actually bad for my health, like I could have a heart attack. It's worse than I ever remember it, this desperation. The game lurches towards penalties. And as they eventually arrive, I know exactly how this will end. Of course I do. Everyone does. This is when Manchester

United win this game of football and we leave with our carefully cultivated hatred, our own martyrish losing secure.

The penalties are taking place at the far side of the ground to us. It lends a further desperation, an even clearer sense of lack of control, watching them from so far away, the banks of players lined up on either side. I do not know what's happening on television, on the commentary, but I already sense the way it is panning out, the way Manchester United are – as always – the heart of the story, feeling ourselves outside our own life. Bruno Fernandes is first for United. He waits, to silence, before slotting the ball left, sending Bernd Leno the wrong way: 1-0 United. Then it is Raúl Jiménez for Fulham. Gloved hands on hips. Hair whipped over to the left. I love Raúl. He suffered such a serious head injury during a game that it nearly took his life and I love that he will run towards any loose ball with his head as if that hadn't happened, as if he would do the same again. He stands dead centre before running to his left, stuttering one, two, three times – waiting for United goalkeeper Onana to commit himself, then placing it left too, the opposite side to the goalkeeper: 1-1. Dalot staggers on the spot for United, running his feet into the ground like a cartoon dog, before running towards the ball. He makes it 2-1. Sander Berge, a humble beating heart in everything Fulham have done well this year, somehow so very Fulham in his understatedness, so fit for our club, takes a breath I can see from where I am, his shoulders going up then down. *If anyone is going to miss a penalty it's going to be someone like him*, I tell myself. Someone who doesn't deserve the pain. He runs up and, as it turns out, my life experience and prejudices making absolutely no difference to how this pans out, he scores emphatically. Top left.

Unsavable: 2-2. My heart is beating out of my chest now. Into my past. Into the future. Casemiro scores for Manchester United. I feel the flooding of my eyes, the absolute reality of being alive and – finally – the absolute admission of wanting something, of needing something, of anything else not being enough, not being able to bare my own need for it. Willian, our Brazilian international seeing out the autumn of his career at Fulham, gently steps up, pauses as if frozen, his kicking leg waiting, waits more, slides the ball calmly to the left-hand side of the goal, close to the centre, the keeper again weirdly wrong-footed.

All the penalties have been without panic, strangely casual in their perspective, the opposite of how I feel. Lindelöf is next for United. From where we are, I can see the line-up of players behind, in view of the goalkeeper beyond the penalty taker. As Lindelöf runs up, Raúl is crouched, as if looking down the barrel of a pool table, weighing up a shot, and then he sticks his left arm out, like he is confidently hailing a cab, summoning it to stop. Lindelöf steps up and puts the ball exactly where Raúl is pointing. I don't know whether Bernd Leno has seen, but he has gone the same way. There is a glorious thud. The thud of safety. The thud of a ball hitting goalkeeping gloves. This somehow makes everything feel worse. I feel like I know we will still lose, and trying to work out exactly how from here, and that it will feel worse when we do. But Antonee Robinson strolls up, doesn't break stride, scores, lets out a roar with both fists clenched to his side. When Zirkzee walks towards the spot, suddenly the expectation of Old Trafford is upon him, all that winning, all that history, standing up and in the air in Manchester, looking down disappointedly at what it is seeing. He puts the ball to the right, my heart sinking slightly into my chest, before Leno, who as a child slept in goalkeeping gloves because they were so comfortable to him, checks his dive and keeps it out with his feet. Fulham have won on penalties. I am jumping up and down. I am screaming – in the midst of something that feels close to exorcism. I am so happy to be alive.

By the time we are walking back over Bridgewater Way, half lost, an earthly feeling is coming back into my body for the first time. It gently continues to reappear until the next morning, on the bus in London, just thinking about the game, I begin to cry. They are the tears that come from somewhere wholesome, from a gratitude for being able to feel things as deeply and as vastly as that, and because Fulham won, and what the future might be.

16

Quarter-final

Saturday, 29 March 2025
Craven Cottage, Attendance: 26,222
Fulham vs Crystal Palace

When my brother Hugo's son, Jet, was born in 2018, my first instinct, the first thing I wanted to give him, was to get him in Fulham kits. His grandad on his mother's side supports Portsmouth, and we had eyed each other suspiciously during Laura's pregnancy, then through smiles loaded with desperate eyes when Jet was a few months old. I knew directing the course of travel for Jet and football was going to be, if not a bloodbath, then a spiritual arm wrestle, and I needed to get in there early. For at least three of his first six birthdays, I took a day off from whatever I was doing to travel to Craven Cottage on a non-game day, resisting that persistent, nagging temptation at that bridge to throw everything out of my pockets and overboard, returning with a Fulham kit, each year a size bigger, with his name and a number on the back. At first, it was just a joke. It was funny, the same way taking a photo of a baby and a pint is funny or putting them in band T-shirts or Adidas shoes. If only a joke and a sincere intention were as separable as we would like them to be. In my late twenties, years before Jet, I would often end up at parties after games of football, wearing my Fulham scarf, the one with the old badge, bought on those early solo missions in 1997. I would drape it on my closest friends one by one, when the party was really going, and take photos of them. There was something moving about it to me, something almost piercing, to see a Fulham scarf on people I loved. It was like they both made sense of each other, even if they did not support Fulham or even like football. Most seemed happy to be wearing the scarf, to take photos with it, to walk around bars in it. The scarf took on a kind of golden quality on each of them, almost as if it was actually lighting up their faces. It is an amplified version of this with Jet, attempting to pass Fulham on to him in a way it had not been passed to me, seeing a future for him in which he would not have to do all that complicated, bruising and shameful defecting to get there.

When Jet reached the right age – for some reason the consensus was four years old – I started taking him to Fulham games with Hugo. His first game was Fulham at home to Huddersfield in the Championship. He had to climb the steps of the Johnny Haynes Stand to get up to his view of the pitch, each concrete slab like a hike, hauling himself up one foot at a time before placing both hands on the next step, climbing one after another, creating a queue behind him, of people carrying Bovril and burgers, watching his journey up. It was quite an emotional experience for me, to see Jet setting eyes on Craven Cottage for the first time, looking out onto it. Fulham were beaten 2-0 that day and he asked to leave half an hour before the end. Though he got the impression that Huddersfield Town were the Galácticos, he was proudly telling everyone when he got back that he had just been to see Fulham, that they play at a place that sounds a bit like a farm, and they had lost to Huddersfield Town.

There are more trips, one or two a season, all with tiny little moments in them where he seems like he might actually be into it, but mainly they are treated like days out to Legoland, very little focus on the football, him using them as brainstorming sessions for constant running commentary on everything he is seeing, asking why the number next to Fulham on the scoreboard is still on 0 while the other one seems to be moving. As the *Fulham Fix* podcast is added to the list of jobs that give me both a feeling of meaningful determination and seasickness, where I get to talk to Fulham legends and current players and stare lovingly into their eyes, telling them how much they mean to me, one of the benefits is that I can get us tickets in the press box. The entrance, hidden behind the statue of Johnny Haynes next to the cottage itself, is small, and inside it reveals Fulham as almost exactly the club I hoped it would be – despite now being back in the Premiership, a sense of a small, local club full of very caring people. Jet says to the surprised woman serving the food, that yes, he would like pie and mash, before turning around to the club employees, and announcing to them, very loudly, that "Fulham never win". He spends each game just talking and talking. It has sparked some curiosity in him where he can't sit still, his brain flooding him with information and questions at the sight of the game. Each week that he comes, the interest gently, almost imperceptibly, increases. He wants to stay longer and longer every time until, one week, he does not want to leave before the end. He wants to stay to see the score at the final whistle.

And then, like someone sparking a match without knowing that fuel has been going into a rocket for years, or those illustrated reinterpretations of the Beatles first finding drugs and their imaginations exploding into multicoloured thoughts, a football obsession takes flight extremely rapidly. Jet can suddenly name every goalkeeper in every team in the Premier League and the Championship. He can, from memory, list the entire Fulham squad and squad numbers. He watches every game of football that is available to him, without exception and whatever it is, through my Sky Sports subscription, and then he watches highlights of every game, memorising every goal and how they happened. He starts to leave voice notes via his parents on my phone, asking me questions about football, telling me what position we are in the league table, where we will be if we win and whoever is above us lose. There are infinite permutations every week. I send him messages back immediately. It very quickly becomes my favourite communication. Sometimes he is falling asleep, and I just get voice messages where he wants to tell me what the Fulham team should be, or simply lists pairs of names in the squad that have no connection to each other. He says weirdly specific, football-y type things that people who have watched football for decades say to try to sound intelligent, like Sander Berge playing in the middle is a good idea because he "really gets Fulham playing". Football lexicon sweeps across him. Top bins. Megs. Tekkers. That's a banger.

In real time, we are suddenly witnessing football unlock

something in him, a first serious passion, a choice he is making for himself, tangibly joining him to the adult world, and it is like witnessing the human capacity to learn something when the information is not a chore. He is learning to read and write, the pronunciation of foreign players' names, all kinds of maths through the endless permutations of the league table every week should certain results go certain ways. He is learning how to speak to everyone and anyone on the street, "Who do you support?" becoming a one-stop shop to get to know almost anyone in England. When the Lionesses win the Euros, he celebrates wildly and begins to walk around practising Chloe Kelly's penalty hop. When he sits down, he does so like a footballer does on a bench, leaning forward slightly, hands on his chin, as if he is analysing a non-existent game. He randomly walks around as if he is clapping a crowd and has just been substituted. He looks at old videos of Craven Cottage that I show him, gawping, looking me in the eyes and saying, "It looks exactly the same." He voice-notes me while I am at games, saying very adult things in a very childlike voice like, "What's the atmosphere like down there, mate?" Before long, he is playing football with every second he has, Laura and Hugo watching their house turn into a walking, interactive museum for the game. At Christmas, I give him and his cousin Lana Fulham kits with slightly left-field names on the back – Kenny Tete and Alex Iwobi – handpicked for them, and hats and scarves. I am anticipating them opening the presents more than they are, and when they do, there is a sort of mania that takes hold of them for a second, excitedly putting them on, euphoria. I teach Lana "Come on Fulham", which she says across the course of the day, strangers occasionally smiling at the two-year-old girl in full Fulham

Alex Iwobi kit getting on the bus in Peckham, the odd Fulham fan opening the door for her or making space for her on a train because she's one too. Jet, meanwhile, is walking around everywhere in two different Fulham kits, one on top of another, and a training top. He comes around to ours on a Sunday, in full kit, looking like he's about to be substituted onto the field of play, and says to me when I answer the door, "I feel it in my heart and" – tapping the badge by his heart – "that's because the badge is here."

All of this handing down of Fulham sends me a sense of unprecedented gravity in my life – it is becoming a family thing that my niece and nephew are inheriting. I love that they support Fulham. It suits them both. You know, in my opinion, that is. We share it and we are all into it together. Jet, of course, does not have the same history as me, though. He does not, or does not seem to, have some sort of internalised desire to suck in loss and pain. He has no real cause to. He wants Fulham to win. That is what he is coming to games to see, his team winning. He also has no concept of this being almost the best Fulham season in the club's entire history, landing us roughly mid-table in the Premier League. His friends support teams like Arsenal and Chelsea. They are walking into school on Monday more buoyant more often than Jet. This sparks a needy, probing anxiety in me that Jet will decide at some point that while Fulham might work for me, it does not work for him. After all, why would you choose to be less happy, less satisfied, less excited, more often, if you could help it? Occasionally, he tries it out for size. He tells me he supports Fulham with his heart but Arsenal with his brain. Then he checks himself, maybe seeing the look on my face that I am trying to hide, and says he supports Fulham with his brain as well, actually. He goes on holiday to Thailand and, in the liberation of being in another country, tries out being another person too. He asks his parents to buy him counterfeit versions of other team's kits. He tries a different one every day with players' names – Manchester City and Haaland, Arsenal and Saka, Bayern Munich and Lewandowski. He wears the kits the same way a child would wear a Superman or Spider-Man outfit – channelling these people, becoming them. He goes to sleep listening to a documentary about Phil Foden's life. When he comes back, holiday behind him, he tells his mum, "OK, I'm Jet and I support Fulham, got it?", as if he is a married man returning from an affair, making sure everyone has their story straight, sliding the ring back on the finger.

I take Jet, for his seventh birthday, to see Nottingham Forest at home. Where the other games, pre-football explosion, used to be essentially just something to do, this game takes on a much deeper, analytical, significant meaning. We speak almost every day about what the score is going to be. Nottingham Forest have beaten Brighton recently 7-0 and he voices his concerns, regularly, about the same happening to us. He says he knows that Nottingham Forest are very good. They are fourth in the Premier League. He would even take a draw, he tells me a few times a week, over a few weeks.

He's had a football party that morning too, and the traffic has been a nightmare getting there, so he and Hugo are late. Fifteen minutes into the first half, Fulham are winning 1-0 and Jet runs down the stairs, past the wooden seats in the Johnny Haynes Stand, forcing the row to get up one by one, squeezing side-on past all the men's knees, as if he is a detective going down an extremely tight space between two walls. When he reaches me, he is speaking in tongues about football, saying so much stuff about the game in front of him that his mouth can hardly keep up. He's asking about the goal. He knows Emile Smith Rowe scored the goal, and asks urgently about the assist, and how the goal came about. Adama Traoré, I tell him. It was a really good ball. He points at the Nottingham Forest fans and says they are "as quiet as a mouse". Calvin Bassey heads Fulham back into the lead, after they have been pegged back for half an hour, and Jet is an explosive, irrepressible, firework of euphoria, almost to the point that it looks like his head is going to pop off. The woman behind him is laughing constantly, listening to everything he says, extremely invested in his experience too. In the dying seconds of the game, he turns to me, when the ball is booted free from a final Forest attack, whispering, "Wait, so we won?" And almost exactly on cue, the referee blows the final whistle. Jet is uncontrollably happy. Happy in an extremely pure way. I have to hide that I almost have tears in my eyes, seeing how happy it has made him. I am happy we won too. He voice-notes me that evening. "I'm so happy Fulham won," he says. "I thought that it was me being bad luck, but it was just the players being rubbish."

These mystical things are almost immediately at play with Jet. How can I affect this? What did I do to make this better or worse? There are anxiety loops too. He comes downstairs one morning crying, saying that Bernd Leno and Calvin Bassey have left Fulham. His parents look this up and can't find any proof of this information, before asking him again, and he realises that he might have just imagined it, and then forgotten it wasn't real. I am only told, in passing, when I enthusiastically tell news of this new Fulham Football Club obsession to my friend's mother, that she mentions that seven is "the age of reason". It suddenly makes sense how football harnesses this moment in a child's life – the age very specifically linking its arms with football. The expanding capacity for rational thought at his age is meeting a new, internalised sense of right and wrong, and a more astute ability for impulse control. The age, internet wormholes tell me, facilitates new neural pathways and enhances connectivity between different brain regions, making space for heightened emotional processing.

Jet is insistent we go to watch Fulham for his dad's birthday too. I look at the dates, secretly working this out and tell him, via his mum's WhatsApp, which is now being used as a tool for constant communication between the two of us, that the date lands on an away fixture at Brighton, sadly. Don't worry, says Jet down the phone, Laura's thumb on record, away at Brighton is fine. We will travel. And so, we travel. Away. Jet is wearing a Fulham kit when I arrive at their house in South-east London, which I say he might have to cover up when we walk into the ground. He nods, confused. He has not yet learned how who you support is often something you disguise at away games, that they are trips where you try to blend in, covert, as if you are part of the home team's surroundings, until the first moment you walk into the away area where, matching your tribe, you burst into song. Jet rolls up his sleeves and says to his mum, "Go on, then", and she writes our phone numbers on each arm in pen, in case he gets lost. On our way into the ground, he is absolutely pumped, just at the idea of seeing another football ground, that we are travelling the same roads the Fulham team have and, mid-conversation, when we arrive and walk in a crowd, suddenly says to me, apropos of nothing, "I can't believe you used to support Chelsea."

He lets that land for a second, me checking no one else in the crowd has heard, before he adds, "I'm always going to support Fulham." I am part proud, part relieved, part humiliated. For unrelated reasons, I am nervous about Jet being in the Fulham end – knowing that he will likely be exposed to more swearing than he has ever heard in his life within a matter of seconds – and as we queue for the turnstiles, you can hear the sound, the guttural, beery sound of men meeting. We go through the turnstiles one at a time, him being separated from my brother and me for a second and, as we join again the other side, he hears it, the low, long, South-west London birdsong of "Yooouuuuu whhiiiiiiittteeesss." Without a moment's thought, as if he has done it a million times before, he repeats it, loudly, as low as he can manage: "Yyyoooouu whhhiiitttes."

We are in the very front row of the away end. Jet studies all the chants very observantly and wilfully, watching my lips as I sing the wordier ones, pulling himself onto the barrier when Raúl Jiménez opens the scoring for Fulham, punching the air. A security guard, sat facing the crowd, ringed around the touchline, half motions to move towards him, working out if he is technically any sort of threat. When Brighton dominate the rest of the game, equalising, and eventually, on the far side to us, win a penalty with the very last kick of the game, there is a sudden stillness in him. In the kerfuffle of pointless complaints and clearing of the penalty area, he is processing what has happened. And that it's exactly the opposite of what he wanted to happen. He is confused, disturbed. "But we've come all this way," he says. There is time, in the sorting out before the penalty is taken, to try to explain to him that it's not the end of the world if Brighton score here. That it is not that important, in the scheme of things.

We've got an FA Cup quarter-final with Crystal Palace too, which is more important. He is nodding, staring into the distance. The same security guard notices this exchange, and his eyes soften, smiling at Jet, almost as if he wants to go and tell him the same thing. Bernd Leno guesses the right way for the penalty, diving full stretch to his left, but can only land half a glove on the ball. Brighton score. As we watch the entirety of the Amex Stadium erupt in unified gloating, that sickening thing of watching other fans celebrate, he is very still, his eyes not moving anywhere but forward. In the car home, the processing moving from his initial sense that he is going to "tell all Brighton supporters he hates them", he is just sat in his seat, eyes drifting out of the window. "I just can't stop thinking about it," he says. I know, I say. Me too.

Watching Jet go through all these feelings for the first time makes me realise, for tiny windows of time, what it must be like to be a parent. To be helpless to what the world will offer for your child, but having the impulse to ring-fence it, to give them only positive reinforcement. To witness your own desperation for things to be safe and everything to work out how you want it to, only to be dealt the continuous blows that there is nothing you can do to ensure this. To have to watch them hurt and yearn and deal with disappointment. The world is moving beautifully slowly for Jet. He is up at five in the morning, each day seeming like it lasts for ever. It does not matter to him that football happens every season, it has not all blurred into the shrugging merry-go-round that it eventually becomes. There is not always next season to him. Everything that happens now is the only thing that happens. Everything that happens in this moment is the absolute be-all and end-all. This feeling, this sudden desperation for Fulham to make him happy, spills into my life too. I know other clubs are waiting – that Arsenal will offer him a higher probability of winning more often – that he might choose this. I am preparing myself to take it like an adult, not a child, if he makes that call for himself. Allowing him to make his own decision. But, with the FA Cup, for the first time in a long time, suddenly feeling wide open, with all the big teams apart from Manchester City knocked out and Fulham still in the competition, I am choked into a black hole of awful, awful anticipation. This merges in the build-up with the fantasy of control in my mind, the same one Jet has begun to have activate in his age of reason. It is exactly fifty years since Fulham reached their only FA Cup final. I begin to believe, to hope, that something was calling me to do this pilgrimage, that I was channelling a higher calling unwittingly, and Fulham are destined to reach the FA Cup final again. That would be such a lovely, neat story, wouldn't it, for everything in life to land in place like that, and Jet to be at Wembley this year.

It is unbearable, this sudden open wound of hope that I must harbour daily about the FA Cup quarter-final. All the admission of wanting to win, of needing to feel good, opens itself into absolute vulnerability. I feel like trying to find a way to tell the players and the Fulham manager, Marco Silva, that they are really aware how important this game is, right? I talk about the game often, as if some things might come true if I say them enough, or some fears will be dispelled if I cast them out into the world. I message everyone I know, working out ways that Fulham win this game. This accumulates and accumulates in my head until I am on my knees the night before the game, a forty-year-old man, again praying to a god I do not believe in, that Fulham win tomorrow. I do believe maybe, actually? I would believe if they just answered this one thing for me. After all, it worked last time. I am praying for a theoretical ball to land in favour of a theoretical Fulham player, for them to theoretically take that theoretical chance. That we get a moment. That we can all go to Wembley. I know Jet has already chalked down the dates. He has told me when the semi-final will be and when the final is. He has inked Fulham in for both of these games. It does not matter that we have not reached a domestic cup final since 1975. It does not matter to him that the last time we made a semi-final was when I was nineteen, going up on a coach to Villa Park to see us lose to Chelsea, and that I have lived more than my entire life again since then. It does not matter that all this points to the sheer unlikeliness of it working for us. None of that history is his. This season is his only footballing map. The rest are boring old war stories to him, embellished and drawn out to total insignificance. As I close my eyes for the final time before the game the next day, I see disturbing images, not the ones I have ordered from that deity, but catastrophic ones, of a stillness at Craven Cottage, and the opposite side of the ground to us, the Crystal Palace end, awash with red and blue, celebrating.

The next day, on the same walk over the bridge, nothing thrown overboard, I am still having images, flashes of Crystal Palace fans celebrating. Soon I will be released from this feeling, at least. Worst case, this sickening sense of need will be gone. Then I remember that there will be no relief. Because Jet will not be insulated from it. I want to stop him before we go in; tell him he's walking into a trap.

It's too late, he is saying out loud, "I'm ready to win." We have tickets in the back of the Hammersmith End, that promised land turned *Wizard of Oz* illusion, back there as a family, even my dad in tow, for the first time since that first game. There has been a lot of push from the club to make sure that the atmosphere is not lethargic or drifty, and everyone has got the memo to will this thing true. It is as loud and exciting and raucous as Craven Cottage gets. Everyone is on their feet, from the front of the Hammersmith End to the back, so Jet has to stand on top of the folding seats to see. He is on tiptoes, stretching himself to his furthest possible reach to see over the tops of the men's heads.

Fulham start very well. Rodrigo Muniz beats two Palace defenders, the exact sequence not particularly visible from the other side of the ground. As his shot fizzes past the post, we both look at each other, eyes wide, hands on our heads. The sun is out at midday, the new Riverside Stand more than twice as big as the one I first met in 1995, casting its chequered shadow halfway across the pitch. Crystal Palace have beaten Fulham 2-0 a few weeks previously and, although Fulham dominate much of the first half-hour, their presence here is ominous. They are organised and fast, a self-confidence and composure in most things they do. As they find themselves into the game, Eberechi Eze receives the ball on the right-hand side of the penalty area, as we look at it. He turns at a right angle, sharp and purposeful, parallel to the penalty area as Saša Lukić stretches to keep up with him. Then, us with a cruel line of sight of this movement, he strikes the ball, clean and flat, beyond Bernd Leno and into the bottom right-hand corner of the goal. It's a stunning goal, sharp and painful. And with it, in its aftermath, there is first silence, and then that sound, that delayed sound, of the celebration behind the goal. Minutes later, just as me and Jet are talking about how that's not the end of the world and there's a lot of time left, Palace break again. Ismaïla Sarr is on the end of an Eze cross. It's directed off his head. The net is rippled again. It's 2-0. As we watch the same thing unfold as minutes before, the sound at the far end, the silent processing of our new reality, I can almost hear the sound of Jet's heart breaking too. I can almost chart it, like a scene in *The Simpsons*, but much more brutal. The moment the net has rippled. The brief checking for any reason it hasn't happened or might be ruled out. And then the dawning that what has been done, cannot be undone. That no one can change that. The world will not be the same again.

For the rest of the game, we are stunned into a very slow zoning out, as Fulham try to get back in the game, with much possession but little sting. Jet is yo-yoing between tears, heavy tears, despondence and small rays of optimism. In the latter, he turns to me and says, "I believe in Fulham." He pauses. "It's just that my heart will break if we lose." By the time, on the break with fifteen minutes left, Eddie Nketiah has made it 3-0, the seats around us are being vacated. It is truly like witnessing a first heartbreak, seeing him sitting there, staring out into middle distance. The absolute injustice of life not working out for you is playing out for him in its ruthless first form. For the last ten minutes, the rest of the game a depressing procession, we just discuss, in broken sentences, how sad football is and how this is the worst day of Jet's life. A trapdoor has opened for both of us that only football knows how to open, where you feel so desperately sad you can't conceive of how you'll get over it. After the final whistle, we are almost the last people to leave the Hammersmith End, as if there is a heaviness in our legs suddenly, anchoring us all to this moment. On the far side, there it is, my anxiety loop, that worst fear manifesting, the Crystal Palace end, red and blue, having the moment that we dreamed would be ours.

As we leave the ground eventually, I am feeling as if those shirts I constantly gave Jet, on those walks, were not jokes or belonging, but that I have simply handed him a big box of sadness. I am embarrassed about all that hope now, about how much I realised I wanted it, and by how much Fulham were clearly beaten. And as my phone begins to vibrate and ping, with that weird, almost exclusively male, sending of texts football fans do to commiserate with someone when they have lost a big game, I feel the sensation again of wanting to just eat. To eat fast food, to be pinned down, to forget the world. Somehow, it's football that brings this out of me, this rawness of feeling. I am entering a comic darkness with Jet. The final person we see, as we are walking back to the car with our heads bowed, is a man in a jumper that says, "Life is pain". We walk past him, wordlessly.

Jet has gone home with us, told his mum that "it's been a bit of a rough day", and then we run outside to play football immediately. As I watch him play, occasionally saying how Fulham were not "super Fulham" like the song goes, but more "medium Fulham" today, I realise he is definitely going to be OK. That today has been an adult experience for him, a little thunderbolt of the untethered laws of the universe, and a childlike one for me. I might have given him a box of sadness today, but also maybe the absolute gift of caring about something very trivial too. And that, through him, I have finally learned to face what might not be *his* hurt, but mine, and he has finally brought out in me, not a self-defence internalised mechanic of needing Fulham to lose for strange grief fuel, but being face to face with the pure stuff of life, where you simply admit to yourself that you want something, that you might not get it, and either way, you will still survive just fine.

17

Semi-final

Sunday, 27 April 2025
Wembley Stadium, Attendance: 72,976
Nottingham Forest vs Manchester City

It is one of those days in London, late April, where everything is calm, the weather unusually placid and oddly perfect. There was a time when FA Cup semi-finals were in neutral venues in the middle of the country – Hillsborough, Villa Park, Maine Road – those types of places. The last time I was at one was that game my whole lifetime ago, when the whole of West London decanted to Villa Park to watch Chelsea beat Fulham 1-0, John Terry doing an impression of Terry Butcher, head bandaged after a clash, scoring the winner with a header at the Fulham end.

Today, and for a long time since, the semi-final is at Wembley. I don't know anyone who thinks this is a good idea, who doesn't think that a semi-final at Wembley somehow entirely diminishes the whole premise of the FA Cup being a road to Wembley. Still, Wembley is where it is held and, in its own way, it does at least lend itself to teams of losing semi-finalists having some sort of day out, a feeling of having got there, even if there, it turns out, is nowhere. Crystal Palace beat Aston Villa 3-0 yesterday. I found this hard to watch on a rare day off – dripping with what might have been for Fulham, what I had dreamed it to be, and instead lying on my sofa staring slightly off-centre of the screen, scrolling and scrolling my phone looking at god knows what, getting my fill of little jealousies and triggers of things I should maybe buy or people that look like they are doing better than or are happier than me. The screen in the background, Palace running away with this semi-final, sets a foundation to all these petty resentments that make up modern living, the red and blue end full and vibrant, waving flags, making noise.

That evening, I go to a birthday dinner and Mark Stephenson – the same Mark who had a bash at being a lower league football reporter in his youth before realising how unwelcoming it was – walks in like a football fan extra in a quite poorly conceived drama. There are unopened, warm cans of Kronenbourg in his pockets, a red and blue Palace shirt under his zipped-up jacket, and he is off-loading the cans onto a table that is otherwise laden with Prosecco and wine. He's weirdly understated, given how euphoric it all must have been, mumbling, saying it's the best Palace performance of his lifetime. I'm checking my phone on the sly for no reason during dinner and Matt de Jong, a Villa fan who was at Wembley, messages me, saying "for some reason it hurts more now we're older" as Mark mumbles platitudes. For some reason, it really does.

Chris Eubank Jr fought Conor Benn last night too – an intentional throwback to the two fights their dads took part in back in the nineties. It reminds me that we watched one of those fights in a pizza restaurant down the road. My dad does not remember this. I remember it clearly. The TV in the corner of the room, the way the waiters were constantly turning to watch it. The brutality and the danger and the not being able to watch anything else.

I have this strange relationship with time now. The reunion of the band has been throwing me back to random spots in my life that I had otherwise forgotten from fifteen years ago, but now appear to remember extremely clearly. Then I try to remember what happened last week and it is like walking back into a room you have only just left, finding it is suddenly full of haze, flooded with dry ice, impossible to see anything clearly. And I have this strange sensation where 1994 is for some reason closer than 2024, or an argument in an old relationship in my mid-twenties suddenly muscles its way into my brain, asking me to question whether I should get back in touch with her, say she was right about that, actually, and I hope she's well. This mindset lends itself to travelling towards Wembley – the kind of place that you are led to believe is at the end of a rainbow. I think of all the trains that have taken me across England, but my mind replaces what has happened in reality with a fantasy – boarding them and seeing everyone I'd ever known on these trains, staring out of the windows, in their little groups and conversations, and me just sitting there and becoming used to their presence, the same way I have done with all the strangers on these journeys, momentarily soaking in who they are via football or tattoos on their arms. The vision you are sold of Wembley is a bit like this – some sort of glorious holding pen where all your childhood recollections are held, where some sort of finality, some sort of clarity and definition of your life should be made.

It's funny how it first happens in London on the Tube: at first it's the odd person – the couple with the nineties Forest shirts on with Shipstones on the front, the woman waiting with the replica shirt that does not look official, its shape tugging at her. Then the woman with big ear defenders on and a Haaland shirt. These tiny appearances of sky blue and red break up the London monochrome, the still sunshine somehow making the shirts bounce with an extra hyper-reality. It is like the tap is being turned on, the first drips of colour, a deluge waiting to happen.

As the red becomes more and more commonplace, shirts from every era suddenly outside pubs or walking the streets, I have an impulse to find a Forest shirt and buy one. The very footballish desire to be someone else for the day, or the very footballish yearning to blend in and be part of the pack, swells in my system. I would like, just for today maybe, to become someone else entirely. It is almost as if I have begun to reimagine Wembley as a less arty Berghain in Berlin, an exclusive club where there will be bouncers looking me up and down, making sure I fit the bill, even though I have a ticket. Today is an empty canvas in which only pure possibility exists. I could be a Forest fan if I like. I do not buy the shirt. I keep walking.

I meet three friends in the centre of London for Sri Lankan curry – a strange choice for lunch in the heat – and they have a table outside the front, their backs to me. As I walk towards them, there is a woman walking towards me. She has had an altercation with a cyclist on the pavement and in a thick American accent she shouts at him: "You fucking asshole!" As she shouts it, I walk into view of my friends at the table, it appearing to them like she has screamed it directly at my face. "FA Cup weather, this," Mannie says, as I arrive. I'm not sure it's ever been specified what FA Cup weather is, but I know exactly what he means.

We have pints in town, finding a pub that is empty, save a handful of Forest fans. They already have quite faraway looks in their eyes, like they have been out for a never-ending weekend. One man is sat hunched over the bar vaping, yellow old away kit on, a pink glowstick around his neck. It is ten to three in the afternoon. Kick-off is at four thirty. I am leaving the men's when he walks in, a man side by side in the urinals with him, eyeing his Forest shirt and saying, "I hope you smash them today." That's the kind of levels of reaching out and sweetness that men reach in pub toilets, your equivalent of "Babe, you are living your best life." I keep thinking he is looking at me, as if he has sensed I'm masquerading as a Forest fan, while I warily watch him back. Instead he eventually asks if he can have a photo, tells me that he listens to *Tailenders*. I'm not sure exactly why, maybe it's relief, but I ask him if I can have one for me too, handing my phone to my friend Frank. Frank takes the photo with the look of a man who knows that it will never be looked at again, back in the camera roll with everything else, where memories go to die. Sixteen of them have come down in a minibus, the Forest fan with a glowstick around his neck says. I wish I had the afternoon ahead of me that he has – all that potential euphoria in the sky. The conversation, as will be par for the course when four men get together before watching football of this magnitude, is all about football in the old days and loaded sentimental feelings about growing up with the FA Cup. Nottingham Forest is a good club to be revelling in this feeling with, the specific age we are. We all remember the dawning of the Premier League, its first season, and the haunting vision of Brian Clough leaving the City Ground for the last time with Forest relegated. There was some deep sadness in him, obvious even to us who had not known the Clough who had won two European Cups and the league with Forest in the eighties. As he left, walking back down that tunnel for the last time, he gave some strange indication about wrestling your way through life, how, no matter what you achieved, no matter how far you got, you might still leave it with a cloud over your head. Brian Clough conversations in the pub, old Nottingham Forest teams in the nineties – these are triggering things for four of us to be talking about and Frank, with the barest of threads between one topic and the other, gesticulating with a pint in hand, says that he was once so excited to go to Disney World Florida, had worked himself up into such a state of overexcitement, that on walking through the gates he got a nosebleed that would not stop.

Entering Wembley is akin to that. All renovated, of course, the entire area still has the essence of something just built in the wreckage of the stadium that it leads to, like the waves of stories from the stadium have squashed everything in its immediate vicinity to be small, insignificant, bowing in its wake. Walking into the ground, through the half anticipation of a largely unpopulated Wembley Way, into the open, strangely popcorn-orientated concourses, is a bit like getting a nosebleed at Disney World Florida. It's as if the anticipation cannot match reality, turning the occasion into something inaccessible, something with innate pressure built into it. Walking into the Forest end, there are men upon men upon men with generally fazed looks in their eyes, like they've been drinking for four days. It's almost as if Forest, in their first FA Cup semi-final here since the early nineties, when they reached the final and were beaten courtesy of a Des Walker own goal in extra time, have had their day by just reaching here, as if the summit is being here at all, clambering to the top of those steps like Jet did at his first Fulham match. Me and Joel Gunter are in the second row, blending cautiously into the sea of red, me on the right-hand side of a mother with her son, maybe eight years old, who spends the entire game, from the moment the teams walk out, with his mouth agape, eyes like moons and his fingers in his ears. He is not looking anywhere but dead ahead at the pitch, his view fixed on nothing in particular, as if there is too much input to the senses to make any sense at all out of anything.

From our view, pitch-side, by the halfway line, everything to our right and then sweeping across the entire southern half of Wembley, is bathed in pure, brilliant red. It's like the tap, all those drips of colour that bled into the day from the Tube stations outside, is now fully rushing or a puzzle of pieces, minibuses of sixteen people and the like, has now come together to make sense of itself. To our left, there is a strange, less momentous feel. There are huge gaps in the top tier of the Manchester City stands, some people clearly sitting in pairs on their own, rows and rows of seats between them and others. It brings up some sort of sensory memory of Penrith and Crawley and Cray, where solitary figures sucked in football like it was a fire before having to be spat out back into the cold. It's odd to be reminded of a scene that, apart from the dimensions of a football pitch, bears absolutely no similarity to the present whatsoever. Manchester City, having won the Premier League four times on the bounce, won the FA Cup for the seventh time in 2023, and surprisingly were beaten finalists in 2024. If you ever need proof that constant winning does not bond people in the same way shared failure and loss and ordeals do, just look to your right and then to your left. When Fulham were in the old League One, the third tier of English football, with Manchester City, their games regularly sold out, as if their struggle in some ways made people more committed to turning up to see it, to will some new truth on their club in person. Now, the club is so convinced of their greatness, so sure of their involvement in games like this, people so stung from the literal cost of the club's success, with trips to London costing hundreds of pounds, that some people who twenty years ago would have sold their houses to be at something like this do not show up at all.

The event is scary in its scale, as the teams line up, then run towards their respective ends, each to applause. Like the boy next to me, I find it hard to focus on any one thing, to make it real, to contextualise what is happening. This, however, is put to bed within two minutes, when Rico Lewis, the Manchester City defender, turns his man and slots into the corner of the Forest goal. There is that strange silence, the split second where everyone is processing what they've just seen, then, an even better exploration of how light and sound travel at different speeds than any so far, the roar from the Manchester City end. Two minutes have been played, and the Forest end where we are is stunned into nothing. An acclimatising takes place from that moment on, an hour and a half of gently coming to terms with the fact Manchester City will just inevitably dominate this game. It's like the whole red end is having the same conversation me and Jet had for those last ten minutes at Craven Cottage – tens and tens of thousands of people from Nottingham just in hushed communication about how sad football is. Being so close to the side of the pitch, the Manchester City players, so far away in the Salford game in the third round, are demystified in some way. It is as if you have to be this close to understand that they are actually real, taking in their figures and constant running amid the awe-striking depth perception of Wembley.

The semi-final spills out into a foregone conclusion, the second-minute goal almost acting as if Wembley has been surrounded in a giant bubblegum bubble, then burst on impact, with the entire Forest end recognising they are suddenly either very drunk or very hungover or both and that the best part of the day might be already gone. In the weird silence, I start to contemplate that I must be the only person who has been to this completely random confection of games this season. In the daydream, in the not knowing whether I am proud of this fact or slightly worried about myself, I drift into thinking about how nice the pitch looks, the players becoming just shards of light running left and right as I do. *I would like to sleep on that one day,* I think. That's all I would like to do, sleep. Preferably on the pitch at Wembley. My fantasy is broken towards the end of the second half when a Forest fan shouts in my ear, not at me, but for the benefit of everyone, "I hate Jack Grealish with a passion, fuck off", and he raises two fingers at Grealish who has the ball and then is giving it and turning, City keeping the football in these little squares that I have become accustomed to listening to and talking about, but do not completely understand.

I miss the second City goal at the start of the second half; I am holding a pint and queuing up for a coffee that I will drink simultaneously. The Forest fans in the queue with me just hear it and their body language darkens, less out of shock, more like a lilo losing air on impact. When Morgan Gibbs-White's volley with the inside of his left foot loops and hits the post, the first of three times Forest will do this while weirdly never looking like scoring, the two women behind me in matching Forest shirts and blue jeans, their arms folded, sink lightly further into their seats, digging their knees into our backs. I turn around, not out of protest, but just to take in this sunken feeling in my back, and they are watching their football team with expressions on their faces as if they are looking at a child they are extremely disappointed in. When we leave, breaking for the exit a minute ahead of time only to realise that either way we will be stuck in a crush on Wembley Way, so we should stay and drink, there is a man in a yellow top who is being chased out of the view of the pitch. He is engulfed by security men who put their full weight on him, the lower part of his belly spilling out of his replica shirt and making contact with the cold concrete. "All right," he is shouting, "it's over, I'm done." As they hold him there, unsure of what the next moves might be, he makes a couple of sounds, close to *argh* and *urgh*, and then gives up, his chin on the ground, eyes like a sad dog looking out onto the concourse, the whistle blowing in the background. The day at Wembley is done. Forest will not be back here this season.

18

Final

Saturday, 17 May 2025
Wembley Stadium, Attendance: 84,163
Crystal Palace vs Manchester City

The day of the FA Cup final is as close as you will find to a collective birthday for the whole country. Here it is again, the most baked-in, universal footballing metric for another year gone by. Once they rolled by slowly for us, counting the days towards the final, wishing for the next one with a sharp focus on it. But now, time does its cruel thing, speeding up until you can't keep up with it, while you beg it to stay still just for a moment. The contrariness of memory continues to do its thing, especially, for whatever reason, with football. I can remember every detail of the FA Cup rounds of the early nineties, thirty years ago. I can tell you the teams and substitutes. I can tell you the way the ball fell to certain players in certain minutes of certain games. I can recall internal feelings against footballing images. Chris Woods only managing to parry the ball, Graham Hyde helpless to clear the ball in the last minute, lying stretched face down on the floor after the fact as Arsenal win the FA Cup in 1993. Neville Southall making save after save in 1995 to help Everton win it and then, when asked if they were the best of his career, telling the entire country, "Not really, no." And then, on how he would be celebrating: "I'm going to go home. When you've been with these lads as long as I have, you'd want to go home as well." Rob Jones of Liverpool on the goal-line trying to contort his body towards an Eric Cantona volley in the eighty-fifth minute in 1996, before his teammates around him sink to their knees. By contrast, even though I watched just as much of the FA Cup last season, I would genuinely have to stop and search for it to tell you Manchester United won it. This year too, like a birthday that you would rather forget, one where you don't want anyone to know your age, the final seems to catch everyone by surprise.

In the days that somehow linger in the memory despite their distance, the FA Cup final was the standout showcase, the absolute appointment to view in the country. The event that presaged social media in all its gloriously mundane build-up, like a warning sign of how addictive an everyday life lived through a screen might be. This year, though, with the world absolutely flooded with this sort of thing on any given day whether it be a cup final or not, every moment of everyone's daily activity documented for all to see like cup final coverage, it turns up almost unannounced among all the other content. It is in the middle of the penultimate weekend of Premier League football – shoehorned between league games on a Friday and a Sunday. As I listen to the build-up the night before the game, BBC 5 Live's Darren Fletcher says it feels like English football is "sticking the FA

Cup final in the shed". Every footballing voice makes a version of this point. It really is not what it used to be. It really is such a shame. Even the fact that it kicks off at four thirty rather than three o'clock sparks its own outrage. What universe are we living in where an FA Cup final doesn't start at three o'clock, everyone says. This is often – no, always – followed by "but it is what it is", before they get onto the next news item. This is how football works now. We complain that it isn't like it was. Then we shrug and we keep watching. It's interesting how this all plays out in a footballing year, the annual fetishisation and myth-making of the FA Cup, now turned into an annual playing out of qualms about footballing civil rights and traditions being stripped away.

But the sense of occasion, however much it is squeezed, will not be wrestled from the FA Cup final this year. Crystal Palace are here – with genuine and not completely misguided hope. You are going to need a massive shed to put all that in. This, for everyone apart from the top four, is an absolute relief amid the everyday begrudgery of watching the usual teams involved in the tournament every season. Crystal Palace have never won the cup, or for that matter, any major trophy and, with a team this year hardwired with sharp, breakaway communication, shared commitment to the cause and moments of regular inspiration, carry a torch for the rest of the country to the cup final saying, it does not have to be the same teams that win this every year, it could be us. It's like that Jamie Donley strike earlier in the tournament, cruelly chalked down as an own goal eventually, before Manchester City eventually beat Leyton Orient. Something everyone can get behind. Palace have similarities too, if evolved ones, to the characters and teams that came so close for them in 1990 and 2016, losing both times to fucking Manchester United of course.

In 1990, a young, exciting Crystal Palace drew 3-3 with United thanks to two goals from substitute Ian Wright. In the replay, they were allocated slightly more tickets than the first game, where people queued overnight for tickets – four for everyone at the front of the queue and two for everyone at the back. There were little scuffles, with touts having commandeered tickets that deserving fans could not access. Geoff Thomas, the Palace captain, does a television promo run before the final, looking slightly stunned and staring down the lens of news cameras on local and national television, his words only coming after his eyes have widened significantly. "The grass is [cut] very close, so the ball doesn't run very smoothly," he tells ITV. "It seems like it gets caught up on it, and your legs do the same." He could be forewarning the heaviness that will befall Palace when they lose the final later that week, but just as easily, twenty-six years later, when, after a Jason Puncheon goal in the seventy-eighth minute, the remaining twelve appear to be sudden, insurmountable quicksand for them, and they lose in extra time.

Dan Cook has been running the HLTCO YouTube channel and social media accounts for over a decade. He supports Crystal Palace because of his dad, whose dad supported Crystal Palace because of his dad. Dan has been on his YouTube channel a couple of days before the final, saying that he "loves Crystal Palace with every fibre of his being". He describes the ninety seconds after the Jason Puncheon goal in 2016 as the most surreal of his life, that he "genuinely felt as though I was floating, levitating, whatever you want to call it". As a South Londoner who has chosen to support Palace, he says, you have chosen to shun the success that is easily obtainable on your doorstep in Chelsea, Arsenal, or any of the big teams that many Londoners are minded to support. He explains that supporting Palace at his age, from where he was from, was a "measure of resolve and spirit", choosing to align yourself with a club that went through administration twice and was a last-minute goal from being relegated out of the Championship, over easily accessible, glossy happiness. If you support Palace, he says, you believe in representing something that is local to you. Alongside Fulham, Crystal Palace are the biggest team in the country to have never won a major trophy. In almost every way imaginable, from statistics and outlook to geographical location, they are defined by their nearliness. They are not meant to win major trophies – all the laws of physics and history deny them this. And so their mere presence today, the absolute sense of a moment to be grabbed, a moment to be happy to be alive, turns any of the usual bemoaning of the FA Cup down to the point of non-existence. They shake the attention away from the gloom and, on the other side of the build-up, make the FA Cup feel like it once did. There is a song, there are poems, there are stories of hurt and pain and meaning and people who are not here to see this and would have done anything to be. As Dan puts it, as if speaking on behalf of every Palace fan since 1861, "Life is short, life is dull, life is full of pain, and this is a chance for something special." This sentence alone articulates as sharply as any meandering ramble the meaning of the FA Cup this year to Crystal Palace fans, turning it back into that twitching, aspirational reality show we once knew.

As a supporter of a similar-sized club, one with a similar feeling about itself, watching Crystal Palace have a moment like this is a complicated feeling. The lesser clubs, resigned to living for small victories and little moments rather than any sustained periods of dominance or, god forbid, silverware, understand how these highs in the spotlight are given once-in-a-lifetime significance. It is almost part of the job description to enjoy it when it lands somewhere else. I feel like I do really want Palace to win. I want that for football. I want that for them. And yet, reinforced by that vision of their supporters celebrating at Craven Cottage that became true, sitting next to Jet's heartbreak while knowing I will be incognito among them today, it is impossible not to be also confronted with my own ugly, petty jealousy.

Manchester City, to my knowledge, have no poems or songs this year. They are accustomed to trips to Wembley, almost to the point of it being a chore. This is coupled with a disorientating season of harsh disappointment for Pep Guardiola and his quadruple-winning Manchester City team. They are in the final for the third consecutive season, but after a year of harsh burn-out and a severe drop in form, they come with their invincibility complex dented. "I want to feel alive while I'm living," says Pep the day before the final in response to a question about his feelings on this season's disappointments, "and I felt alive this season." It is only a few months since he was spotted in his dugout, in an exposing and alarming period where Manchester City suddenly could not win, scratching at his eyes and his head, leaving red marks of self-flagellation everywhere. It was not so much reassuring that football could do this even to Pep Guardiola, it was more a life lesson of significance. One that said however much you win, it might not be enough for you if you can't maintain it for ever, and no one can maintain it for ever. It was like that parting sight of a despondent Brian Clough walking down the tunnel, relegated. Pep's version is sitting on the bench, clawing at his own eyes. On the

FA Cup final and its fighting against the dying of the light, he says something extremely poignant too: "You have to be there," he says, "to feel it."

And so we travel, all these people aching to be there to feel it, all with our different reasons to feel, en route to Wembley. The weather is the exact perfect London summer heat, a nostalgic summer heat, the type that triggers some very distant, washed out, early memory. It's the kind that makes you remember oddly specific things, a holiday or a paddling pool in a garden. I remember – for whatever reason – that my mum loved white Magnums, and we used to talk in detail about how nice white Magnums were. And for a second, not in a particularly heavy way, she is real again and on the earth, talking about how it's because the chocolate on the outside is kind of crisp and the ice cream is soft. It's the sort of heat that you know to cherish in London, because in a couple of days it will probably get to the point that there are hot weather warnings and people passing out at train stations, with automated messages everywhere you go telling you to make sure to drink water, as if that doesn't occur to Londoners at any other time of the year. There is that little breeze too, the one that helps with small, regular sensations of relief alongside those flashes of razor-sharp memories, that tells you something is in the air, relenting to let the heat to bake us all while we are on our phones, before arriving again, touching the air, like the sea laps the shore.

The first Crystal Palace fan I see is at Denmark Hill station, with his legs crossed, looking into his phone like it is a crystal ball, AirPods in. He has the TDK kit on that Palace wore at some point between the 1990 and 2016 FA Cup finals. It is a famous kit, a memory as distant but as close as the one the heat is evoking. This TDK kit specifically says this is where I'm from, somewhere you might know, the land of disappointment, the land of nearly, the land of Crystal Palace, from Selhurst Park. I am leaving South-east London, the home of Crystal Palace, to go to Wembley, fleeing with all the same people to the same point.

But still, no matter how big a thing is, or your life is, London has a way of patting you on the head, reminding you that you are not that important, that it does not need you or any of your dreams. On the Overground into Canada Water, two men in their late twenties are talking, half-facing each other. "We should put money on the game," one of them says. "What game?" "The final is today, isn't it?" "Is it?" "I'm pretty sure it is?" They do not resolve this, they just shrug at the two Palace fans, their kits painting faint red and blue flashes into the train carriage, and the conversation goes on. "There was a fight outside Cartier the other day," the one wanting to place a bet excitedly says. Someone had nicked something. "Someone got whacked over the head with a dustpan and brush." "Do you think it hurt?" asks the man who doesn't believe it's cup final day today. "Well, I'm not sure, I think it was very plasticky. That's the problem with a dustpan and brush; it looks good and funny but you're sacrificing a bit of oomph." The man considers the impact, solemnly nodding, looking into the distance, as if he is registering this information for future notice, should he ever need a dustpan and brush as a weapon.

On the Jubilee line from Canada Water, the cup final has still not completely revealed itself. An American woman sits opposite me on the train. She is wearing headphones, talking to someone. "Yeah, the songs are shit, but I'm super happy with the team and everything," she says. She squints her eyes as if it will help her hear the reply in the not particularly good but still miraculous reception on an Underground train. She does the nod that I have learned some record label people do, a vacant, patronising smile and nod. "Yeah, super happy," she says. She listens, squints again. She's losing signal. Gets the signal back. She's frowning a lot now and shaking her head. The sort of solemn, sincere one that old men do when defenders for their team are not picking up their corresponding runners. "Yeah, but I guess that's why they're number one." Then she's shaking her head again. "I covered his ass so much." She shares a laugh about someone in the office. "Well, that's all well and good if all you have to do is staff people. I'd be the best in the world if all I had to do was staff people." The woman next to her in training gear and big glasses laughs, maybe at the podcast she is listening to, maybe at the conversation she is overhearing.

At Waterloo, the record label woman gets off and the ingestion of Palace fans into the Jubilee line train finally tells you what day it is. It's cup final day. There is a man wearing a rosette and a trilby, with thick-rimmed glasses. He looks as if he has been preserved from the 1990 final, ageless since then in fashion and in shape. The area of Wembley tends to do this, shows you people that look they have been preserved in cryo chambers just for these occasions, stuck in a non-specific time. There is a boy next to him with straight long hair and brown boots, draped in a Palace flag like a cape. It is unclear whether these two know each other: they are standing very close and not speaking, their only definitive stylistic similarity their colours. When the boy turns around to check the Tube map, he looks like something out of *The Lord of the Rings*, like he is going into battle against evil for the good of the future of the planet. And in his own way, he sort of is.

The Palace fans stand in a huddle, vibrating away on the Tube to Wembley. The Perspex screen that designates the end of a row of seats separates them from a couple of Manchester City fans, two men in sky blue. They begin a conversation and, like the two Palace fans standing, they are oddly separated in all ways but their colours. They are opposite each other, a similar age, maybe mid-fifties. One of them has a heavy Mancunian accent, and the other a London East End one. It is a big unspoken part of their conversation for long chunks of the journey, that one of them clearly is not from Manchester. He goes slightly red when they start talking. "I was there against Wigan," he says, referencing the FA Cup final that Man City were shocked in and lost twelve years ago. The man opposite says, "Me too." The Londoner City fan says, "And that was a banker, wasn't it." It's almost like they are willing a loss their way, as if Manchester City's season this year, a kind of crumbling of a dynasty, has been in its own way comforting to them. The Londoner searches for dark days and reels them off, parading them like trophies: "I remember losing 5-0 to Charlton, things like that." There is an unwritten negotiation of a conversation between them, one where the Londoner is desperate to flag his credentials to this stranger, to make it very clear he is not a Johnny-come-lately tourist-style glory supporter. "I was the only City fan in my school," he says, so gently that you can almost hear small violins. "There was a shop where they had to order the kits. I had to try a Watford one on for the size so they could order the kit." They look across to a farther part of a train, where another child with a London accent is wearing full City gear, talking about the game. The man sitting down, the Londoner, shoots him a look as if he doesn't even know he was born. The Londoner then points at the Manc's blue kit, one from the 1970s, with absolute, gooey compassion. "I was about seven," he says. The other man looks down at his shirt, turns around and shows him the number on the back. It's a number 8. "Colin Bell," they both say at the same time. "What do you think of the new kit?" the Londoner asks. The Manc says he likes it. The Londoner agrees. "Eighty-five quid for a shirt, though," the Colin-Bell-shirt-wearing man says. "And that's before you print anything on it," the Londoner adds. They both roll their eyes.

I am torn watching all this jostling for depth of personal history on the Tube – partly envious and partly relieved not to be about to go through the feelings that I would be. If I could hardly bear to open my eyes for ninety minutes during an FA Cup quarter-final in which Fulham were soundly beaten, could I even watch them in the final? Would that be in any way a nice experience? Would I even survive that?

Football encourages people who are prone to catastrophise situations that are not even real and as I consider these completely theoretical, inconsequential things that, given they have never happened in my lifetime, are extremely unlikely ever to be a problem for me, the Jubilee line Tube dives out from underground, light suddenly shines into the carriage, illuminating the difference between red and blue and light blue. As the train pulls up at Wembley Park station, the carriages ready to spit each of us out here and into a mass where everyone will be unidentifiable from the next, the two Manchester City fans stand side by side, ready to leave. "Well, then," the Manc-born man says, "let's see what we can see." The Tube doors open and the first thing they not so much see but hear on entering the station, already stacked with bodies slowly climbing the stairs of the station, is the Palace fans, now not lonely AirPod figures on tubes in

TDK shirts, or singular trilbies or *Lord of the Rings* capes, now a throng, just making the sound "Eeeeaaaagggglllleeeeesss".

As we walk out of the station, there is a heart-racing sense of anticipation. A woman, sixty, with a Ray Wilkins shirt, walks over the horizon beyond me, and there is Wembley Way. She walks past a man with a megaphone, the only person facing the opposite direction, carrying a sign saying, "There is one god and one mediator, Jesus Christ." Nobody even acknowledges him, as if he has not noticed that there are already uncontrollable natural forces in operation. Some Palace fans I know say that they haven't slept for a week. I've texted all of them this morning – such is etiquette when you support teams like Palace and Fulham – earnestly telling them that I'm thinking of them and I hope they win. I almost actually mean it.

I am early enough to watch people arrive at Wembley. This is a conscious decision. Not just because age has planted in me, year by year, an anxiety about being late or being in a rush, sitting in airports four hours before I need to be, but also because I want to see the tens of thousands of people flood into Wembley with reasons, mostly unarticulated, of why today means something to them. A dad walks hand in hand with his daughter who has dyed half her hair red and the other half blue. Teenage friends walk side by side, half in their phones, draped in Palace capes and kits. A ten-year-old girl is entirely half blue and half red, from clothing to painted skin. She walks past Man City fans who ask if they can have a photo with her, before they notice that her brother and her dad are exactly the same, and invite them into the photo too.

I am so early that while everyone else stops at bars on Wembley Way, I am literally the first person queueing up to get into the ground.

The handful of Palace fans behind me help me feel less trainspotterish, but not much. I am the only one not in red and blue. I keep my head down, anxious someone will notice me as the guy that does the Fulham podcast, going in stealth as a Palace fan, taking a ticket that has been robbed from the hands of someone who deserves it more. This complex guilt is going to rub itself into everything that unfolds in the next two hours, I can just feel it. And yet, I am flush full of a sort of childlike giddiness, that I am at a cup final.

They open the doors. I remember these moments as a teenager, from going to see Oasis, in the years when they offered me a lifeline, where there was so much hope in those songs, that I carried them everywhere with me, to the front of queues to get in, before I would run to the front of the barrier, needing to be exactly at the front, exactly in the middle, eyes unblinking, hoping to meet theirs. A version of this teenage me pushes itself to the front of who I am as we are let in, and my stride becomes hurried. I have not predetermined this, but I am doing that strange, rushed walk people do, that is not quite a run, more of an urgent walk, but is almost the same speed as sprinting. The pitch at Wembley opens up in front of me, the seats entirely red, totally unoccupied. The PA just turned on, the television crews on the side of the pitch. There is just one other man in the stands here, walking out immediately, and – just like I did when I was young, when I used to decide I was in a race with an unknowing member of the public walking down the street and beat them to some imaginary finish line – I notice no one is sitting down yet and that I could be the first. It somehow becomes important to me that I am that person. I am urgently finding row 16, seat 236 of block 142. I win. I sit down first, before he or anyone else has taken a seat at the cup final. Then there's this satisfaction. One completely internal. Mine alone. I made it. I have made it through this entire FA Cup campaign. I'm at the top of this extremely weird, self-imposed, partly solitary journey through football. A strange sort of Everest climbed, I scan the ground, looking around, the cameras and media melee in place. Just to the left is the FA Cup. It sits unguarded on a red box, everyone preoccupied with their televisual duties. There is nothing much closer to football spirituality, surely, than seeing the FA Cup on its own, glimmering, on the afternoon of the FA Cup final, while being the only person in their seat two and a quarter hours before kick-off. It is quite an emotional thing to witness, oddly, an emotion that I'm not sure is sadness or happiness or rediscovered youth or a journey ended. It is just an unspecified, all-encompassing emotion, to see it there, unattended, waiting for someone to grab it.

Slowly a handful of people come in, mouths slightly agape, just like the Forest fan who appeared not to be able to focus on anything. A teenage boy in a Palace kit, a block to the left, looks across at me, a big smile on his face. We both put our thumbs up at each other. Nedum Onuoha is doing TV across the barrier, yellow microphone in hand. I like listening to Nedum Onuoha. He is next to Mark Chapman and Michael Brown. Then there is Shearer and Troy Deeney and more and more football names, Lineker and co., probably saying stuff like "the first fifteen minutes are massive here". As they do their jobs, the atmosphere that surrounds them this early in the day is almost cathedral-like. Palace fans are slowly walking in and – from here – it feels like everyone is whispering. There is almost no point filming it or taking photos. Some people attempt to, and then quickly put away their phones, as if they were in a museum and specifically told not to take pictures. There is no way of capturing the feeling, size or depth of it.

Back in the foyer by the strangely American pick'n'mix and confectionary that Wembley now offers, a child in a yellow kit pretends to score a goal and then runs in front of his parents, two fingers to the sky, eyes to the ceiling, celebrating. A man with white hair and a South-east London accent, a typical Crystal Palace-y, I've-drunk-quite-a lot-of-lager-but-am-pretty-sweet type of guy, sits against a wall, his legs stretched out, next to a child sitting cross-legged. The child has glasses, long hair, and is pointing at every page of the programme, asking loads of questions, which the man is fielding. It's actually very beautiful, should you choose to look for beauty here – everywhere you look, this level of dreaming is permeating through the generations.

Being in Wembley before so many other people, before it's carnage in the toilets, as it soon will be, is like being in someone else's house at night, not intent on stealing anything, just imagining what it's like to be them for a second. A couple kiss. The exact type I don't like seeing. A volt runs through me. I want to drink. Blur the edges. Slip into the lovely, brief non-anxiety softness that those first two or three pints allow before you start feeling tired and heavy and sad. I might need to drink now, just to slip through this sense of being an undercover Fulham fan witnessing something actually quite intimate and special from inside the lair of the faithful. I get a pint on my own. I feel oddly emotional still, unsure whether I might cry at some point at something very small. It's even the very sense that people have all come here to feel something, they have come here knowing they might be very hurt, just opening themselves up to the universe, asking it to answer them this time. I'm having a moment, on my own, drinking this pint, my pores open to this condition that only football really gives, this jeopardy, where I realise maybe I could let go of all the stuff I have been holding onto in my life, that all those little quirks and grudges and triggers that once served me might not anymore. I realise, the way the travelling through this competition has sometimes gifted me a perspective just from the sheer nature of moving away from London, that I am still ushering things around in life to bring back to the teenage version of myself, staying totally faithful to that person, only to neglect the one that is actually real and here today. These are quite intense thought loops to be having while pretending to be a Crystal Palace fan inconspicuously. But just witnessing them here in their moment, back again at Wembley, I start to imagine how my own life might be different the other side of this, just as they wish something true, surrounded by such communal suspense.

Mark Stephenson, the same Mark who had a crack at non-league football reporting before finding it broadly inhospitable, locked inside the ground at Crawley Town, the one who arrived after the semi-final with beers in his pockets, is in the concourses with his entire family and a group of close friends. His mum, his dad, his sister, his nephew, his cousin ("probably the only person who grew up in Doncaster supporting Crystal Palace") and another cousin he hasn't seen for nearly twenty years are all with him. He has bought tickets for most of these people, hunting them down individually when little batches were released by the club before games, working out who can sit with who, trying to make sure everyone gets in. When I meet them, it strikes me as being potentially the first time I've ever seen a large group of family and friends all together like this, many generations all sharing something, other than at a wedding or a funeral.

Both Mark's parents already supported Crystal Palace before they met. His mum's dad had been a Palace fan since the 1930s and took her to games when she was a child. She was one of very few female supporters and they learned to get seats close to the only women's toilet in the entirety of Selhurst Park at that time. Mark was at the 1990 cup final at the age of five with his dad. His mum couldn't get tickets, but because she was by now a police officer, she managed to work the game and meet them in their seats before the heartbreak ensued. He was at the 2016 final too, before the inevitable heartbreak ensued again. The build-up this time has not so much made him excited but incredibly nostalgic and wistful for the past, watching back the final in 1990, unsure if the memories are his own or the television replays. Many of the clips being shared before the game reduce him to tears. Crystal Palace is something that he and a huge percentage of the people in his life have always had in common, a shared interest that has kept them connected and in contact. He has two boys, who are finding their way into football via bedtime re-watches of *Match of the Day* with him. His sister drifted away from the club for a while, but her son has become so obsessed that he's been on two tours of Selhurst Park this year, and it's reignited the spark in her. Now, her friends know not to try to make plans with her on matchdays. Palace are playing.

Mark doesn't like to drink before a game. He has found that he won't be able to focus on it if he does, and he has spent his Tube journey in today with noise-cancelling headphones on, like the TDK man at the Tube station, not joining in with the singing. "I see people being so happy and think how sad they will be soon," he explains. He says this with an entire lifetime of experience that suggests it's best not to get carried away, and that the thing you desperately want to happen, ultimately will not. The singing before a game makes him stressed. He tries to block it all out. Nonetheless, Mark spends almost all his spare time, all year round, reading about, listening to or watching football, and he is disturbing himself by being objectively confident. "I think we have a chance," he says, half-jogging on the spot in nervous anticipation. "Glasner is good at working out teams, and City look readable, especially the way we counterattack." I've always listened intently to Mark's football analysis, not just because it is considered and comes from genuine thought and perception, but also because when I first met Mark in 2004, he would walk around the halls of residence at the University of Sussex in full Palace kit for no reason other than he was playing *Football Manager* and it helped him focus. When Mark got married to Jess, who lived in the room opposite mine in the same halls, he started his speech by proposing a toast to Steve Coppell. The former Palace manager was definitely not at, or aware of, the wedding; Mark just wanted to make sure that Steve Coppell was the first person he thanked.

In the concourses, "I Gotta Feeling" by Black Eyed Peas plays. Of course it does. It is not the most romantic of threads, but nonetheless a thread that has tied Penrith, Haywards Heath and MK Dons to this. Exactly the same music. The constant four to the floor. Quite bad dance music, as vague and generic as possible. All of it about having the best night of your life. Best freaking night of your life.

Tonight's going to be a good night. Every day, every pre-kick-off being piped in with the promise of the best night of your life. Freed from desire. Mind and senses purified. And then everyone sings loads of "na na nas".

As it builds, for the last time in this FA Cup, on the other side of the "na na nas" as we get closer to kick-off, there is that strange thing I hate and am drawn to, the part of men's football that is what the territory demands. The guttural voice. The men shouting obscene stuff. That adrenaline rush of threat. The collection of noises is rising and rising before it all becomes that smell again of beer and burgers and breath and the sound of chanting, thousands of voices merging into a pack of sounds and strut. God, I hate that I am a Fulham fan in here, the silent sense of being an imposter or an outsider. If I feel like this now, in what is actually a very family friendly football environment, how must it feel to be a spy, to spend your life blending into the background? Or someone genuinely not welcome, just for where they are from? And that's the strange part of this entire experience, the constant toing and froing between wanting nothing but to blend in, be totally unremarkable, just safe and sure, and the feeling that keeps me working through my daily existence, keeps me fuelled, keeps me trying, like a devilish tick, saying, *What you are doing is not enough, do more, be seen more, stay alive in the minds of everyone.*

When I get back from the bar, my seat is still down, like it's asking me back to it. I go to sit there, one drink in, and now set up directly in front of me is a TV bench with Mark Pougatch, Roy Keane, Ian Wright and Joleon Lescott. I know all these people bizarrely well just from television. I look at them and think, *They look happy. They look complete. Do I wish I was them? Maybe I sometimes wish I was them.*

As they joke between takes, I have that same sense of longing as I once did for slip cordons in cricket or for bands. The desire to be inside the in-joke, in the middle of an all-encapsulating glare. They look like they're glowing. My brain does not do the maths here that it's probably the TV lights, that they are literally illuminated. I just see them glow, wish that I glowed too. The song we named 86TVs after, the I Am Kloot song, runs through my head: "I saw you laughing on a TV show, what did I think you'd know?" I must have listened to that song ten thousand times but, for the first time, I understand it. What do I think they know? I feel heartbroken for myself, strangely, that I've spent a whole life trying to get inside that glow, sort of succeeding, and that maybe that was always about never really feeling enough, never really feeling happy, only accessing all these dopamine hits constantly, assuming that someone laughing on a TV show must genuinely know some secret that I didn't.

Matt Horan, one of my *Tailenders* co-hosts, is joining me for this one. I offered him a ticket a couple of days ago and he has dropped everything to be at his first FA Cup final. He supports Bristol City and says this is likely, no, definitely, his only chance to ever be at one. It's hard to disagree with him. He has come from Bristol today, and apparently lots of Manchester City fans have been making the same journey. The last time he came to Wembley it was still the old one, after winning a competition where you got a tour of the stadium if you pulled a certain colour ring-pull off a can of Coke. His mum took him and his two brothers to Wembley, where he insisted on dominating the Q&A with questions about John Barnes. He was "flabbergasted" that the tour guide did not immediately know John Barnes's boot size.

As Matt tells me this story, the this-is-your-life feelings that cup finals inspire playing out in him and me and everyone else here, my eyes wander to a Crystal Palace fan meandering around with a large popcorn in one hand and three quarters of a pint in the other. He looks quite lost, as if he's lost his central navigational system, like a cat without its whiskers. It turns out that Matt's story might have gone on slightly too long, because when we get back to our seats, now three pints deep, we have missed the ceremonial singing of "Abide With Me". Wembley is completely full now – overwhelmingly so. Prince William has walked out of the fireworks that smell like there has been a bonfire the size of Wembley, which there sort of has. He is shaking hands with people, making conversation, while the pitch is flooded with soldiers. Red tape now gates off the trophy in a triangle in the middle of the pitch, as William faces the players, making small talk. The military influence seems slightly odd to me, slightly incongruous, and when it clears, something as close to an English Super Bowl serenade as you are likely to see just gone, the smoke dissipates into the air, as if on timely cue, and we are left with Palace goalkeeper, Dean Henderson, walking around stamping on stray balloons. The man to my left appears to be extremely high on something more than alcohol and has seemingly forgotten about the football, while the woman to my right eyes him wearily. They both wear Palace kits and, without looking at me, the man hands me a blue flag. As I look out onto Wembley, the Crystal Palace end is making a reverberating sound, the sound of sheer, lifelong, transgenerational collective anticipation and forcing away of another hurt. It is a cacophony of noises, of absolute assured belonging. I am inside it. As inside it as an outsider can be.

Manchester City – as expected – dominate the ball in the first ten minutes. But outside the pitch there is a genuine sense of them being squeezed by every Crystal Palace fan inside Wembley. It is as if having the ball here is inconsequential against the deafening will of all these people, pushing the ball away from the Palace net with sound.

Sixteen minutes in, it does not feel like Crystal Palace have had the ball, but they have also not been seriously threatened. I know from the Fulham quarter-final, from the flashbacks I still have of it, that they break with telepathic, intense, sharp speed when the moment allows. City lose the ball in the Crystal Palace half and they sense their moment. Until now, all the football has taken place in the shade and comparative darkness, where Wembley's roof casts a shadow. As Mateta receives the ball, he holds it up on the lip of the Manchester City half and, as if for the first time, he looks across to the other half of the pitch. There is sudden light, bright and vivid, from underneath his feet to the other end. It is bright in the way that cathedrals are built to inspire, to leave you with little choice but to believe in forces above and beyond. Wearing protective headgear after being knocked unconscious by a tackle in the fifth round, he looks out into the sun and then finds ongoing fullback Muñoz, running into space on the right-hand side of the pitch, which is back in the shade. He finds a ball that is perfectly in his stride, onrushing, the Manchester City players running back towards their own goal. There is some sort of inevitability to the way they seem in flight, every Palace player synchronising like fighter jets or birds or, as cheesy as it sounds, eagles. Muñoz is sprinting, ball in his control, before shimmying back into the light, and passing the ball into the bleached-out Manchester City area. Eze is there. Whenever Eze is there, there is a holding of breath, or the sound of thousands of people standing up, their seats clattering as they flip back. The ball is landing exactly in his stride too and, with one composed, clinical, smooth touch, he strikes it into the bottom right-hand corner of the goal. From the other side of the ground there is all the usual sequence that huge goals in huge grounds give. The strike, the distant sound of the thud of the boot on ball, then the ripple of the net and, as if a momentary glimpse of disbelief, a moment of silent processing, before all around me, people are flying over seats, screaming into the sky, hugging anyone and everyone.

From the seventeenth minute of the game, it is like the FA Cup final is operating with the panic and desperation and ferocity of the last kick of the game. Manchester City will feel like they have the ball for ever now, and the Palace team, arranged and resolute, alongside the force of all the shared history in the Palace stands will attempt to force them out. Being inside the desperation of feeling, without it being *my* team, is suddenly a privileged situation to be in. Without not being able to watch, I stand among it, slightly detached, almost awestruck, like I am watching a game of football for the first time, witnessing the madness of how human beings will put so much of their wellbeing and happiness into something they are totally at the whim of. Everyone is in a world where we are trying desperately to shape whatever is happening, to sniff out where the threat might be coming from, without being able to affect it in any way. There are lots of little events that play out in a mad rush of feeling. Dean Henderson should probably be sent off for a foul outside his area. He then saves a penalty, which Erling Haaland has bizarrely handed over to Omar Marmoush at the last minute, diving to his right, the same delirium playing out as his outstretched glove pushes the ball away and then catches the ball from Haaland on the rebound.

At half-time, I walk back into the concourse where one man is telling another that "he felt it in his bones" that Henderson was going to save the penalty. And as me and Matt huddle in the corner, blurring more edges with more pints, I look out into the Palace throng. It's strange how every team seem to have some sort of "look". It's not always completely pin-downable what that look is, but there is definitely a certain look a Palace fan has. The side partings of the adults and the dads are more punctuated in the glow of being forty-five minutes away from winning the FA Cup, all of them variations of a theme of the club owner Steve Parish, so sure of who they are, so proud to have stuck it out, so close to reaching footballing nirvana.

When we get back to our seats, past a woman in a leopard-print wheelchair eating a burger, there is a new, very big and bald man occupying the standing space in front of our seats. We squeeze in next to him, all of us standing, to accommodate us all. He has a Crystal Palace scarf wrapped around his head and he is swaying, like he has been drinking for the entire time that my Palace friends have told me that they haven't been sleeping this week. He is the kind of drunk where you can see the alcohol filling up to his eyes, rocking in his pupils like little oceans. He is standing on his heels like a drunk computer character, blowing strawberry vape smoke across Wembley, eyes not focusing on the football at all. He will not really notice or engage with the fact the second half is going to play out like a continued training drill, where Manchester City have the ball and Crystal Palace line up in front of it, pure resilience and organisation, saying, you will not pass.

Dean Henderson, now in the half of Wembley which shoots reverent light, operates for the second half in a baseball cap. I'm looking around for faces. There are 84,163 people here and each one has a story about why and how and what it means to them. Some stories do not even need to be told. When eighty-eight minutes are gone, I look to my right and a woman my age is looking directly at me, crying. There are ten minutes of added time, each playing out like every single minute has done bar that one from the gods in the sixteenth. And when Kevin De Bruyne, in the ninety-ninth minute, lifts the ball past the goal and into the crowd for the last time, with his last kick for Manchester City, there is a sudden, disbelieving lull. Crystal Palace are actually going to win? It's like no one has thought this far ahead, no one knows what this will feel like, or where they go from here. And when the final whistle blows, I turn around, through the strawberry haze, past the drunk man with a Palace bandana around his head, who is suddenly so shot full of adrenaline it is as if he is focusing for the first time, just repeating "That's unreal", and see an old man sobbing so much that it almost feels like an invasion of privacy to be witnessing it.

There is a lot of face-holding. A lot of checking the score. People are holding each other, not letting go of each other. There is another man, having a moment to himself, looking down at the floor, almost shaking. When he looks up, he catches my eye, and I wink at him, the sort of wink you do to your friends to say, *I notice you're in your element* or *I love you* or *Are you OK?* He shakes his head at me and then breaks down crying, his face in his hands. The word "Winners" is spelled out on the screens at Wembley, but with one extra *n*, so it reads "Winnners", as if the result has even spun this very simple sentiment out too. The light catches Oliver Glasner's face as he and the rest of the squad walk up behind us to receive the trophy. The total stranger I have just exchanged a slightly over-intimate moment with is turned away, looking at the screen, everyone else turned towards the players, so when Joel Ward and Marc Guéhi lift the cup together, I am looking back at him, arms aloft, the same TDK shirt as the one I'd walked past this morning at Denmark Hill that screams *I am from the land of disappointment*, with white hair and tears in his eyes.

There is some beauty in the fact that in football, you can be without the ball for almost the entirety of a game, and still deservedly win the match. Dean Henderson is already telling TV cameras that he felt like his dad was with him. In this moment, it feels like everyone who has been lost is here too. It is an extremely supernatural moment. And, as the Crystal Palace players go back onto the pitch, in front of a very quickly built stage, one half of Wembley is singing "Freed from Desire", the song that I have heard at every single ground since Penrith, the unromantic connective tissue of this whole tournament, mushing every team and fan base into a chorus of "na na na na na na nas". It does, undeniably, feel really good. On the other half, the Manchester City end is vacated. There may be even fewer people left in that entire stand than the 210 that were there against Penrith. The players lift the trophy on the pitch, and my imposter syndrome has turned into a rare sense of gratitude just to be a witness at what most people here will call the best day of their lives. Something truly magical has happened. An entire history of hurt turned worthwhile inside one game of football.

Mark is half-running through the empty concourses while

everyone celebrates in view of the pitch. He did not celebrate the Eze goal until about five seconds after it happened, finding himself in a "weird, emotional state" on even seeing it. He spent the remainder of the game watching the clock, large chunks of action missing from his memory even without the drinking beforehand. The friends he is with all cried at the end of the game, as if a multi-generational curse had been broken on the blow of one whistle. It is only now, though, mid-stride and with no one around, that the sensation breaks through for him. He starts to cry. No Crystal Palace fan in history before this moment has ever had this feeling. He will be crying intermittently for the next week. "I know this sounds crazy," he tells me later, "but it was the same feeling as when my boys were born." Given that I inexplicably cried on a bus the day after Fulham simply reached the quarter-final of this campaign, this does not sound crazy to me, even if I do not yet know how it feels to have a child. "Obviously, my boys are the biggest thing in my life, but it was a similar sensation, the only thing that I can come close to comparing it to. The difference was, that's a very intimate thing, it's you and your partner. Today, there was this collective outpouring of joy and elation, with all these people I'd known my whole life. It was a very, very powerful feeling."

The stage is dismantled almost as quickly as it was built, revealing most of it to be cardboard, like a joke from an episode of *Trigger Happy TV*. As the ground empties out, I stay. Others, like Mark and his family, are doing their own version of hanging onto this moment, waiting in the ground as long as they can. It's as if people are unsure what the world looks like on the other side of this. They are not sure how to move back into the world as the actual winners of the FA Cup. There is no guidebook for this feeling. One that isn't cruel hurt. The weird disorientation of actually getting what you want and the world outside not really changing at all. Confetti is cleared off the floor by ground staff, wearing black like it's the end of a theatre show and they are resetting the stage for tomorrow. They have hoovers and dustpans and brushes, and they clear while the sounds of seats folding back up and balloons popping go off like soft artillery in the background. I was the first to sit down here and I want to be the last to leave. I wait until nobody else is left, just a security guy asking for the twelfth time if we can leave via the exit, please. The last essence of the FA Cup of 2024–25 that I will take in is not the trophy, long since disappeared down the tunnel, or the mass celebrating, behind me and on its way down Wembley Way, but the sudden smell of freshly cut grass. It is the first time I have noticed the smell of grass the entire tournament. It's almost the first time that I've even stopped to consider that football takes place on grass, grass that must be grown and cultivated and taken care of, grass that needs all types of weather to survive. It smells really comforting – there's something deeply nostalgic about it, exactly like the weather on the way in – something that reminds me of being seven, when everything felt like it was where it should be.

And with that smell, I feel an ache of melancholy, that this will never happen again, in this order, from Penrith to Pep to Palace. That although the FA Cup repeats and fades every year, it won't repeat and fade again like this. I could have been from any of those places. I could have been in love with any of those teams. You can, after all, be whoever you want to be.

19

Six weeks later, The Maccabees are about to walk on at Glastonbury. It is a Sunday and the evening is setting in, the sun hiding behind the opposite side of the stage. Minutes before we go on, it is as if we are all the versions of ourselves that we have ever been, all rolled up into one new, nervous ball of energy. The history and flood of shared feeling that can be carried in songs is about to carry us into that longed-for state too, the world about to be simplified. As we move towards it, deep breath upon deep breath, up the incline to the stage and then out onto a field where darkness is setting in among smoke and flares and flags, there is a moment amid the immediate chaos where that feeling that I thought I had lost forever returns. The stage slows, everything stills and I look first out towards the crowd, able to pick out individual faces from tens of thousands of people. Inside this sudden slowness, the glow of it warm and vivid, my hands frantically playing, my feet switching pedals on and off, my lungs screaming parts without needing any conscious thought, I look out to people in the far distance and into the surrounding hills and have a crystal-clear, tiny revelation. In the uncatchable nanosecond,

I have a crystal-clear reflection – I see suddenly how all these little rituals have been to keep sadness and solitariness at bay. How the path that the FA Cup has taken me on from Penrith to Wembley has been some parallel road from Kendal to Glastonbury too. In the moment, there is just a lightning flash of a thought, a piercing revelation, about how spine-tinglingly beautiful and fragile being in a band is. How rare it is to be able to find a group of people that all agree on a thing before time splits you back up again. How we are all, just like everyone at every one of those games towards Wembley, dreaming of reaching something beyond just ourselves, landing our hands on as close to the same places at the same time as we can manage. Knowing that on the other side, when the feeling has gone, you will expect to be in some way complete, but that you never quite are.

It won't ever give you exactly what you want. But, if you're lucky, it will show you what you need next.

Acknowledgements

———

I would like to thank the following list of people who worked on this book. Without them, it would simply not exist.

Trevor Davies, for his trust and belief in me and the project. Nick Walters, for his continued work, support and encouragement, from the very inception of the idea until now. Mel Four, for her absolutely fantastic work on the design. Alex Stetter, yet again for all her time and expertise in the edit and beyond. Megan Brown, who I love working with, for everything she has done to get the book out into the world with love. Matt Grindon, for everything online. Sarah Parry, the production controller. Also Annie Bowes, John English, Gill Phillips and Clare Hubbard for their contributions, time and fortunate football fan-ish knowledge!

There are many people who are in this book that gave their time and shared their personal history with real generosity. Thank you to all the friends old and new who turn up in these pages.

Outside of those who have worked on this book or are in it, this is the product of many, many conversations with almost everyone close in my life. I would like to thank you all, but I am not going to make a big list for fear of inevitably forgetting someone important. (I hope) You know who you are! I love you!

And as much as anything or anyone, thank you to Fulham Football Club, just for being there.

Que sera, sera.

About the Author

—

Felix White is a British musician, originally best known as the guitarist of the indie rock band The Maccabees. His life has widened to many disciplines since, taking in broadcasting, writing, film composition and presenting. He is the co-presenter of both the loosely cricket-based BBC podcast *Tailenders*, with Greg James and Jimmy Anderson, and the official Fulham Football Club podcast *Fulham Fix*, as well as the founding member, guitarist and vocalist of 86TVs. He has composed music for multiple feature-length films, including the Emmy Award-winning *McEnroe*, and presents the baseball coverage on the BBC, appearing every Sunday throughout the season on *Bases Covered Live*. His first book, *It's Always Summer Somewhere: A Matter of Life and Cricket*, was a BBC Radio 4 Book of the Week and a *Sunday Times* Bestseller. *Whatever Will Be, Will Be* is the highly anticipated sequel.